UNDERSTANDING SONET/SDH AND ATM

Books of Related Interest from IEEE Press . . .

FUNDAMENTALS OF TELECOMMUNICATIONS NETWORK MANAGEMENT
Lakshmi G. Raman
1999   Hardcover   368 pp   IEEE Order No. PC5723   ISBN 0-7803-3466-3

PLANNING TELECOMMUNICATION NETWORKS
Thomas G. Robertazzi
1999   Hardcover   208 pp   IEEE Order No. PC5755   ISBN 0-7803-4702-1

TELECOMMUNICATIONS NETWORK MANAGEMENT: Technologies
  and Implementations
Edited by Salah Aidarous and Thomas Plevyak
1998   Hardcover   352 pp   IEEE Order No. PC5711   ISBN 0-7803-3454-X

UNDERSTANDING NEURAL NETWORKS AND FUZZY LOGIC: Basic
  Concepts and Applications
Stamatios V. Kartalopoulos
1996   Softcover   232 pp   IEEE Order No. PP5591   ISBN 0-7803-1128-0

SONET/SDH: A Sourcebook of Synchronous Networking
Edited by Curtis A. Siller, Jr. and Mansoor Shafi
1996   Hardcover   404 pp   IEEE Order No. PC4457   ISBN 0-7803-1168-X

UNDERSTANDING SONET/SDH AND ATM

Communications Networks for the Next Millennium

Stamatios V. Kartalopoulos

Lucent Technologies, Inc.

IEEE Communications Society, *Sponsor*

**IEEE
PRESS**

IEEE Press Understanding Science & Technology Series
Dr. Mohamed E. El-Hawary, *Series Editor*

The Institute of Electrical and Electronics Engineers, Inc., New York

Printed in the United States of America

10   9   8   7   6   5   4   3

ISBN 0-7803-4745-5
IEEE Order Number: PP5399

Library of Congress Cataloging-in-Publication Data

Kartalopoulos, Stamatios V.
    Understanding SONET/SDH and ATM : communications networks for
the next millennium / Stamatios V. Kartalopoulos.
        p.   cm.—(IEEE Press understanding science & technology series)
    "IEEE Communications Society, sponsor."
    Includes bibliographical references and index.
    ISBN 0-7803-4745-5
    1. SONET (Data transmission)   2. Synchronous digital hierarchy
(Data transmission)   3. Asynchronous transfer mode.   I. IEEE
Communications Society.   II. Title.   III. Series.
TK5105.415.K37   1999
621.382'75—dc21   99-10012
                                                        CIP

To the Uncreated Light

Φῶς ἐκ φωτός

CONTENTS

PREFACE

How can two tin cans and a string be a lot of fun? In my childhood, these items could be used to make a "toy" telephone. Each end of the tin can was connected to the string, which was stretched by pulling away the two tin cans. These tin cans were used for both a microphone and an earphone.

As we grew older, we "graduated" from the tin-can communication system and discovered that walkie-talkies were a better solution. Now, there were no strings and no cans, but pocket-size "miracle" electronic devices using earphones, microphones, oscillators, antennas, and electromagnetic waves to do the job. Telephones were also installed virtually at every corner, and for a token we could dial a number and be connected with a friend anywhere almost instantly—that was an amazing thing! In Marvel Comics, we read about a science-fiction policeman who had a wrist "telephone" with which he was able to talk to anyone! We also read in illustrated classics that people of the past communicated using light or smoke signals and that thousands of years ago someone tried to answer the question: Does light propagate in a transparent medium following its curvature or does it travel in a straight line? He discovered the former and used a bucket of water to prove it—how simple!

Yesterday's science fiction is today's reality. Simple experiments of the past have helped us to understand the nature of things. Three crystals fused together created a transistor, which revolutionized the way we live. The wrist-size communicator is not fiction any more. Pocket-size powerful computers and credit-card-size communication devices are a reality. Satellite communication networks are not "pie in the sky." At the click of a button, one can access virtually any source of information around the globe. Wireless telephony and data, Low Earth Orbit Satellite (LEOS) systems, and fiber-optic communications are realities. Direct-to-satellite communications enable wireless connectivity anywhere at anytime in the world and also provide global positioning within an accuracy of a few feet. A single optical fiber can transport the contents of hundreds of thousands of volumes within a second. We are on such a "technological roll" that we cannot even guess what the next 20 or 50 years will bring. Hopefully, however, technology is advancing solely to serve humanity, and we will never allow it to control humanity, as some science fiction predicts. Otherwise, what is the point?

For the last few years, I have been working on both the Synchronous Optical Network/Synchronous Digital Hierarchy (SONET/SDH) and the asynchronous transfer mode (ATM). In addition, my work on mapping ATM over SONET/SDH payloads for my company's proprietary systems has led me to several innovations. My work in this subject culminated into a set of notes and viewgraphs that had educational value to both me and my colleagues. As a result, I decided to give an introductory tutorial at a public forum, the International Communication Conference, 1998. The tutorial far exceeded our estimated attendance. It was received with enthusiasm, and many attendees suggested publishing my notes. The intention of this book is to provide an introduction to SONET/SDH, ATM, and ATM over SONET, and to also touch on the subjects of the Internet, dense wavelength division multiplexing (DWDM), and convergence—all subjects related to optical communications. This book is not meant to replace related standards; readers interested in further details of SONET/SDH or ATM are strongly recommended to consult the latest version of them prior to design work, as these are the official recommendations. I wish you happy and easy reading.

Stamatios V. Kartalopoulos
Lucent Technologies, Inc.

ACKNOWLEDGMENTS

Throughout time, few achievements of note have been the product of individual effort. Instead, they have been accomplished through the efforts of many. Similarly, the fruition of this book would be impossible without the cooperation, diligence, understanding, and encouragement of a number of people. Among them, I would like to extend my thanks and appreciation to my wife Anita for her patience and encouragement; to my colleagues for creating an environment that fosters learning and collaboration; to the anonymous reviewers for their comments and constructive criticism; to the IEEE Press staff for encouragement, suggestions, creativity, and project management; and to all those who diligently worked on all phases of the production of this book.

Stamatios V. Kartalopoulos
Lucent Technologies, Inc.

INTRODUCTION

HISTORY

An ancient philosopher said, "Humans are social animals." The natural need for socializing led mankind to form communities, marketplaces, or agoras, and places where they got together and socialized. There, people exchanged ideas and information about themselves and others and about current and past events. People were curious to know what happened, and this curiosity combined with inventiveness led them to build networks to facilitate information exchange and communication.

The first communications channel was "word of mouth" as long as the "talker" and the "listener" were in proximity to hear each other. When peoples started communicating with peoples of distant communities, different methods were developed: a messenger with a verbal or written message on foot, riding a horse or a chariot, or sailing the unpredictable sea. However, these methods required time, and critical messages could not afford delays or could not depend on the "health" and "integrity" of the messenger. Thus, the need for a better method led to establishing a network of watchtowers across the land. Guards, using the light of a torch and a secret code, "signaled" the message from tower to tower, and since light travels fast, so did the message. Ancient mid-Eastern cultures, the Greeks, and the Romans applied the watchtower method. Native Americans followed a similar practice using the smoke of a fire on top of a hill or mountain. In both cases, messages were "visible," and if an enemy had knowledge of the secret code, a message could be intercepted or deciphered.

DISRUPTIVE TECHNOLOGIES

Ancient practices were simple and efficient and, in the absence of a better method, they were applied until the nineteenth century when a significant invention was made.

The *telegraph,* taking advantage of electricity, was able to send "invisible" coded messages. This was a technology that changed the old paradigm of communicating, or a disruptive technology that caused a revolution in communications but also led to extensive copper mining and deforestation. The telegraph, in addition to electricity, needed long copper-wire cables that had to be supported by wooden poles. Thousands of miles of cable were installed to form a network connecting many cities. Deforestation and mining was a socially acceptable penalty that had to be paid to meet the communication needs of the social animals. However, the telegraph had shortcomings: It was a one-way communications system, and a response to a message was not warranted; it was not a real-time communications, channel; the message had to be short and the cost was high (charging by the word); and the method was inconvenient (the sender had to physically go to the telegraph station, typically to a post office or a train station). Thus, the method made sense for long-distance emergency communication, and sending longer messages (letters, documents, etc.) was still the job of the pony express, the train, and the post office.

Telephony was the next disruptive technology that eventually replaced the telegraph. Using the already established infrastructure, telephony was able now to offer real-time two-way voice communication. This technology converted the analog voice into an analog electrical signal and eliminated the distance between the caller and the calling party. However, this technology was purely analog, and many people had to attend the network in order to establish long-distance connectivity. Major telephone exchanges had so many operators and were physically so large that many dispatchers used roller skates to bring the connectivity messages fast from one operator to another.

Digital electronic technology was a disruptive technology that led to the development of electronic (logic) computing machines. Digital technology replaced analog telephony and displaced the phone company's roller skaters. At the same time, many new digital services emerged that were added to the network, each with different characteristics, requirements, and profitability. For example:

> *Telemetry data* are used for monitoring purposes and are transmitted at very low bit rates. Telemetry data services last on the average a few seconds.

> *User data,* using a modem device, are presently transmitted at 56 kilobits per second (Kbps) or lower over traditional networks. High-speed modems are also used on a limited basis. Modem data may last from a few minutes to a few hours.

> *Video data,* real-time digital, is compressed according to a standard algorithm known as MPEG-n. Video services last for many minutes to a few hours.

> *Voice data* has been the traditional telephony service at 64 Kbps (and the compressed derivatives at 32 or 16 Kbps or lower). Telephone calls last on the average several minutes (if my children are not home).

Figure I.1 illustrates the relative characteristics of many services, old and new. What is not mapped however, is the *revenues per service;* presently traditional telephony dominates the revenues.

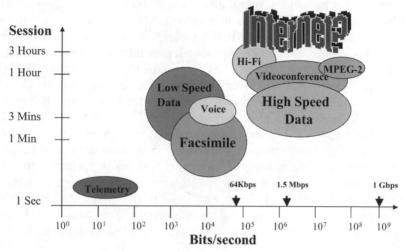

Figure I.1 Characteristics per service.

TODAY

Today, the ubiquitous computer and sophisticated fast digital transmission techniques have created new needs for fast data communications and new services. Low-cost, book-sized powerful computers have replaced the high-cost dinosaur computers of the 1970s. The race for more computing power and memory at less cost is on. As soon as one type of personal computer becomes available, a new one is advertised at about the same price that is faster and has more memory and storage capacity with faster communications interfaces and more features (based on personal experience).

Over the last 20 years, the cost of a computing-power unit has been dramatically decreased by many thousand times. However, over the same period the cost per minute of voice services has remained pretty flat. The market observes and analyzes these trends and makes predictions, typically not in favor of the old telephony services. For the time being, the voice traffic far exceeds the data traffic (e.g., computer communication services), and thus voice-based networks and services dictate the cost. However, as more and more computers become part of the communications network and particularly with the exploding Internet services, it is reasonable to expect that data traffic will influence the network structure and the cost of services. Predictions have it that future tariffs will be on a kilobit-per-second basis, and voice (at 64, 32, or 16 Kbps) will become the lowest cost service (or may be offered almost free).

THE NEXT CHAPTER

When digital telephony was developed, it quickly replaced the analog communications network and formed a *synchronous communications network* infrastructure that has set the foundations upon which all succeeding networks were based, apart from local area networks (LANs). Consequently, before we embark on our main subject, in Part I we explain some of the fundamental concepts. The reader who knows digital or legacy telephony may go directly to Part II, where the fundamentals of Synchronous Optical Network (SONET) and Synchronous Digital Hierarchy (SDH) are described. Part III describes the fundamentals of the asynchronous transfer mode (ATM) and, briefly, wireless over ATM as well as Internet over ATM. Having covered both SONET/SDH and ATM, Part IV describes ATM over SONET, and finally Part V describes convergence—that is, voice, video, and data mixed together and sent over the same network. Convergence, as many predict, is the direction where the industry is moving to and, along with ultrahigh transmission speeds and ultra broadband optical networks, it will trigger the next communications revolution. At the end of most chapters there are exercises. However, references are listed at the end of each part to avoid substantial duplication.

STANDARDS

SONET, SDH, and ATM communications systems are specified in detail in documents published by various international standards bodies. These documents are official and voluminous and, as such, our book is considered only a *tutorial* to help understand how these systems work. In addition, several issues are still being worked on, such as Voice over Internet Protocol (VoIP) and Video over IP (VoIP) mapped in SONET/SDH and in ATM, issues on wireless over ATM, dense wavelength digital multiplexing (DWDM) related to SONET/SDH issues, and others. Consequently, we strongly recommend that system designers consult the latest issue of these standards for details. These standards are available for a fee to interested parties through several publishing companies or the standards organization itself. Some international standards bodies are as follows:

- *ITU-T and ITU-R*—International Telecommunications Union—Telecommunications Standardization Sector, and International Telecommunications Union—Radio-communications Sector, respectively. ITU has published several documents identified by "ITU-T Recommendation G.nnn," where nnn is a number that refers to a specific aspect of the system. For example, ITU-T Recommendation G.774.01 describes the Synchronous Digital Hierarchy (SDH) Performance Monitoring for the Network Element.

- *CCITT*—Consultative Committee International Telegraph and Telephone is the former name of ITU. Thus, documents published prior to changing the name to ITU bear the CCITT initials.

- *ANSI*—American National Standards Institute. ANSI has published several documents identified by "ANSI T1.nnn," where nnn is a number that refers to a specific aspect of the system. For example, ANSI T1.105.02 describes the Synchronous Optical Network (SONET) payload mappings.

- *BSI*—British Standards Institution. Similarly, BSI BS ISO/IEC 13246, 1997 describes the Information Technology—Telecommunications and Information Exchange between Systems.

- *DIN*—Deutsches Institut fuer Normung EV. DIN has published several documents referred to as DIN ETS nnn. For example, DIN ETS 300493 describes the Transmission and Multiplexing of the Synchronous Digital Hierarchy (SDH) information model of the subnetwork.

- *AFNOR*—Association Francaise de Normalisation. AFNOR documents are identified by AFNOR NF Z NN-nnn. For example, AFNOR NF Z 82-300 describes the Broadband Integrated Services Digital Network (B-ISDN); Synchronous Digital Hierarchy (SDH).

- *ECMA*—European Association for Standardizing Information and Communication Systems. Similarly, an ECMA document is identified as ECMA NNN, such as ECMA 265—Broadband Private Integrated Services Network (B-PISN), InterExchange Signaling Protocol—ATM.

- *IEEE*—Institute of Electrical and Electronics Engineers. IEEE technical groups known as task forces have developed several standards.

- *Bellcore*—A U.S.-based organization that has contributed to standards and has also published recommendations.

- Other known standards bodies are ATM-Forum, Electronics Industry Association/Telecommunications Industry Association (EIA/TIA), European Telecommunications Standardization Institute (ETSI), Frame-Relay Forum (FRF), Internet Engineering Task Force (IETF), Motion Picture Experts Group (MPEG), International Standards Organization (ISO), Telecommunications Information Networking Architecture (TINA) consortium, Comit Europ en de Normalisation Electrotechnique (CENELEC), Personal Computer Memory Card International Association (PCMCIA), World Wide Web Consortium (W3C), and others.

SECTION I
LEGACY COMMUNICATIONS
SYSTEMS: CONCEPTS

In this part, we review principles applicable to traditional communications systems and traditional services that have helped shape the modern high-speed fiber-optic and wireless communications network, and it also influences the network of tomorrow. Chapter 1 reviews the basic communications technologies and services, Chapter 2 reviews hierarchical multiplexing in U.S., European, and other systems and Chapter 3 reviews traditional, or legacy, communications systems and networks.

CHAPTER 1

BASIC TECHNOLOGY AND SERVICES

1.1 PULSE-CODED MODULATION

Voice has been one of the primary services in the communications industry. Voice, by nature, is an analog signal. First, an acoustic wave is generated as the vibrating vocal cords and the mouth cavity modulates it into recognizable and distinguishable compounded sounds that we call words. This acoustical signal is converted to an electrical signal by a *transducer* known as the microphone. The generated electrical signal is also analog; that is, it changes value in a continuous manner with respect to time. At the receiving end, this electrical signal activates the electromagnetic coil of a speaker, another transducer, which reproduces the original acoustical signal.

Initially, telephony entailed few basic functions such as *ringing* and *call initiation* (and number dialing), and an analog signal was transmitted over the telephone network. This service became known as *Plain Old Telephone Service (POTS)* and the telephones were known as *POTS telephones*. Soon thereafter, the analog signal was converted to a digital one, known as *pulse-coded modulation (PCM)*, to form a binary (or digital) bit stream at 64,000 bits per second, known as *digital signal level 0 (DS0)*.

The circuitry responsible for converting an analog electrical signal to PCM and vice versa is known as a *coder/decoder*, abbreviated *CODEC*. Figure 1.1 illustrates an analog voice signal propagated over a twisted pair of wires (left side), also known as tip-and-ring (T&R); it passes through the CODEC circuit and on the right side we obtain a digitally encoded signal.

A CODEC periodically samples the analog signal, and based on a conversion table, it translates each sampled value into a binary representation. There are two different representations or conversion tables. The one, known as the μ-law (mu-law), is used in the United States, and the other, known as the α-law (alpha-law), is used in Europe.

The acoustical signal of speaking voice, for all practical purposes, has a maximum frequency of under 4 kilocycles per second, or kilohertz (3.4 kHz).

3

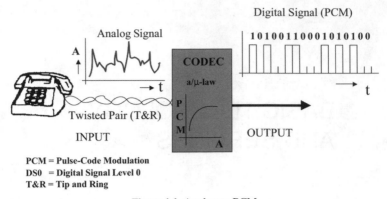

PCM = Pulse-Code Modulation
DS0 = Digital Signal Level 0
T&R = Tip and Ring

Figure 1.1 Analog to PCM.

Although voice (depending on the speaker) may contain higher frequencies, filters remove the frequencies above 3.4 kHz. It is proven that in order to decode PCM perceptually back to the (almost) same voice signal, the analog signal must have been sampled at least twice its maximum frequency content. This is known as *Shannon's theorem,* developed and proven by Shannon while working at Bell Laboratories. Thus, a CODEC samples the electrical equivalent of analog voice 8000 times per second (2×4000), or every 125 μs, and it converts each sample into 8 bits PCM. Consequently, in every second there are generated $8000 \times 8 = 64,000$ bits, or a bit rate of 64 kilobits per second (64 Kbps); see Figure 1.2. This is a 64-Kbps channel and the bit rate is termed DS0.

1.1.1 Adaptive PCM

Besides the 64 Kbps, methods have been developed that use sophisticated digital signal-processing algorithms to compress the 64 Kbps to 32 Kbps, or to 16 Kbps, or even to lower than that. These methods, known as differential

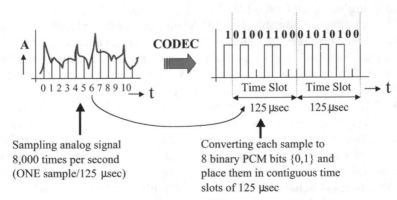

Sampling analog signal
8,000 times per second
(ONE sample/125 μsec)

Converting each sample to
8 binary PCM bits {0,1} and
place them in contiguous time
slots of 125 μsec

Figure 1.2 DS0 rate.

PCM (DPCM), adaptive DPCM (ADPCM), and sigma-delta PCM ($\Sigma\Delta$PCM), are compression techniques, each identifying the particular algorithm used.

1.1.2 Local Loop

In traditional telephony, the user's equipment is a POTS telephone that transmits an analog signal over a pair of twisted copper wires to the service provider equipment, where the CODEC is located. This pair of copper wires is also known as a *local loop* cable. Copper wires may be placed underground or on poles. These cables are susceptible to environmental electrical interference and noise, and in long loops and legacy systems chokes or filters had been placed to filter out the high-frequency content (above 3400 kHz) of the analog signal.

1.2 TIME-DIVISION MULTIPLEXING

Since the "digitization" era, all communications systems and networks that support voice transport are based on the 8-kHz sampling rate (or an integer multiple of it), on 64-Kbps channels, and on the 125-μs "quantum" interval.

In a traditional digital network, the POTS telephone converts the acoustical signal into an electrical signal. The electrical signal is then transmitted over a pair of copper wires to a communications system where the CODEC function is performed. From that point on, the network does not know of analog signals but only of digital, and this is what constitutes an *all-digital communications network*.

Now that the network has become all-digital, in addition to voice, we can also pass through it digital data (raw digital data, encoded video, encoded sound, etc.). An earlier data service is the *Digital Data Service* (*DDS*). This takes advantage of the 64-Kbps channel and uses 56 Kbps for data and the remaining 8 Kbps for "in-band" signaling, that is, bandwidth allocated to the network for its needs and not delivered to the end user.

Another service is the *Basic Rate Integrated Services Digital Network* (*BRISDN* or *BRI*). The BRI uses two 64-Kbps channels, known as channels B, and a 16 Kbps subrate channel, known as channel D, to support a combination of voice and/or data services over a single pair of wires. BRI is defined to support, at the end user's request, any of the following modes: two B channels for voice and a D channel for data; one B channel for voice and the B + D channels for data; two B channels for data and the D for signaling; all channels for data. Notice, however, that BRI can only be supported if both the user has Integrated Services Digital Network (ISDN) equipment and the communications system supports ISDN. The CODEC in this case is located at the end user's equipment. Table 1.1 lists the DS0 services and the various formats per service. The formats listed in the table will be explained in a subsequent section.

Table 1.1 DS0 Rates and Line Codes

Source	Format, Overhead Line Code
Voice: 64 Kbps	Frame, bit robbed
DDS 56 Kbps + 8 Kbps signaling	64 CCC
	B8ZS
B-ISDN 64 Kbps	64 CCC
B channel (2B + D)	B8Zs

Abbreviations: CCC, clear channel capability; B = 64 Kbps voice or data channel, DDS, digital data services; D = 16 Kbps signaling or data channel.

The *user-to-network interface* (*UNI*) is the interface where the user signal, a 64-Kbps data stream (organized in 8-bit bytes), first meets the network. At the UNI, however, signals from many users arrive. These signals are synchronized with the system clock, 8 kHz or a multiple of it. Then, based on a round-robin principle (a periodic, sequential and circular polling scheme), the signals are sequentially polled one byte at a time and placed one after the other in a fixed order, a process known as *byte interleaving,* and the bit rate is upped. The location of each byte source in this ordered digital signal is known as *time slot.* This process is known as *time-division multiplexing* (*TDM*), see Figures 1.2 and 1.3. At the receiving end, *time-division demultiplexing* takes place. That is, based on the round-robin mechanism, the time slots in the received TDM signal are extracted and each is distributed to its destination.

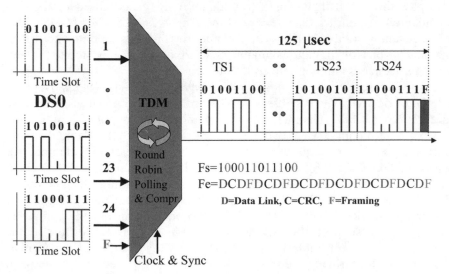

Figure 1.3 DS1 rate—M1 Mux.

1.3 DS1 RATE

When 24 bytes (a byte from 24 different signals) are time-division multiplexed, the beginning of the byte sequence must be marked to distinguish it from the previous 24 bytes. Adding a single bit, the F-bit, does this. The 24 bytes and the F-bit together construct a *DS1 frame*. In a DS1 frame there is a total of $24 \times 8 + 1 = 193$ bits and all 193 bits are transmitted within 125 μs, or at a bit rate of 1.544 Mbps, known as digital signal level 1 (DS1). The F-bit constitutes a subrate channel of 8 Kbps. The function of this time-division multiplexer is known as a M1 multiplexer (Figure 1.3).

Although a single bit (the F-bit) cannot mark the beginning of a single frame, 24 bits over 24 frames, or *a superframe,* can. Thus, the F-bit becomes meaningful when it is collected over 12 or 24 frames (depending on the system). The basic function of the F subrate channel is threefold: to mark the beginning of a frame (a function known as framing), to provide a data link over which *network data* are sent between the transmitting and receiving end, and to provide error control. Table 1.2 lists the DS1 services and the line coding per service. The formats listed in the table will be explained in a subsequent section.

1.3.1 Superframe and Extended Superframe

Depending on the application, the F-bit may have different interpretations. In addition to the framing function, which is the same for all applications, the data link may be interpreted in different ways, known as the superframe, or SF (Fs), and the extended superframe, or ESF (Fe).

1.3.2 DS1 Formats

A DS1 frame consists of 24 time slots and the F-bit. Depending on the application, all 24 time slots may be allocated for user data. In a different configuration, such as, for example, the primary rate ISDN (PRI), 23 time slots are allocated for 23 B channels (at 64 Kbps each) and 1 time slot is allocated for four D channels (at 16 Kbps each). The F-bit is again part of the PRI frame.

Table 1.2 DS1 Rate and Line Codes

Source	Format, Overhead Line Code
Voice: 24XDS0	SF, ESF, AMI
DDS 23XDS0 + sync + frame	SF, ESF
	B8ZS
P-ISDN 23B + D	SF, ESF
B channel (2B + D)	AMI

Abbreviations: SF, superframe; ESF, extended superframe; AMI, alternate mark inversion.

1.3.3   DS1 Signal

Depending on the application, the DS1 signal is encoded and transmitted using what is known as the *alternate mark inversion (AMI)* technique or the *bipolar with eight-zero substitution,* also known as *bits eight-zero suppression (B8ZS).* B8ZS belongs to a family of codes known as *bipolar with n-zero substitution (BnZS).* These coding techniques are artifices to create in the transmitted signal a guaranteed minimum number of 1's even if, in the original digital signal, a very long string of 0's exists. This minimum number of 1's is translated to a minimum amount of energy that the receiver requires so that the clock circuitry sustains its frequency within certain limits of accuracy.

1.3.4   Going the Extra Mile

The DS1 signal is transmitted over a pair of wires (typically a 22-gauge pulp-insulated cable) known as a T1 line. One pair of wires is used for each direction. As the transmitted electrical signal travels down the cable it is attenuated and the longer it travels the weaker it becomes. A weaker signal is more susceptible to external electromagnetic influences that may distort it and corrupt the digital information. As a consequence, when an attenuated binary signal arrives at the receiver, it may or may not be correctly recovered. That is a 1 may be perceived as a 0 or vice versa, and hence signal errors may occur.

Communications systems at the DS1 level are designed with an error objective of 10^{-6} or better, that is one or less bit error for each million bits transmitted. As it turns out, to assure that this error quality is maintained, a regenerator is placed (providing an amplification function) after 3000 ft from user and every 6000 ft between regenerators; see Figure 1.4.

However, regenerators are circuits that also may fail. Consequently, a regenerator every 6000 ft places a maintenance and troubleshooting overhead that in the long run is translated to increased operating cost. It is obvious that if a system could provide the same (or more) service at the same length (or longer) with the same transmission quality (or better) and with fewer (or none) regenerators, then it would offer a great benefit to the user and to the service provider.

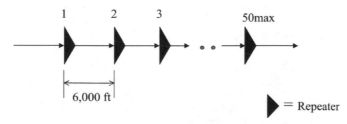

Figure 1.4 T1 characteristics.

1.4   xDSL

The copper twisted-pair cable that connects most homes (the user or sub-scriber equipment) with the telephone service provider equipment, known as the local loop, is the traditional transmission medium for analog signals up to 4 kHz (actually, up to 3400 kHz). When the transmitted information over the loop is in digital form, such as the BRI, the loop is known as a *digital subscriber line (DSL)*.

Multimedia and Internet services drive the need for high bit rates (several megabits per second) to the home. Although this need may be addressed with other media, such as coaxial and fiber-optic cable, there is already a huge cap-ital investment made in copper loop (twisted-pair) cable that will not disap-pear quickly.

DSL is a digital technology that can deliver high bit rates of 1.544 Mbps and in some cases up to 7 Mbps over existing twisted-pair copper cable. How-ever, DSL is possible only on loops that are not "loaded." That is, there are no inductors or coils on the loop cable. Loaded cables were used in traditional telephony to choke, or filter out, the high-frequency content of the (voice) analog signal that is perceived as noise. Consequently, DSL can be used only if the coils are removed from the loop copper cable. DSL digital signals, being at high bit rates and transmitted over an unshielded twisted pair, dissipate faster than analog low-frequency signals. Thus, the effective distance of a DSL signal shortens as the bit rate increases. For example, a DSL signal at about 1.5 Mbps can travel as far as several miles, but at about 25 Mbps it can travel as far as half a mile.

The digital subscriber line is also referred to as xDSL. The x in the xDSL refers to one of many DSL formats and rates. For example, VDSL means very high-bit-rate DSL, HDSL means high-bit-rate DSL, ADSL means asymmetric DSL, and SDSL means symmetric DSL. RADSL means rate adaptive DSL; RADSL-based systems typically run in the autorate adaptive or in the manual mode and adapt to a variety of bit rates as required by the user. MSDSL means multirate symmetric DSL; MSDSL-based systems build on the single-pair DSL technology offer one of many rates and thus one of many loop lengths. For example, MSDSL on a 24-gauge unloaded copper pair can provide service at 64/128 Kbps up to 29,000 ft (8.9 km) or 2 Mbps up to 15,000 ft (4.5 km).

Having described what xDSL can do and what it cannot do, xDSL may be deployed in all digital transmission services as well as in many new ones that require high-speed digital transmission, including Internet. However, xDSL is a technology that requires terminating devices at both ends of the loop, at the user and at the service provider, to terminate the upstream (user-to-provider) and downstream (provider-to-user) digi-tal signals.

A digital signal transmitted over xDSL requires modulation. Such modulation techniques are the *two-bits-to-one quartenary* (*2B1Q*), the *discrete multitone* (*DMT*) modulation, and the *carrierless amplitude phase* (*CAP*).

- The 2B1Q translates a 2-bit binary code in one of four voltage levels, $-3, -1, +1$, and $+3$. Its transmitting power is superior to that of AMI (used in T1 lines at 1.544 Mbps), but its bit rate is limited to 392 Kbps, which is suitable for upstream transmission on the loop. 2B1Q coding is used for BRI signals.
- DMT modulation divides the bandwidth into frequency channels onto which traffic is overlaid. With DMT modulation, when a certain (frequency) channel is detected to have inferior transmission characteristics, the traffic is assigned another frequency channel, a technique known as *frequency hopping*. DMT modulation has been the official standard of the ANSI T1E1.4 Working Group to support up to 6-Mbps services (this includes up to four MPEG-1 or a single MPEG-2 compressed video data, where MPEG stands for Motion Picture Experts Group).
- CAP is a derivative of the quadrature amplitude modulation (QAM) technique. CAP translates a 4-bit code in one of 16 voltage phase points. One may think of the CAP as a 2B1Q two-dimensional approach, where on the vertical axis is amplitude and on the horizontal is phase. Its transmitting power is superior to that of AMI and 2B1Q; however, its effective bit rate is in the range of 10-175 Kbps. Although DMT has been the standard of choice, CAP has been the de facto standard that by 1996 was deployed in almost 97% of all ADSL applications.

Depending on the application, the upstream/downstream signals and the cable lengths may differ. More specifically, for a 24-gauge wire with no repeaters:

- *ISDN:* Two pairs, downstream bit rate 144 Kbps, upstream bit rate 144 Kbps, maximum length of loop 18,000 ft.
- *HDSL two pair:* Downstream bit rate 2.048 Mbps, upstream bit rate 2.048 Mbps, maximum length of loop 13,000 ft. Compare with a T1 line that requires two repeaters.
- *HDSL single pair:* Downstream bit rate 768 Kbps, upstream bit rate 768 Kbps, maximum length of loop 12,000 ft.
- *ADSL DMT:* Single pair, downstream bit rate 1.5 Mbps, upstream bit rate 176 Kbps, maximum length of loop 12,000 ft.
- *ADSL CAP:* Single pair, downstream bit rate 6 Mbps, upstream bit rate 640 Kbps, maximum length of loop 12,000 ft.
- *ADSL CAP:* Single pair, downstream bit rate 1.5 Mbps, upstream bit rate 64 Kbps, maximum length of loop 18,000 feet.

1.5 LVDS

Low-voltage differential signaling (LVDS) is a transmission technique once defined for high-speed data transmission over relatively long cables. LVDS is now used as a high-speed, 155.5-Mbps, low-power, general-purpose data transmission technology at the board and at the bus level, that is, at short distances over printed circuit boards, board-to-board interconnections, and short cables.

The LVDS is specified by the TIA/EIA-644 standard (Telecommunications Industry Association/Electronic Industry Alliance). The LVDS differential voltage swing is between the voltage levels V_{OH} = 1.4 V and V_{OL} = 1.0 V.

One form of LVDS is the scalable coherent interface LVDS (SCI-LVDS) specified by the IEEE 1596.3 standard. SCI-LVDS uses unidirectional point-to-point links, from a transmitter to a receiver.

1.6 1000BaseT

The 1000BaseT is an evolutionary standard that derives from the 100BaseT used in LANs. The IEEE 802.3ab task force is working on this standard. 1000BaseT allows for transmission of a balanced digital signal at 1 Gbps over category 5 unshielded twisted-pair cable (UTP-5) and for 100-m link segments. Because of the limited link distance, the majority of the 1000BaseT applications are expected to be in the LAN.

1.7 CODING SCHEMES

A number of coding techniques are used in communications systems to transmit a signal. In the following we review some of them.

1.7.1 Unipolar and Bipolar

A unipolar is a two-voltage-level signal that typically swings between zero voltage and +1 V (Figure 1.5).

A *bipolar* signal is a three-voltage-level signal that typically swings between a positive and a negative voltage. Bipolar signals may *return to zero* (*RZ*) or *nonreturn to zero* (*NRZ*). In a digital bipolar signal, the 1's alternate between the two voltages, positive and negative. This results in a zero DC component on the transmission line.

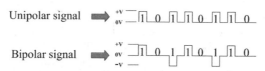

Figure 1.5 Unipolar and bipolar coding.

A *unipolar* signal and a NRZ bipolar are considered to be on-off signals, and they may be applied to either electrical or optical signals (Figure 1.5). In electrical transmission, assuming that statistically there is an equal number of 1's as 0's, then there is a DC component that may reach half the peak positive voltage. For transmission over long distances this DC component is undesirable.

Another category of signals is a *multilevel* signal. In this case, several voltage levels (e.g., eight) may be used, each level corresponding to one of eight codes. Although multilevel signals are attractive because of their inherent code compression properties, nevertheless they are not used for transmission in communications networks.

1.7.2   Return to Zero and Nonreturn to Zero

Figure 1.6 illustrates RZ and NRZ coding. With either method, the signal alternates between a positive $(+V)$ and a negative $(-V)$ voltage. Logic 1 is when the signal is at positive voltage and logic 0 when at negative voltage. However, in the NRZ method, transitions between logic 0 and logic 1, and vice versa, are directly crossing the zero voltage level, whereas in the RZ method, transitions stay temporarily on the zero voltage level.

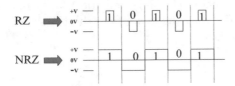

Figure 1.6 RZ and NRZ coding.

1.7.3   4B/5B Coding

The 4B/5B code translates 4 bits into one of 16 predetermined 5-bit codes. Thus, even if the original 4-bit code is 0000, it is translated to a 5-bit not-all-zero code.

1.7.4   Bipolar Violations

The bipolar signal is a three-level signal where consecutive 1's in the bit stream are alternating polarity. When two consecutive 1's do not change polarity, then we have a *bipolar violation* (BV); see Figure 1.7. A bipolar viola-

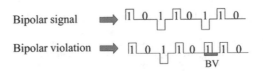

Figure 1.7 Bipolar and bipolar violation.

tion can be used to either detect errors in the bit stream or mark a specific bit manipulation (coding) in the bit stream.

1.7.5   B8ZS and HDB3 Coding

The B8ZS code (bit eight-zero suppression) recognizes eight consecutive 0's in the bit stream and substitutes them with a bipolar violation (Figure 1.8). At the receiving end, the bipolar violation is detected and the bit stream is restored to its original form.

B8ZS

Polarity of the preceding pulse	Substitute 8 consec. Zeroes by:
−	000-+0+1
+	000+-0-+

HDB3

Polarity of the pulse preceding the 4 zeros to be substituted	No. of bipolar pulses since last substitution	
	Odd	Even
−	000-	+00+
+	000+	-00-

HDB3: High Density Bipolar 3 zeros

Figure 1.8 B8ZS and HDB3 coding.

The HDB3 code substitutes four 0's by a code that contains a violation (Figure 1.8). Similarly, at the receiving end, the violation is detected and the bit stream is restored to its original form.

EXERCISES

1. An ADPCM circuit is able to compress eight DS0 channels to eight Kbps each.
   a. How many bits per compressed channel (in 125 μs) are there?
   b. How many compressed channels could fit in a DS1 signal?

2. Consider the following signal: . . . 110100000100110000000010110111000000110.
   If BnZs coding were used:
   a. How many times would the B8ZS have been applied?
   b. How many times for the B6ZA?
   c. Make a bipolar graph using B6ZA coding.

3. A local loop used for POTS services consists of a twisted-pair copper cable. The user needs to upgrade the home equipment to transmit data at higher bit rates. What would you recommend if:
   a. The new bit rate is at 56 Kbps?
   b. It is 144 Kbps?
   c. It is 1.5 Mbps?
   d. It is 10 Mbps?

Answers

1. a. 1, b. 192
2. a. 1, b. 2
3. a. Use a 56-Kbps modem.
   b. Use B-ISDN (call your local telephone company).
   c. Use xDSL (call your local telephone company).
   d. Call your local telephone company.

CHAPTER 2

HIERARCHICAL MULTIPLEXING

In the previous chapter we examined how a higher bit rate (e.g., DS1 was constructed by the confluence of several lower rate bit sources (e.g., DS0). In communications systems, the point of confluence of several similar sources and their organization into a stream of higher bit rate is known as a *multiplexer.*

If we examine how a large river is formed, we find that small tributaries meet to construct larger ones, and several of them confluence to become a river. That is, there is a hierarchical organization from small tributaries to main streams. Similarly, in communications networks there is a logical and hierarchical organization. As a matter of fact, the hierarchical organization of communication systems uses *flow principles* extensively.

2.1 IN NORTH AMERICA

In North America (and perhaps some other countries) 24 DS0 signals (plus a bit known as the framing *F-bit*) are time-division multiplexed by a level 1 multiplexer (M1) to construct a DS1 signal (see previous chapter). Four DS1 signals (plus a control bit, the C-bit, every 48 payload bits) are bit-interleaved (multiplexed) by a level 1-to-2 multiplexer (M12) to construct a DS2 signal. Then, seven DS2 signals (plus a bit every 84 payload bits, known as the control *C-bit*) are bit-interleaved by a level 2-to-3 multiplexer (M23) to construct a DS3 signal. This type of multiplexing from DS1 to DS3 is known as *two-stage* multiplexing (Figure 2.1).

Although the DS2 signal has been defined, it is not popularly used. Instead, an M13 multiplexer is used that multiplexes in *one-stage* 28 DS1 signals and the appropriate (F and C) bits to construct a DS3 signal at a bit rate of 44.736 Mbps.

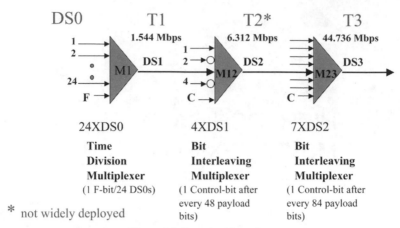

Figure 2.1 T-carrier hierarchy.

2.1.1 Stuffing Bits

A DS2 signal is formed by *bit interleaving* four DS1 signals; that is, in a recurrent manner, a bit from each of the four DS1's is placed in a sequential order. However, each constituent DS1 signal may be at a slightly different bit rate than the expected 1.544 Mbps. Stuffing additional bits in specific time slots of slower DS1 signals so that the composite DS2 signal is exactly 6.183 Mbps compensates for this difference.

Figure 2.2 illustrates the frame organization, control bit positioning, and stuffing bit opportunity in a DS2 signal.

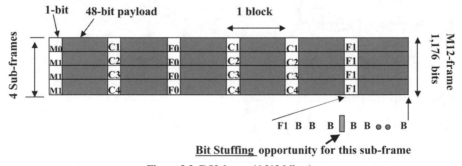

Figure 2.2 DS2 frame (6.312 Mbps).

2.1.2 T1c Rate

Another known format in legacy systems is the T1c. Two DS1 signals and a control bit (C-bit) are multiplexed by a M11c bit-interleaved multiplexer to construct a DS1c signal. Such a signal uses a duo-binary modulation and in effect doubles the bandwidth capacity of a T1 line (Figure 2.3).

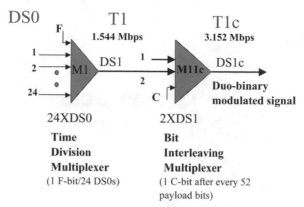

Figure 2.3 T-carrier hierarchy.

2.1.3 DS3 Rate

Figure 2.4 illustrates the frame organization, control bit positioning, and stuffing opportunity of a DS3 signal.

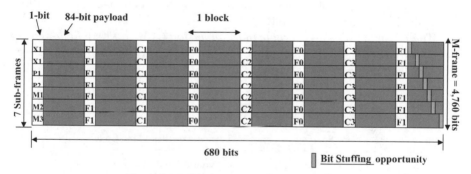

Figure 2.4 DS3 frame definition (44.736 Mbps).

2.2 MULTIPLEXING IN EUROPE

European systems time-division multiplex 30 user time slots and one time slot for every 15 user time slots (for framing and signaling) to yield an *E1* (or E11) frame with 32 time slots (Figure 2.5). Here, we use the term *European* for brevity and with the understanding that many countries around the world use the same or similar multiplexing schemes. The functions of the multiplexer are round-robin polling, byte interleaving, and time compression. In the reverse direction, a received E1 signal is demultiplexed; that is, the 30 user channels are separated from the two added channels for

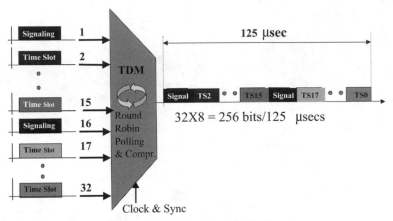

Figure 2.5 E1 rate (2.048 Mbps).

framing and signaling, and each channel is decompressed to 64 Kbps. Voice channels pass through a CODEC function to regenerate the analog signal of voice.

Again, each frame is transmitted within 125 μs, or at a bit rate of 2.048 Mbps. Notice the different bit rates between the E1 and DS1 (1.544 Mbps) and also the absence of the F-bit.

The E1 signal uses an *alternate mark inversion (AMI)* with a *high-density bipolar three-zero (HDB3)* technique to assure a density of 1's for the receiver clock to sustain the proper accuracy (Table 2.1).

Table 2.1 E1 Rate and Line Code

Source	Format, Overhead Line Code
Voice: 30 × DS0 + two 64-Kbps channels	Out-of-band signaling HDB3 (AMI)

As with the multiplexer hierarchy in the United States, there is a similar hierarchy of multiplexers in European communications systems. Thus, 30 DS0 channels plus two 64-Kbps channels for framing and signaling are time compressed and byte multiplexed by a level 1 multiplexer to construct an E1 signal. Then, four E1's plus four 64-Kbps channels for signaling are bit interleaved and time compressed by a 1-to-2 multiplexer to construct an E2 signal at 8.448 Mbps. Four E2 signals plus nine 64-Kbps channels for signaling are bit interleaved and time compressed by a 2-to-3 multiplexer to construct an E3 signal at 34.368 Mbps (Figure 2.6).

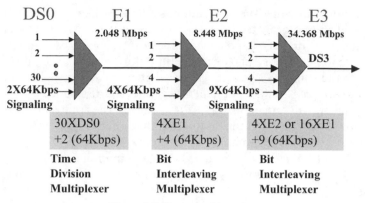

Figure 2.6 European hierarchy.

2.3   LEGACY RATES: SUMMARY

Although many similarities exist between the various standards (e.g., bit rates), there are enough dissimilarities to make life challenging. Table 2.2 captures the variety of bit rates in three major areas of the world.

Table 2.2 Legacy Rates

Facility	United States	Europe	Japan
DS0	64 Kbps	64 Kbps	64 Kbps
DS1	1.544 Mbps	—	1.544 Mbps
E1	—	2.048 Mbps	
DS1c	3.152 Mbps		3.152 Mbps
DS2	6.312 Mbps		6.312 Mbps
E2		8.448 Mbps	32.064 Mbps
DS3	44.736 Mbps	34.368 Mbps	
DS3c	91.053 Mbps		
			97.728 Mbps
E3		139.264 Mbps	
DS4	274.176 Mbps		
			397.2 Mbps

2.4   PROS AND CONS OF LEGACY NETWORKS

Legacy networks were initially designed to carry voice signal from many sources to many destinations. Imagine a node in a network at which many source signals arrive. Each arriving signal needs to be routed to a destination, not necessarily the same. The destination is defined when the telephone number is dialed and before a telephone connection is established. When the telephone number is dialed, the receiving node, a *switch,* makes a determination of the route to be selected and assigns a time slot on a DS1 signal. That is, the signal from the source is switched. This is what classifies a switched service (as opposed to services that are permanently connected and hence nonswitched). This assignment will remain the same for as long as the connection is active. In the meantime, ringing alerts the destination that a caller requests connectivity. When the destination answers the call, then connectivity is established and customer data (digitized voice or data) can flow in either direction. This connection will remain active for as long as both source and destination are "off the hook."

Now, legacy systems have some fundamental advantages. Time slots are assigned to a particular user for as long as the connection is active. Therefore the system is deterministic and its design simpler. However, assigned time slots have the disadvantage of bandwidth underutilization. That is, when a connection is established, data do not always flow continuously. For example, voice connections have long periods of silence, and other data may come in bursts. In addition, legacy networks do not cost-effectively accommodate high-bit-rate services. Consequently, cost-effective bandwidth utilization became the primary motivator to redefine the communications network to the networks that we will examine in Parts II and III.

EXERCISES

1. Calculate the DS1, E1, T1c, and E3 rates.
2. Assume that the F-bit consists of the repetitious code 10010110. Assume also that a synchronization function tries to find this pattern in the data stream so that it can frame synchronize with it.
   a. Is there a probability that this pattern may also be emulated in the data stream?
   b. If the answer to part a is yes, comment on whether synchronization may be achieved.

Answers

1. DS1: $24 \times 8 + 1 = 193$ bits/125 μs
         $193 \times 8000 = 1.544$ Mbps
   E1: $32 \times 8 = 256$ bits/125 μs
         $256 \times 8000 = 2.048$ Mbps
   T1c: 2×1.544 Mbps $+ 64$ Kbps $= 3.152$ Mbps
   E3: 16×2.048 Mbps $+ (16 + 9)$ 64 Kbps $= 34.368$ Mbps
2. a. There is a probability, but it is very small.
   b. A synchronizer expects to find the same pattern every 125 μs. As such, the probability is almost zero.

CHAPTER 3

LEGACY DATA NETWORKS

Legacy synchronous communications networks, described in Chapters 1 and 2, do not address the requirements for voice and data applications in an equitable manner. What we mean by this is that, in voice communications networks, *short delays* of the signal through the network were the primary concern whereas for many data applications it was *high bit rates* and *low cost per unit of time*. Examples of such data applications are banks, stock-brokerage firms, publishing companies, and image transmission. The contrasting needs of these applications brought to bear a data network able to transport chunks of data, up to about 9000 bytes, known as *packets*. Such systems are the *local area network* (*LAN*), the *metropolitan area network* (*MAN*), the *wide area network* (*WAN*), and the *switched multimegabit data services* (*SMDS*).

The *asynchronous transfer mode* (*ATM*) network is also a packet-based network, where packets are 53 bytes long, known as ATM *cells* (later we will see more of this).

3.1 LANs

The network that was first deployed locally or in a limited area (building, campus) was the local area network. Many terminals were connected on a LAN *backbone*, and based on a LAN *communications protocol*, terminals were able to communicate among them.

LAN networks are of two major types: *Ethernet* and *ring*. Ethernet LANs are hierarchical and the transmission rate is at 10 or 100 Mbps (a 1-Gbps standard is also emerging). Ethernet 10BaseT denotes 10 Mbps over a twisted pair of wires.

The FDDI (*Fiber Distributed Data Interface*) is a counterrotating fiber ring LAN specified at 100 Mbps effective data rate. However, the FDDI employs 4B/5B coding and thus the actual bit rate is 125 Mbps.

The IEEE specifies both types (Ethernet and FDDI) in the 802.1 to 802.5 specifications.

Soon after the LAN deployment, LANs were expanded to cover a city or a metropolis and the *metropolitan area network* (*MAN*) evolved.

Traffic from one data network was brought to another via a function (or circuit) known as a bridge. In addition, LAN/MAN traffic was routed on the communications network so that connectivity between two (or more) remote LANs/MANs could be established. If high traffic between two LANs/MANs is sustained 24 h/day, then it may be more efficient to establish a dedicated link between them and form a private data network. Else, it could be more efficient to establish semipermanent links.

3.2 SMDS

The SMDS is a public MAN service developed by Bellcore® primarily for LAN interconnections. SMDS is based on the *distributed queue dual bus* (*DQDB*) transport and multiplexing mechanism and is defined in IEEE 802.6. The use of the DQDB format is based on a 53-byte cell structure that is similar to the ATM cell. SMDS is a connectionless technology specified over synchronous carriers like the DS1, DS3, E1, and E3 lines.

3.3 FRAME RELAY

Frame relay (FR) is a packet service. Frame relay may be viewed as a highway with ramps on and off. At the ramps, any car, small or large, may approach the highway at a slower speed, but once on the highway, one can travel any length of the highway and as fast as the limit. That is, the highway is equally accessible and shareable by all. The more lanes in the highway, the more cars it can contain. In FR, the ramps are the access points and the number of lanes determines the bandwidth of the FR system. As such, FR is a shared-bandwidth solution that takes advantage of traffic pattern variability and oversubscription to provide a cost-effective data service.

At the access points, or the user-to-network interface, circuitry concentrates the packet traffic from a number of users, typically over leased lines (T1/E1). The concentrated traffic is switched by means of a FR switch and it is put on a common backbone (the highway). A number of FR switches are interconnected to form a FR network.

EXERCISES

1. Determine why the bit rate of the F-bit in the DS1 signal is 8 Kbps.
2. What is the rate of a superframe?
3. The 4B/5B coding in FDDI increases the transmitted bit rate from 100 to 125 Mbps. Discuss why.

ANSWERS

1. It is $\frac{1}{8} \times 64$ Kbps $= 8$ Kbps.
2. A frame repeats every 125 μs. Thus a superframe repeats every 24×125 μs $= 3$ms.
3. Adding a bit to 4 bits results in increasing the bit rate by 25%, i.e., 125 Mbps.

SECTION I

REFERENCES

[1] P. Black and T. Meng, "A 1-Gb/s Four-State Sliding Block Viterbi Decoder," *IEEE JSSC*, vol. 32, no. 6, 1997, pp. 797–805.

[2] J. A. C. Bingham, "Multicarrier Modulation for Data Transmission: An Idea Whose Time Has Come," *IEEE Commun. Mag.*, vol. 28, no. 5, 1990, pp. 5–14.

[3] E. B. Carne, *Telecommunications Primer,* Prentice-Hall, Englewood Cliffs, NJ, 1995.

[4] N. Dagdeviren, J. A. Newell, L. A. Spindel, and N. J. Stefanick, "Global Networking with ISDN," *IEEE Commun. Mag.,* June 1994, pp. 26–32.

[5] O. Edfors, M. Sandell, J. J. Van de Beek, D. Landstrom, and F. S. Joberz, "An Introduction to Orthogonal Frequency-Division Multiplexing," http://www.tde.lth.se/home/oes/publications.html.

[6] J. R. Freer, *Computer Communications and Networks,* IEEE Press, New York, 1996.

[7] R. Handel and M. N. Huber, *Integrated Broadband Network,* Addison-Wesley, Reading, MA, 1991.

[8] G. Hawley, "ADSL Data: The Next Generation," *Telephony,* Aug. 12, 1996, pp. 24–29.

[9] R. D. Gitlin, J. F. Hayes, and S. B. Weinstein, *Data Communications Principles,* Plenum, New York, 1992.

[10] G. H. Im and J. J. Werner, "Bandwidth-Efficient Digital Transmission over Unshielded Twisted Pair Wiring," *IEEE JSAC,* vol. 13, no. 9, 1995, pp. 1643–1655.

[11] R. E. Matick, *Transmission Lines for Digital and Communication Networks,* IEEE Press, New York, 1995.

[12] S. V. Kartalopoulos, "Global Multi-Satellite Networks," *Proc. IEEE Int. Commun. Conf.,* Montreal, Canada, June 1997.

[13] S. V. Kartalopoulos, "Fuzzy Logic and Neural Networks in Communications Systems," Tutorial, Globecom'93, Houston, TX, Nov. 29, 1993.

[14] S. V. Kartalopoulos, "Temporal Fuzziness in Communications Systems," ICCN'94, ICNN, Orlando, FL, July 2, 1994.

[15] S. V. Kartalopoulos, "A Manhattan Fiber Distributed Data Interface Architecture," Globecom'90, San Diego, Dec. 2–5, 1990.

[16] S. V. Kartalopoulos, "Disaster Avoidance in the Manhattan Fiber Distributed Data Interface Network," Globecom'93, Houston, TX, Dec. 2, 1993.

[17] S. V. Kartalopoulos, "A Time Compression Multiplexing System for a Circuit Switched Digital Capability," *IEEE Trans. Commun.*, vol. Com-30, no. 9, 1982, pp. 2046–2052.

[18] S. V. Kartalopoulos, "A Loop Access System for a Circuit Switched Digital Capability," presented at the International Symposium on Subscriber Loop Systems, Toronto, Canada, Sept. 20–24, 1982.

[19] S. V. Kartalopoulos, "A Plateau of Performance?" Guest Editorial, *IEEE Commun. Mag.*, Sept. 1992, pp. 13–14.

[20] S. V. Kartalopoulos, "Signal Processing and Implementation of Motion Detection Neurons in Optical Pathways," Globecom'90, San Diego, Dec. 2–5, 1990.

[21] S. V. Kartalopoulos, "Micro-computers in Real-Time Processing of Information," paper presented at the Twenty-Third Midwest Symposium on Circuits and Systems, Toledo, OH, Aug. 4–5, 1980.

[22] S. V. Kartalopoulos, *Understanding Neural Networks and Fuzzy Logic*, IEEE Press, New York, 1995.

[23] S. V. Kartalopoulos, "The Architecture of the Facility Access Device in the SLC™ 5 Carrier System," Globecom'86, Houston, TX, Dec. 1–4, 1986.

[24] K. Maxwell, "Asymmetric Digital Subscriber Line: Interim Technology for the Next Forty Years," *IEEE Commun. Mag.*, Oct. 1996, pp. 100–106.

[25] Members of the Technical Staff, "Transmission Systems for Communications," Bell Telephone Laboratories, Holmdel, NJ, 1982.

[26] J. Nellist, *Understanding Telecommunications and Lightwave Systems*, IEEE Press, New York, 1996.

[27] B. Petri and D. Schwetje, "Narrowband ISDN and Broadband ISDN Service and Network Interworking," *IEEE Commun. Mag.*, June 1996, pp. 84–89.

[28] S. U. H. Qureshi, "Adaptive Equalization," *Proc. IEEE*, vol. 73, no. 9, Sept. 1985, pp. 1349–1386.

[29] W. D. Reeve, *Subscriber Loop Signaling and Transmission Handbook*, IEEE Press, New York, 1995.

[30] W. Stallings, *Local Networks: An Introduction*, Macmillan, New York, 1987.

[31] W. Stallings, *ISDN & Broadband-ISDN*, Macmillan, New York, 1992.

[32] W. Y. Zhou and Y. Wu, "COFDM: An Overview," *IEEE Trans. Broadcasting*, vol. 41, no. 1, 1995, pp. 1–8.

STANDARDS

[1] ADSL Forum TR-001, "ADSL Forum System Reference Model," 1996.

[2] ANSI/IEEE 812-1984, "Definition of Terms Relating to Fiber Optics," 1984.

[3] Bellcore, GR-1110-CORE, "Broadband Switching System (BSS) Generic Requirements," 1995.

[4] Bellcore, GR-1111-CORE, "Broadband Access Signaling (BAS) Generic Requirements," 1995.

[5] Bellcore, GR-1112-CORE, "Broadband ISDN UNI and NNI Physical Criteria Generic Criteria," 1994.

[6] Bellcore, TA-NWT-077, "Digital Channel Banks—Requirements for Dataport Channel Unit Functions," April 1986.

[7] Bellcore, TA-NWT-418, "Generic Reliability Requirements," 1992.

[8] Bellcore, TA-NWT-1042, "Ring Information Model," 1992.

[9] Bellcore, TA-NWT-1250, "File Transfer," 1992.

[10] Bellcore, TR-NWT-233, "Digital Cross Connect System," Nov. 1992.

[11] Bellcore, TR-NWT-499, "Transport Systems Generic Requirements (TSGR): Common Requirements," issue 5, Dec. 1993.

[12] Bellcore, TR-NWT-782, "Switch Trunk Interface," Oct. 1992.

[13] Bellcore, TR-NWT-917, "Regenerator," Oct. 1990.

[14] Bellcore, TR-NWT-1042, "Ring Information Model," 1992.

[15] Bellcore, TR-TSY-303, "Digital Loop Carrier System," Oct. 1989.

[16] Bellcore, TR-TSY-496, "Add-Drop Multiplexer," May 1992.

[17] ITU-T Recommendation G.701, "Vocabulary of Digital Transmission and Multiplexing, and Pulse Code Modulation (PCM) Terms," 1993.

[18] ITU-T Recommendation G.702, "Digital Hierarchy Bit Rates," 1988.

[19] ITU-T Recommendation G.704, "Synchronous Frame Structures used at 1544, 6312, 2048, 8488 and 44736 Kbps Hierarchical Levels," 1995.

[20] ITU-T Recommendation G.711, "Pulse Code Modulation (PCM) of Voice Frequencies," 1988.

[21] ITU-T Recommendation G.726, "40, 32, 24, 16 Kbps Adaptive Differential Pulse Code Modulation (ADPCM)," 1990.

[22] ITU-T Recommendation G.731, "Primary PCM Multiplex Equipment for Voice Frequencies," 1988.

[23] ITU-T Recommendation G.732, "Characteristics of Primary PCM Multiplex Equipment Operating at 2048 Kbps," 1988.

[24] ITU-T Recommendation G.733, "Characteristics of Primary PCM Multiplex Equipment Operating at 1544 Kbps," 1988.

[25] ITU-T Recommendation G.734, "Characteristics of Synchronous Digital Multiplex Equipment Operating at 1544 Kbps," 1988.

[26] ITU-T Recommendation G.736, "Characteristics of Synchronous Digital Multiplex Equipment Operating at 2048 Kbps," 1993.

[27] ITU-T Recommendation G.741, "General Considerations on Second Order Multiplex Equipments," 1988.

[28] ITU-T Recommendation G.805, "General Functional Architecture of Transport Networks," Nov. 1995.

[29] ITU-T Recommendation I.113, "Vocabulary of Terms for Broadband Aspects of ISDN," June 1997.

[30] ITU-T Recommendation I.121, "Broadband Aspects of ISDN," April 1991.

[31] ITU-T Recommendation I.211, "B-ISDN Service Aspects," March 1993.

[32] ITU-T Recommendation I.311, "B-ISDN General Network Aspects," Aug. 1996.

[33] ITU-T Recommendation I.321, "B-ISDN Protocol Reference Model and Its Application," April 1991.

[34] ITU-T Recommendation I.327, "B-ISDN Network Functional Requirements," March 1993.

[35] ITU-T Recommendation I.371, "Traffic Control and Congestion Control in B-ISDN," Aug. 1996.

[36] ITU-T Recommendation I.413, "B-ISDN User-Network Interface," March 1993.

[37] ITU-T Recommendation I.432, "B-ISDN User-Network Interface—Physical Layer Specification," March 1993.

[38] ITU-T Recommendation I.580, "General Arrangements for Interworking between B-ISDN and 64 Kb/s Based ISDN," Dec. 1994.

[39] ITU-T Recommendation I.610, "OAM Principles of B-ISDN Access," Nov. 1995.

[40] ITU-T Recommendation Q.931, "ISDN UNI Layer 3 Specification for Basic Call Control," 1993.

STANDARDS ON LOCAL AREA NETWORKS

[1] IEEE 802.1 to 802.6, Local Area Networks.

[2] IEEE 802.3ab, 1000BaseT.

STANDARDS ON XDSL

[1] ANSI T1E1 Working Group.

[2] ANSI T1E1.4 Working Group.

[3] ANSI T1.413 ADSL.

[4] ANSI T1E1.4 Working Group DMT.

[5] IEEE 1596.3 SCI-LVDS.

[6] ITU G.DMT ADSL.

[7] TIA/EIA-644 LVDS.

STANDARDS ON FACILITIES

[1] ITU Recommendations G.703 and G.704 (on E1).

SECTION II
SONET AND SDH

In this part, the fundamentals of SONET and SDH are reviewed. Chapter 4 provides an introduction to optical networks, particularly SONET and SDH, attempts to define SONET and SDH, and discusses how they differ from legacy networks. Chapter 5 provides a brief description of the major optical components that make SONET and SDH possible. Chapter 6 describes the SONET and SDH network and network topologies and defines the concepts of tributaries, path, line, and section. Chapter 7 describes SONET and SDH frames. Chapter 8 describes virtual tributaries, groups, and capacities. Chapter 9 continues with the description of SONET and SDH frames, overhead definition, pointers and pointer processing, scrambling, and SDH multiplexing. Chapter 10 describes the various models for timing and synchronization of SONET and SDH networks, stratums, timing accuracy, timing stabilization, jitter, and wander. Chapter 11 describes maintenance in SONET and SDH, alarm surveillance, performance monitoring, testing, and the operations communications interface. Lastly, Chapter 12 reviews the Internet Protocol (IP) over SONET and also reviews some novel concepts in dense wavelength division multiplexing (DWDM).

CHAPTER 4

INTRODUCTION

The evolution of the optical fiber to a high-speed, low-cost transmission medium led to the *Synchronous Optical Network* (*SONET*) standard in the United States and the *Synchronous Digital Hierarchy* (*SDH*) in Europe. Prior to SONET and SDH systems, the fiber had already been proven as a transmission medium in precursor fiber systems in the United States, Europe, and Japan. Since its first deployment in the 1980s, SONET and SDH have almost replaced all long-haul copper cable and thousands of miles of new fiber are being installed each year. The optical fiber has responded to an unexpected increase in traffic demand and the much-touted "superhighway" is history in the making.

4.1 WHAT ARE SONET AND SDH?

In this chapter we will address both SONET and SDH in detail. First, however, it suffices to identify some of their most important characteristics, similarities, and differences:

- SONET is a set of standard interfaces in an optical synchronous network of elements (NE) that conform to these interfaces.
- SONET interfaces define all layers, from the physical to the application layer.
- SONET is a synchronous network.
- SDH is also a synchronous network with optical interfaces.
- SDH is a set of standard interfaces in a network of elements that conform to these interfaces.
- Like SONET, SDH interfaces define all layers, from the physical to the application layer.

From the above definitions, at first glance it seems that SONET and SDH are identical. However, as we will see, there are many details that make them different.

4.2   BROADBAND NETWORKS

Currently, systems and networks are being developed that can transport any type of traffic. Voice, video data, Internet, and data from LANs, MANs, and WANs will be transported over a SONET or a SDH Network (Figure 4.1). The SONET network is also able to transport asynchronous transfer mode (ATM) payloads. These systems, called broadband, can manage a very large aggregate bandwidth or traffic.

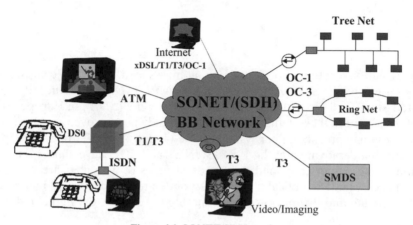

Figure 4.1 SONET/SDH services.

4.3   SONET VERSUS SDH

Although SONET and SDH substantially overlap, they differ enough to make them two separate standards.

Some of the technical similarities between SONET and SDH are:

- Bit rates and frame format organization
- Frame synchronization schemes
- Multiplexing and demultiplexing rules
- Error control

Some of the major differences are:

- The definition of overhead bytes is very similar, but some variations have been introduced to accommodate differences between U.S. and European communications nodes and networks.
- The SDH photonic interface specifies more parameters than SONET.
- SONET and SDH standards have enough minor technical and linguistic differences (i.e., terminology) to add complexity (and cost) in their design [hardware, software (HW, SW)].

Some nomenclature examples (SONET vs. SDH) are:

- Synchronous transport signal (STS) versus synchronous transport module (STM), e.g., STS-1, STS-3, STS-12, STS-48 versus STM-1, STM-4, STM-16, respectively
- Synchronous payload envelope (SPE) versus virtual container (VC)
- Virtual tributary (VT) versus tributary unit (TU)

Here, we try to identify the major characteristics of SONET and SDH so that a comprehensive understanding of both can be gained and we avoid the technical details. It is recommended that the interested reader consult the standard documents as they are the only official documents and they include the latest additions or modifications. Consequently, when we refer to SONET (for brevity) we also mean SDH. However, when there are major differences between them, we will identify each one, SONET and SDH, separately.

4.4 SONET/SDH BENEFITS

It is estimated that a 6–10% shift of telephony traffic from traditional long-distance (LD) services to Internet (IP) may reduce the LD profits significantly (the U.S. LD traffic is about 2000 Tbytes/day; a terabyte is one thousand billion bytes). Therefore, networks and systems that offer low cost per bit per kilometer are very critical in communications. SONET and SDH are such networks. The SONET and SDH advantages are summarized as follows:

1 Reduced cost:
  a. It lowers operations cost.
  b. It has the same interface for all vendors.
2 Integrated network elements:
  a. It allows for multivendor internetworking.
  b. It has enhanced network element management.
3 Remote operations capabilities: It is remotely provisioned, tested, inventoried, customized, and reconfigured.
4 It offers network survivability features.
5 It is compatible with legacy and future networks.

4.5 SONET AND SDH RATES

SONET and SDH rates are defined in the range of 51.85–9953.28 Mbps (almost 10 Gbps or 10,000,000,000 bits per second) and higher rates, at 40 Gbps, are also under study.

When the SONET signal is in its electrical nature, it is known as *synchronous transport signal level N* (*STS-N*). The SDH equivalent is called *synchronous transport module level N* (*STM-N*). After its conversion into optical pulses, it is known as *optical carrier level N* (*OC-N*). In SONET, N takes the values 1, 3, 12, 48, and 192, with corresponding bit rates at 51.84, 155.52, 622.08, 2488.32, and 9953.28 Mbps (Table 4.1). Rates at 39,813.12 Gbps (OC-768) are currently under study.

Table 4.1 SONET/SDH Rates

Signal Designation			Line Rate
SONET	**SDH**	**Optical**	**(Mbps)**
STS-1	STM-0	OC-1	51.84
STS-3	STM-1	OC-3	155.52
STS-12	STM-4	OC-12	622.08
STS-48	STM-16	OC-48	2,488.32
STS-192	STM-64	OC-192	9,953.28
		OC-768(?)	39,813.12

4.6 WHY USE SONET/SDH?

Much has been written about SONET/SDH. The basic differentiator between SONET/SDH and traditional (copper) networks is the transmission medium, the *glass fiber* versus the *copper wire*. Therefore, the question is, Why is glass fiber better than copper wire? The following is a short list of the benefits of glass fiber:

- Higher transmission reliability. Glass fiber is not as susceptible to radio frequency or electromagnetic interference (RFI, EMI) as copper wire unless it is shielded and well grounded.
- Lower bit error rate (BER). Unlike electrical signals in copper cables, light signals transmitted along a bundle of fibers do not interact. This results in lower intersymbol errors and thus fewer transmission errors.
- Higher bandwidth per fiber. A single strand of glass fiber can pass more than 1,000,000 times information than copper wire can. This enables very high capacity systems at lower cost per megabytes per second.
- Fiber can transmit without repeaters at longer distances as compared with copper. This simplifies maintenance and lowers operation cost (per megabytes per second).
- Fiber yields thinner cable (per megahertz or gigahertz bandwidth) than copper.

- SONET/SDH is based on standards, which enables multivendor compatibility and interoperability.

EXERCISES

1. Review the similarities and differences between SONET and SDH.
2. Review the rates between SONET and SDH. What is the OC-3 bit rate and what is the STM-1 bit rate?

CHAPTER 5

OPTICAL COMPONENTS

5.1 THE OPTICAL TRANSMITTER

The optical transmitter is a transducer that converts electrical pulses to optical pulses. The transmitter is characterized by an optical power (the higher the better), a rise time (the shorter the better), a central (nominal) wavelength (the closer centered the better), and a range wavelength minimum/maximum that is generated (the closer these two numbers are, the better).

Laser diodes have better controlled parameters, higher optical power, and short rise times and therefore are better suited for multimegabit rates. Tunable lasers have the ability to transmit a very narrow band of wavelengths. Light-emitting diodes (LEDs) transmit a wider band of wavelengths, are more inexpensive, and are better suited for lower bit rates than laser transmitters. However, as technology evolves, the selection criteria between LEDs and lasers become more challenging.

5.2 THE RECEIVER

The optical receiver is a transducer that converts optical pulses to electrical ones. Optical-to-electrical transducers, or *photodetectors,* can be made with photoresist material or semiconductors. However, the response times of these technologies are very different. For multimegabit rates, detectors must have high optical power sensitivity, very fast response time (fast rise and fall times), and a desirable response to a range of wavelengths that matches the range of transmitted wavelengths.

Such advanced technologies are the positive-intrinsic-negative (PIN) photodiode and the avalanche photodiode (APD).

5.3   THE FIBER MEDIUM

Ultrapure glass *fiber* is the medium used to guide light pulses. Light pulses are generated by the transmitter and detected by the receiver. However, the motivation to use glass fiber instead of copper wire is, as said earlier, the ability to transport a higher bit rate signal more reliably, with fewer errors, and over a longer distance. This is accomplished by controlling a number of factors, such as:

- The geometry of the fiber and particularly its diameter with the smallest possible variation over a long length (many miles) of fiber.
- The density of impurities in the glassy material, as impurities scatter photons and thus attenuate the optical signal.
- The radial distribution of the index of refraction in the fiber so that optical rays do not escape from the fiber surface and they do not disperse the signal. In a dispersion-uncompensated fiber, rays travel faster in a straight axial direction than in an angled direction. Dispersion results in broadening the width of an optical impulse and thus in lowering the bit rate. Fibers able to transmit up to 10 Gbps are already in use.
- The transparency of the glassy material over a wide range of wavelengths. Current single-mode fibers transmit wavelengths in the range 1300–1550 nm and absorb wavelengths in the range 1340–1440 nm. This absorption is due to water molecules trapped in the fiber during the manufacturing process. Lucent Technologies has developed a dispersion-compensated fiber called AllWave™ usable in the entire spectrum of 1280–1625 nm. The AllWave fiber enables higher density in wavelengths over the same fiber (see DWDM) and is suitable for metropolitan and short-haul applications. For long-haul wavelength-division multiplexing (WDM) applications, Lucent's TrueWave™ fiber performs in the range of 1550 nm without dispersion compensation at 10 Gbps over 400 km without amplification.

The glass fiber (or the core) is very thin. To withstand the pulling forces that are applied during installation and to prevent light escaping from the core, a comprehensive manufacturing cable process takes place. A cross section of a fiber cable, viewed under a microscope, would reveal several concentric circles, each made with a different material. The core of the fiber cable is made of ultrapure silica with a well-controlled index of refraction. The core is coated with a lower index-of-refraction cladding to keep the optical signal within its core. The cladding is covered with a buffer coating, and this is enclosed with braided Kevlar to add strength. The latter is wrapped with a plastic jacket. The final cable product looks like a thin common copper cable.

Optical fiber cables are *multimode* or *single mode*. The core diameter of the multimode fiber is 50 or 62.5 μm and of the single mode is about 9 μm. Adding cladding to the core increases the diameter to 125 μm.

Fiber cable is handled differently than wire cable. For example, unlike copper it can be bent with large bending radii. Two fiber cables are not coupled by soldering or twisting together, as done with copper cables. Instead, the fiber ends are polished with specialized tools and specialized connectors are mounted at both ends of the cables. Coupling is made with mating connectors that self-align two fiber cores with extreme precision so that light passing through a connector travels from one fiber to the other with very little and predictable optical power loss, measured in decibels.

5.4   OPTICAL AMPLIFIER

An optical signal propagating in a fiber will be attenuated. As such, the optical signal must be amplified to compensate for losses in the fiber. Amplifying optical signals is a multistep process. Typically, the optical signal is converted to an electronic signal, then it is amplified, and then it is converted back to optical. This function is known as *regeneration,* and it is relatively expensive. Over the span of a fiber link, several regenerators may exist. However, when a regenerator in the link fails, the transmission is interrupted. A system must be able to detect the failure and identify the failed regenerator and in which direction. Consequently, this failure and detection requirement adds a level of complexity to optical communication systems.

Another technique to amplify an optical signal is to use an all-optical-fiber amplifier (OFA). An OFA, in principle, consists of a fiber segment (about 70 m long) doped with erbium (a rare earth) and pumped with light of a wavelength at 980 or 1480 nm. This pumping process excites the erbium atoms in the fiber. When the optical signal, with a wavelength in the range of 1530–1565 nm passes through the fiber, it causes the excited erbium atoms to yield photons of the same wavelength with the signal. This is known as *stimulated emission,* and the result is more photons out than photons in and, thus, an amplified optical signal. Optical fiber amplifiers doped with erbium are also known as erbium-doped fiber amplifiers (EDFAs).

However, excited erbium atoms may spontaneously emit photons even though no optical signal is present. Clearly, this is an undesirable effect, which is minimized with optical components known as *isolators.* Presently, the overall gain of OFAs is in the range of 30 dB with an output power of approximately 10 mW. Better OFAs (shorter wavelength, more gain, and more power) are expected in the near future.

Amplifiers are of three types: single-wavelength digital amplifiers, multiwavelength (or multichannel) digital amplifiers, and amplifiers for analog applications such as CATV. New EDFAs with uniform gain over an 80-nm range, from 1525 to beyond 1565 nm, can support 100 wavelength channels at 100-GHz spacing that makes DWDM technology possible.

EXERCISES

1. How many different fiber modes are there? Comment on the thickness of their core.
2. What is the difference between a regenerator and an optical amplifier?

Answers

1. Two, single mode and multimode.
2. A regeneration converts an optical signal to electronic; it amplifies the signal and converts it back to optical. An optical amplifier amplifies the optical signal directly.

CHAPTER **6**

SONET/SDH NETWORKS

6.1 THE SONET/SDH NETWORK

The SONET/SDH network consists of nodes or network elements (NEs) that are interconnected with fiber cable over which user and network information is transmitted. Information is formatted to comply with one of the standard bit rates and formats, as recommended by the standards bodies (Figure 6.1).

SONET NEs may receive signals from a variety of facilities such as DS1, DS3, ATM, Internet, and LAN/MAN/WAN. They also may receive signals from a variety of network topologies such as rings or trees, for example a LAN at 10 Mbps, 100 Mbps, or higher bit rates. However, SONET NEs must have a proper interface to convert (or emulate) the incoming data format into the SONET format. In subsequent sections we will see how this is done.

In addition, SDH signals may also be connected with a (U.S.) SONET and vice versa. In this case, circuitry translates specific SDH information into its SONET equivalent, and vice versa.

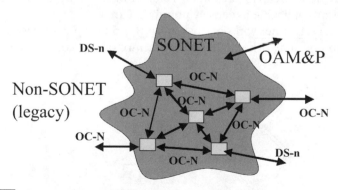

☐ **Network Element (DCS, ADM, Switch, etc.)**

Figure 6.1 SONET network.

41

6.2 NETWORK TOPOLOGIES

In general, networks fall into three topologies: tree, ring, and mesh (Figure 6.2). Each topology has its own benefits and limitations as different networks have different requirements.

The *tree* topology is a hierarchical distribution of NEs and is mostly used in LANs, such as Ethernet. A source is connected to a distribution function, known as a hub, that routes a source packet to its destination node. Typically, a connection between the source and a destination is established for the duration of the packet through the hub. This implies that if another end terminal attempts to communicate with another terminal or with the source, it may not get through, depending on whether the hub is busy or not. Thus, this network is very efficient for asynchronous data transmission but not for real-time data and voice. In addition, if the hub fails, so does any connectivity through it.

The *ring* topology consists of NEs interconnected with a dual fiber, the primary and secondary, to form a ring. One or more NEs in the ring may also be assigned the function of communicating with other rings or topologies. When one of the two fibers breaks, the other fiber in the ring is used. This mechanism provides transmission protection and ring restoration capabilities. If both fibers break, then the network is reconfigured, forming a ring using both the primary and secondary. Information flows in all fibers but the broken ones. Thus, the ring topology offers fast path protection and is widely used in LANs or in applications that are within a (relatively) limited radius (campus, town, and high risers).

The *mesh* topology consists of NEs fully interconnected. In this case, when an interconnecting link breaks, the adjacent NE detects the breakage and reroutes the traffic to another NE. This mechanism provides transmission protection and network restoration capabilities. The mesh network also provides disaster avoidance capabilities when a cluster of NEs may fail. The mesh topology is better applicable in densely populated areas.

SONET/SDH networks are based on the ring topology. However, a typical end-to-end network may consist of a mix of topologies: trees, rings, and meshes.

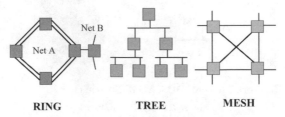

RING   TREE   MESH

Figure 6.2 Ring, tree, and mesh topologies.

6.3   A HIERARCHICAL PROCESS

Any type of non-SONET signal may be transformed into SONET following a *hierarchical* process. From a high-level viewpoint, this process starts with segmenting the signal and mapping the segments in small containers known as *virtual tributaries* (VTs). Once the VTs have been filled with segmented payloads, they are grouped in larger containers that are known as *groups,* and these are mapped in what is called a SONET frame (we will see how this is done in subsequent chapters). Many contiguous frames entail the SONET signal, which is transmitted via an electrical-to-optical transducer, or the optical transmitter, over the OC-N fiber (Figure 6.3).

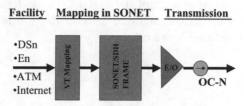

Figure 6.3 SONET hierarchy.

In SDH, the same process follows. However, virtual tributaries are called *tributary units* (*TUs*) and the groups are called *tributary unit groups* (*TUGs*); we will see more of this later.

6.4   BROADBAND SERVICES AND RATES

Each VT (or TU) type or SONET (SDH) frame, although of a different bit capacity, is transmitted within 125 μs. Consequently, the number of bits transmitted per second, or the bit rate, varies. Table 6.1 presents the effective bit rates of VTs (or TU) and the actual STS-N bit rates.

Table 6.1 Broadband Services and Rates

SONET	SDH	Bit Rate (Mbps)	Sample Services
VT1.5		1.728	Voice/high-speed digital services
VT2		2.304	High-capacity digital services
VT3		3.456	
VT6		6.912	
STS-1	STM-0	51.840	
STS-3	STM-1	155.520	SMDS, Broadband-ATM, High-definition TV (HDTV)
STS-12	STM-4	622.080	Uncompressed Extended Quality TV
STS-48	STM-16	2488.320	Uncompressed HDTV
STS-192	STM-64	9953.280	

6.5   PATH, LINE, AND SECTION

A SONET/SDH frame is transmitted from an end user through one or more nodes in the network to eventually reach another end user. As information moves from node to node, certain operations take place to assure the deliverability and integrity of the signal. This means that additional information (bits), or *overhead* bits, must be added to the sending signal to be used for network administration purposes. This is equivalent to a letter that has an address on it, and is packed in a post office bag on which additional information (a label) is added; this bag may also be enclosed in a larger container with more labels on it. This overhead information is *transparent* to the end user; that is, it is not delivered as the tags are not delivered with the letter. In addition, the overhead has been organized hierarchically in the following administrative sectional responsibilities (Figure 6.4):

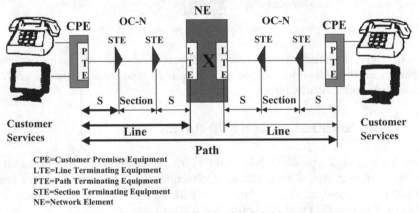

CPE=Customer Premises Equipment
LTE=Line Terminating Equipment
PTE=Path Terminating Equipment
STE=Section Terminating Equipment
NE=Network Element

Figure 6.4 Path/line/section definitions.

1 The *path* deals with overhead added at transmitting path-terminating equipment (PTE), and it is read by the receiving PTE. Path information is not checked or altered by intermediate equipment.

2 The *line* deals with overhead added by the transmitting line-terminating equipment (LTE) to be used by the receiving LTE. At the edges of the network, where there are no LTEs, PTEs play the role of LTEs.

3 The *section* deals with overhead added by equipment terminating a physical segment of the transmission facility. Thus, a segment between two repeaters, or an LTE and a repeater, or an PTE and a repeater, or an LTE and an LTE without repeaters, is also a section. In the following we will see more of this.

Figure 6.5 indicates that a line is also defined between two LTEs with STEs in between.

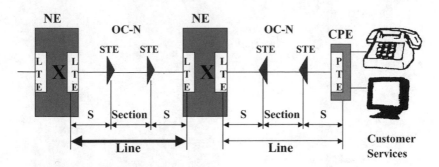

CPE=Customer Premises Equipment
LTE=Line Terminating Equipment
PTE=Path Terminating Equipment
STE=Section Terminating Equipment
NE=Network Element

Figure 6.5 Line/section definitions.

EXERCISES

1. Review the types of topologies. On which topology are SONET networks based?
2. What are virtual tributaries and tributary units?
3. Review STS-N bit rates.
4. What is a path? What is a line? What is a section?

CHAPTER 7

SONET/SDH FRAMES

7.1 STS-1

The smallest SONET frame is visualized as a two-dimensional matrix of 9-row-by-90-column bytes. In SONET, this is known as an *STS-1 frame* (Figure 7.1). Although an STS-1 frame contains 810 bytes, not all are usable by the end user. The first 3 columns of the STS-1 frame contain the *transport overhead,* which is overhead pertaining to section and line.

The byte capacity contained from the fourth column (included) to the last is called a *synchronous payload envelope* (*SPE*). The fourth column of the STS-1 frame (or the first of the SPE) contains *path overhead* information. Two columns in the SPE (columns 30 and 59 of the STS-1), known as *fixed stuff,* do not contain any information.

The actual *payload capacity* is obtained from the space SPE by subtracting 3 columns, the path and the two fixed-stuff columns. That is, a total of 84 columns (or 756 bytes) are used for payload, or 48.384 Mbps effective bit rate.

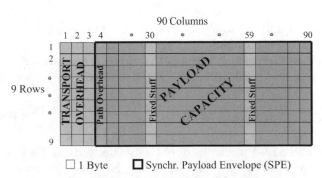

□ 1 Byte   ■ Synchr. Payload Envelope (SPE)

Figure 7.1 SONET STS-1 frame structure.

Based on the above STS-1 description, certain numbers of importance are:

- The SPE consists of 87 columns and 9 rows, or *783 bytes.*
- The first column (9 bytes) of the SPE is allocated for the STS path overhead.
- Columns 30 and 59, known as fixed stuff, do not contain any actual payload. The *756 bytes* in the 84 columns are designated as the STS-1 payload capacity.

7.2   SDH AU-3

SDH does not specify a frame similar to SONET STS-1 (Figure 7.2). However, it specifies a payload container as small as the SONET SPE. The smallest SDH payload container is visualized as a two-dimensional matrix of 9 rows by 87 columns. This is known as *virtual container 3 (VC-3)*. The VC-3 also contains a column for path overhead, called the VC-3 path overhead (VC-3 POH), and two fixed-stuff columns. Thus, the actual payload capacity in a VC-3 is 84 columns (or 756 bytes), similar to the SONET case.

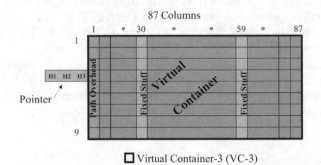

□ Virtual Container-3 (VC-3)

Figure 7.2 SDH AU-3 frame structure.

At the VC-3 and in the fourth row, three additional bytes are added for the VC-3 pointer (H1, H2, and H3). The end result, VC-3 and the pointer, comprises the *administrative unit level 3 (AU-3)*. When three such AU-3's are byte multiplexed, the end result will be the *administrative unit group (AUG)*.

7.3   TRANSMITTING AN STS-1

Consider that an STS-1 frame needs to be transmitted one bit at a time over a transmitting (optical) facility. The question is: How is this done?

Simply, one starts with the most significant bit of the byte in column 1, row

1; then when the byte is serially transmitted, it continues with the byte in column 2, row 1; and so on. At the end of the row, the process continues with row 2, and so on, until all nine rows have been transmitted, the complete frame, or 6480 bits, within 125 μs (Figure 7.3). Multiplying 6480 bits per frame by 8000 frames per second, one obtains the OC-1 rate of 51.84 Mbps.

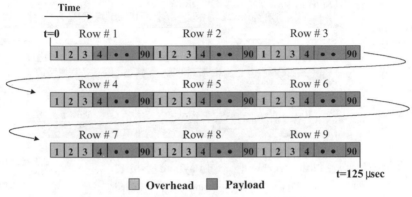

Figure 7.3 SONET STS-1 frame: unfolded.

7.4   FLOATING FRAMES

As said earlier, the SPE is the payload that contains path information and user data. Therefore, when a frame, e.g., STS-1, with overhead (line and section) and SPE is received by a node, the beginning of the frame is not necessarily synchronous with the beginning of the frame that the receiving node generates (Figure 7.4). Moreover, the receiving node may need additional time to process the overhead information, which has nothing to do with user data. If the SPE would have to wait at each node to be resynchronized and also for overhead processing to take place, then it would suffer added delays. In transmission networks, it is of highest importance to minimize and not to prolong delays. Therefore, a method is required to map the SPE in an STS-1 frame with the minimum possible delay. This is accomplished with the floating SPE technique.

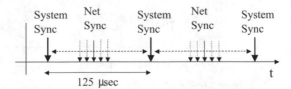

Figure 7.4 Synchronization between system and incoming signal.

Similarly, in order that we can visualize how the floating SPE is mapped in a SONET frame, consider that a received SPE is folding rowwise for all nine rows (Figure 7.5).

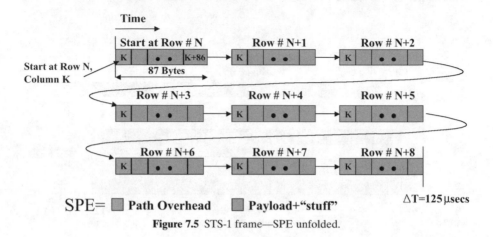

Figure 7.5 STS-1 frame—SPE unfolded.

Having constructed the received SPE, it may be out of phase (in increments of bytes) with the beginning of the STS-1 frame, which is in synchronization with the NE. This out of phase may be viewed as an offset in the STS-1 frame, in terms of columns and rows (Figure 7.6). Thus, the first byte of the receiving SPE (this byte is the first byte of the path overhead) is mapped in the SPE of the current STS-1 frame, say row N and column K.

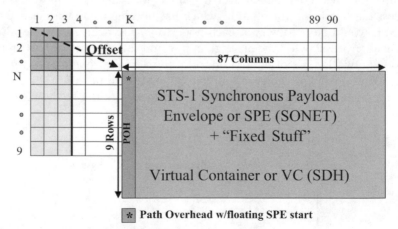

Figure 7.6 SONET STS-1 with floating SPE.

As the SPE is mapped byte after byte starting with row *N* and column *K,* eventually the last byte of the row will be reached (Figure 7.7). Then, the received SPE is wrapped around the STS-1 SPE space. Doing so, the STS-1 SPE space will be filled, the path overhead of the received SPE will be aligned in the *K*th column, but not all bytes of the received SPE will be able to fit in the SPE space of the current STS-1 frame. However, the process does NOT stop but continues in the next STS-1 frame.

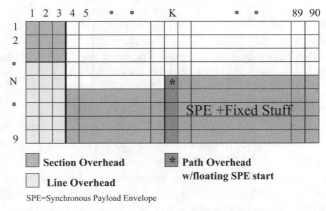

Figure 7.7 Mapping a floating (partial) SPE in an STS-1 frame.

Mapping the received SPE in the next STS-1 frame does not create any time conflicts since both STS-1 and SPEs are synchronous with the 125-μs interval (recall we had said that the 8-kHz clock is an important frequency in communications systems). The end result will be an SPE mapped over two consecutive frames (Figure 7.8).

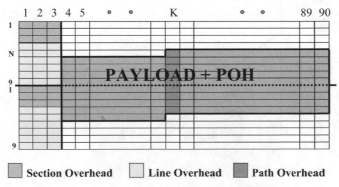

Figure 7.8 Mapping a floating (complete) SPE in STS-1.

7.5   OVERHEAD DEFINITION

7.5.1   Section Overhead: SONET

The first three rows of the overhead space in an STS-1 frame, a total of 9 bytes, carry *synchronization* and *section* overhead information (Figure 7.9).

The first two bytes of an STS-1 frame contain a fixed pattern, known as A1 and A2. This pattern, 0xF628, or in binary 1111 0110 0010 1000, is used by the receiver to detect the beginning of the frame and thus synchronize with it.

The remaining 7 bytes in this overhead section are:

- A1 and A2 contain a fixed framing pattern and are set at the hexadecimal value 0xF628 {1111 0110 0010 1000}. A1 and A2 are NOT scrambled.
- C1 is the STS-1 ID and is defined for each STS-1.
- B1 is a byte used for error monitoring. It is calculated using even parity over all bytes of the previous frame after scrambling and it is placed in the current frame before scrambling.
- E1 is a 64-Kbps voice communication channel for craft personnel. In an STS-N signal (where N STS-1's are byte multiplexed), E1 is defined for the first STS-1 only. The other $N - 1$ E1's are not used.
- F1 is used by the section.

D1 to D3 constitute a 192-Kbps communication channel between STEs. This channel is used for alarms, maintenance, control, monitoring, administration, and other communication needs. In an STS-N signal, this channel is defined for the first STS-1 only. The other $N - 1$ channels are not used.

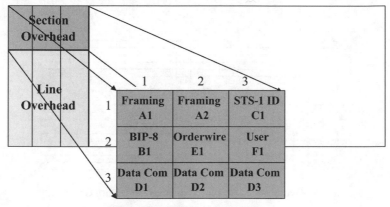

Figure 7.9 STS-1 section overhead.

7.5.2   Line Overhead: SONET

The remaining rows in the overhead space of an STS-1 frame, rows 4–9, or a total of 45 bytes, carry the *line* overhead information (Figure 7.10). These bytes are defined as follows:

- H1 and H2 define the offset between the pointer and first SPE byte.
- H3 defines an action byte for frequency justification purposes. It carries valid payload if the justification is negative.
- BIP-8 is used for locating errors. It is calculated using even parity over the STS-1 of the previous frame after scrambling and is placed in B2 before scrambling the current frame.
- K1 and K2 are used for automatic protection switching; in STS-N this is defined for #1 only (i.e., for the first STS-1 in the STS-N signal).
- D4 to D12 constitute a 576-Kbps communication channel between line termination equipment (LTE) for alarms, maintenance, control, monitoring, administration, and other communication needs; in STS-N this is defined for #1 only.
- Z1 and Z2 are not defined; in STS-N this is defined for #3. Z2 is only defined as line far-end block error (FEBE).
- E2 is an express 64-Kbps communications channel between LTE; in STS-N this is defined for #1 only.

7.5.3   Section Overhead: SDH

The SDH overhead has some small differences in nomenclature. The first three rows of the overhead space are called the regenerator section overhead (RSOH), the fourth row is called the administrative unit pointer, and the remaining five rows are called the multiplex section overhead (MSOH). See Section 9.9 for the definition of SDH overhead bytes.

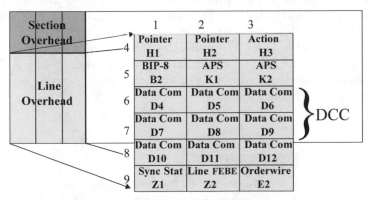

Figure 7.10 STS-1 line overhead.

The first 2 bytes of the RSOH contain a fixed pattern, known as A1 and A2 (as in SONET). This pattern, 0xF628, or in binary 1111 0110 0010 1000, is used by the receiver to detect the beginning of the frame.

7.6   PAYLOAD POINTERS

The two pointers, bytes H1 and H2, contain the actual pointer value (Figure 7.11). However, bytes H1 and H2 contain much more information than a value.

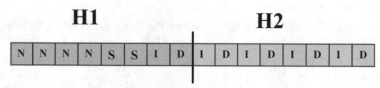

Figure 7.11 Payload pointers—H1 and H2.

The first 4 most significant bits in the H1 byte are known as the new data found (NDF) flag. The NDF may be "normal = 0110" or "set = 1001." When "normal," then one of three conditions may exist: no frequency justification, positive frequency justification has taken place, or negative frequency justification has taken place. "Set" indicates that an arbitrary (and significant) change of the pointer value has occurred due to a change of data position in the SPE.

The next 2 bits are known as the S-bits and indicate the size of the virtual tributary in the payload.

The last 2 least significant bits of the H1 and the 8 bits of the H2 define two bit-alternating 5-bit words. The one is the I-bit word and the other the D-bit word. The I and D are used for incrementing or decrementing the offset and thus, in conjunction with the H3 byte, perform frequency corrections or *frequency justifications.*

Although pointer bytes H1 and H2 define an offset value, the third pointer, byte H3, does not contain an actual pointer value (Figure 7.12). It is merely used as a payload byte opportunity buffer when positive or negative justifications are necessary.

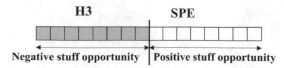

Figure 7.12 Pointer H3—frequency justification.

The function of the H1, H2, and H3 bytes is threefold:

1 Identifies that a change has occurred in the pointer value (NDF = 1001) due to an intermittent synchronization change in the node and where the new start is (I + D bits).

2 Identifies that a change may have occurred in the pointer value (0110) due to a frequency difference between node and incoming frequency. It is possible that the received frequency may be slightly higher or lower than the node frequency. As a result, either more or fewer bits are received than what the SPE can fit. In either case, a periodic resynchronization of the received SPE and STS-1 SPE should take place. If the received frequency is higher, then *negative* frequency justification is required, and if lower, then *positive*.

3 The bits that contain the pointer value, I and D, indicate whether negative or positive frequency justification is necessary.

7.7 FREQUENCY JUSTIFICATION

When the frame rate of the STS SPE is the same as the transport overhead (OH; i.e., NE frame rate), the alignment of the SPE is the same as in the previous frame. This is known as *no justification.* Then, the pointer H1, H2 increments and decrement bits I and D are not inverted and NDF = 0110. In this case, a pointer value of zero would indicate that the first byte of the data is located next to the H3 byte. A value = 10 would indicate that the first byte starts on the 11th byte after H3.

When the frame rate of the STS SPE is less than the transport OH (i.e., NE frame rate), the alignment of the SPE is slipped back by a byte. This is known as *positive justification.* Then, the pointer H1, H2 increments and the *I-bits are inverted.* The NDF still remains 0110.

When the frame rate of the STS SPE is higher than the transport OH (i.e., NE), the alignment of the SPE is advanced by a byte. This is known as *negative justification.* Then, the pointer H1, H2 decrements and *D-bits are inverted.* The NDF still remains 0110.

7.7.1 No Justification

EXAMPLE

Consider that the H1, H2, and H3 bytes are as in Figure 7.13. In this case, the H1 and H2 contain a NDF value of 0110, indicating that no change in the pointer has occurred:

The I- and D-bits have not been inverted, indicating no justification.

The I, D value is (in this example) set to 00 0010 1001 = 41.

The H3 byte is 00000000.   ■

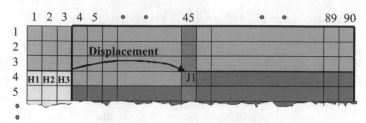

Figure 7.13 STS-1—no-frequency justification.

7.7.2   Positive Justification

EXAMPLE

Consider that the H1, H2, and H3 bytes are as in Figure 7.14. In this case, the H1 and H2 contain a NDF value set at 0110, indicating that no change in the pointer has occurred due to a payload change:

The I-bits have been inverted, indicating positive justification.

The I, D value (after restoring the I-bits) is 00 0010 1010 = 40.

The first byte in the SPE, the byte next to H3, contains zero (i.e., no user payload). The next frame has a pointer value with a noninverted H1, H2 value.

Note: Positive justification is recognized quickly by examining the bit next to the least significant bit (LSB) of the H1 byte (if 1 = positive, if 0 = negative, WHY?)   ■

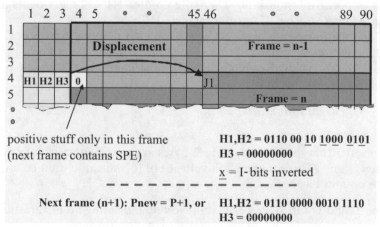

Figure 7.14 STS-1—positive-frequency justification.

7.7.3 Negative Justification

EXAMPLE

Consider that the H1, H2, and H3 bytes are as in Figure 7.15. In this case, the H1 byte contains an NDF value set at 0110, indicating that no change in the pointer has occurred due to a payload change:

The D-bits have been inverted, indicating negative justification.
The I, D value (after restoring the D-bits) is 00 0010 1000 = 40.
The H3 byte contains user payload, in the current frame.

The next frame has a pointer value with a noninverted H1, H2 value and the H3 byte does not contain any user payload (that is, one byte adjustment, positive or negative is only made).   ■

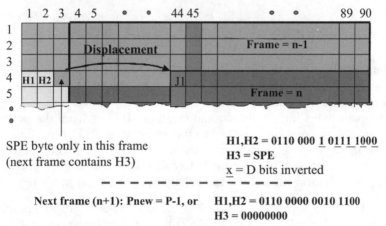

SPE byte only in this frame
(next frame contains H3)

H1,H2 = 0110 000 $\underline{1}$ 0$\underline{1}$11 $\underline{1}$000
H3 = SPE
$\underline{x}$ = D bits inverted

- - - - - - - - - - - - -

Next frame (n+1): Pnew = P-1, or   H1,H2 = 0110 0000 0010 1100
H3 = 00000000

Figure 7.15 STS-1—negative-frequency justification.

7.8 NEW DATA FOUND FLAG

EXAMPLE

Consider that the N bits in the H1 are set at the value 1001. This indicates that a resynchronization has taken place, not because of a positive or negative-frequency justification but because of some system or payload-type change (Figure 7.16).

The I- and D-bits are not inverted. In this case, the NDF value of 1001 and the new pointer value in H1 and H2 must be received three consecutive times for the old pointer value to be replaced.

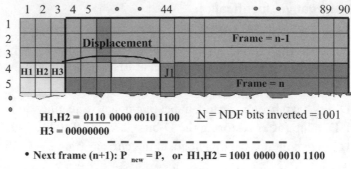

H1,H2 = <u>0110</u> 0000 0010 1100   <u>N</u> = NDF bits inverted =1001
H3 = 00000000

- - - - - - - - - - - - - - -

- **Next frame (n+1): P $_{new}$ = P, or H1,H2 = 1001 0000 0010 1100**

Figure 7.16 STS-1—new data found.

In a different case (not discussed yet), known as *concatenation indication,* the NDF has the value 1001 and the I- and D-bits are set to 11 1111 1111. ∎

7.9   PATH OVERHEAD

As mentioned earlier, the first column of the SPE (9 bytes) is dedicated to path overhead information. Figures 7.17a and b describe the meaning of each byte for the SONET and for the SDH cases.

The path bytes have a directional meaning. That is, from the originating path-terminating equipment (PTE) to the terminating PTE, or vice versa. For example, the byte G1 is used by the destination PTE to indicate the path status to the originating PTE. The list below identifies the path overhead bytes, starting from the top (first row), and briefly describes their meaning:

The first byte, known as the trace byte, or J1, is user programmable. The receiving PTE collects 64 repeating J1 bytes to verify the connectivity with the transmitting PTE. Its default value is 0×00.

The second byte, known as the BIP-8, or B3, is used for error control. The B3 is calculated over all bits of the previous SPE and before scrambling.

The third byte, known as the signal label, or C2, indicates the construction of SPE, that is, asynchronous mapping, ATM, etc.

The fourth byte, known as the path status, or G1, indicates to the originating PTE the status and performance of the terminating PTE.

The fifth byte, known as the user channel, or F2, is allocated for end-user communication purposes.

The sixth byte, known as the multiframe, or H4, is used as an end-to-end generalized multiframe indicator for payloads (a pointer).

The remaining bytes, from seventh to ninth, known as the user bytes, or Z3, Z4, and Z5, are reserved for future use and have no defined values.

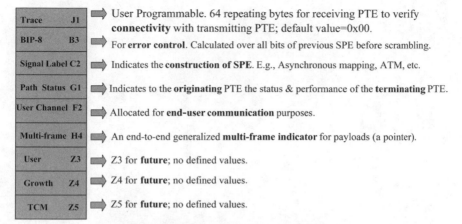

Figure 7.17a SONET STS-1—path overhead.

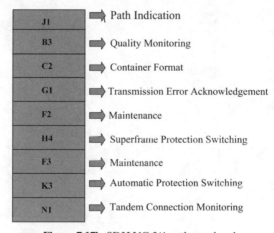

Figure 7.17b SDH VC-3/4 path overhead.

EXERCISES

1. Review the STS-1 frame.
2. Calculate the effective bit rate of any overhead byte in a SONET STS-1 and in an SDH STM-1 signal.
3. Review line overhead bytes.
4. Review frequency justification. What may cause negative justification?
5. Review the path overhead.
6. The path overhead consists of one column. Calculate its bit rate in an STS-3 signal.

CHAPTER 8

VIRTUAL TRIBUTARIES

We have indicated that virtual tributaries (VTs) are small containers that are used to transport user payloads. In SDH, these small containers are called virtual containers (VCs).

Assume that VTs are small containers of certain predetermined capacities and that several of these VTs arrive within a 125-ms interval.

Consider trucks of certain larger predetermined capacities such that a specific number of VTs can fit in them (Figure 8.1). These trucks as moving continuously, each truck every 125 μs. As VT containers arrive, they are stored in the truck; an overhead container is also packed with them in each truck, and the truck departs.

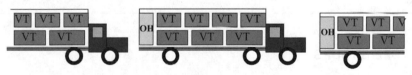

Figure 8.1 VTs—What are they?

The above parallelism is a very simplistic view that does not explain the floating SPE; with a little imagination, this can also be visualized, as already illustrated.

8.1 VT CAPACITIES

VTs come in certain predetermined capacities. A VT with a 3-column capacity, or a total of 27 bytes, is known as a VT1.5 (Figure 8.2). A VT with a 4-column capacity, or a total of 36 bytes, is known as a VT2. A VT with a 6-column capacity, or a total of 54 bytes, is known as a VT3, and a VT with a 12-column capacity, or a total of 108 bytes, is known as a VT6.

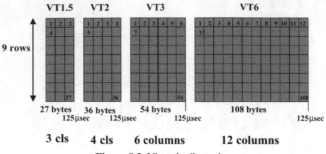

Figure 8.2 Virtual tributaries.

In SDH, a VT1.5 is called a TU-11, a VT2 is called a TU-12, and a VT6 is called a TU-2.

Table 8.1 lists details of all VTs. As an exercise, you are encouraged to verify some of the VT payload rates in the last column.

Table 8.1 Virtual Tributaries and Payload Rates

VT Type	Columna/VT	Bytes/VT	VTs/Group	VTs/SPE	VT Payload Rate (Mbps)
VT1.5	3	27	4	28	1.728
VT2	4	36	3	21	2.304
VT3	6	54	2	14	3.456
VT6	12	108	1	7	6.912

8.2 SPE GROUPS

Now that the VTs have been defined, let us examine how they fit in the SPE. An STS-1 SPE consists of 87 columns (including the path overhead and the 2 stuff columns). The payload capacity, which consists of 84 columns (87 minus the path overhead and the 2 stuff columns), is partitioned in seven groups, each group of 12 columns (Figure 8.3). The number 12 is not magic; it is simply divisible by 3, 4, 6, and 12. This means that exactly four VT1.5's, or three VT2's, or two VT3's or one VT6 fit in a group. Thus, in an STS-1 SPE with seven groups, one can easily calculate how many VT1.5's may fit in it (the answer is $7 \times 4 = 28$).

A very important property of the above is that the seven groups can have a variety of VTs. However, the restriction is that *each group can only have one type of VTs*. This means that although the SPE can transport several types of VTs, each group transports one type only.

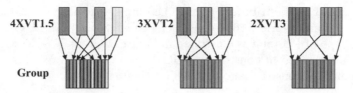

Figure 8.3 SONET—VTs and group structures tributaries.

The above general structure is also valid for SDH, with the exception of the nomenclature. Thus, in SDH one has TUs. That is, a TU-11 has three columns, a TU-12 has four columns, and a TU-2 has 12 columns. There are seven groups, each of 12 columns, called the tributary unit group 2 (TUG-2). When seven TUG-2's are byte multiplexed and two (fixed-stuff) columns are attached to the front of it, one obtains a TUG-3. However, when the seven TUG-2's are byte multiplexed and one path overhead column is attached to the front of it, one obtains a virtual container level 3 (VC-3).

Although we have discussed that a STS-1 SPE is partitioned in seven groups, we have not discussed where in the SPE these groups are. In general, as the VTs are filled with user data, they are byte (or column) interleaved to construct a group. Since each group can have only one type of VT, then as illustrated in Figure 8.3, four VT1.5's are byte (or column) interleaved to construct a group. In a different case, three VT2's would, similarly, construct another group, and so on.

When all seven groups have been constructed, the seven groups are byte (or column) interleaved (Figure 8.4). Notice that during this column interleaving process, the two columns for stuff and one column for the path overhead are also interleaved to construct the SPE. The end result is shown in the next column.

Although we have discussed that a STS-1 SPE is partitioned in seven groups, we have not discussed where in the SPE these groups are.

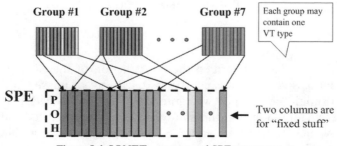

Figure 8.4 SONET—groups and SPE structures.

In general, as the tributary units (TUs) are filled with user data, they are byte (or column) interleaved to construct TUG-2. Since each TUG-2 can have only one type of TU, then as illustrated in Figure 8.4, four TU-11's are byte (or column) interleaved to construct a TUG-2. In a different case, three TU-12's would, similarly, construct another TUG-2 (Figure 8.5).

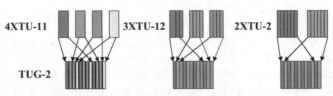

Figure 8.5 SDH—TU and TUG structures.

When all seven groups have been constructed, the seven groups are byte (or column) interleaved. Notice that during this column-interleaving process, the two columns for fixed stuff are added to produce a TUG-3 (Figure 8.6).

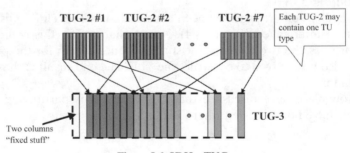

Figure 8.6 SDH—TUGs.

Now that we have described the construction of the SPE (Figure 8.7), imagine that as soon as this is constructed, it is out of phase with the STS-1 frame and should be mapped with minimal delay in a SONET/SDH frame. One can easily envision that the end result is as already discussed, an offset SPE positive/negative justified in the STS-1 SPE space with a pointer identifying the justification and its location.

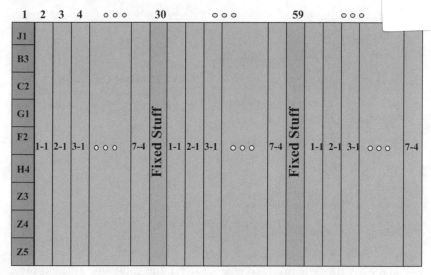

Figure 8.7 VT1.5 mapping in SPE.

8.3 VT SUPERFRAME

As described, an STS-1 frame pointer (bytes H1, H2, and H3) points to the beginning of the floating SPE and provides a mechanism to compensate for frequency differences.

VTs map data from different end users in the SPE payload. As such, end-user data may also be out of phase with each other and to the STS-N frame, and their bit rates may be a little faster or slower. Consequently, a pointer mechanism and a frequency justification mechanism must exist on the VT level, similar to the SPE level.

Consider that each VT is partitioned in a 1-byte *VT overhead* part (V1–V4) and in a *VT envelope capacity* part (Figure 8.8). Clearly, each VT type has a different envelope capacity, depending on the type of VT. For example, a VT1.5 has 26 bytes, whereas a VT6 has 107 bytes envelope capacity; see Table 8.1. Four consecutive VTs (from four consecutive STS-1 frames) that contain data from a single user form a VT superframe. The beginning of the superframe (byte overhead V1) is indicated by the multiframe indication byte H4 in the path overhead of the SPE, that is, by another pointer.

Payloads below DS3 rates are mapped in and transported by VT structures. The H4 byte in the SPE path overhead is used to indicate the phase of V1–V4 (bits B7 and B8) and also 6-, 16-, or 24-frame superframe indication (bits B1 and B2, or B3 and B4, or B5 and B6).

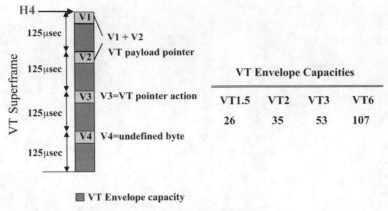

Figure 8.8 VT superframe.

To comply with Bellcore (AR-253-CORE), the following rules apply:

- X is set to 1, or
- bits B1 and B2 count from 00 through 11 over 24 frames (00 for 6 frames, then 01 for the next 6 frames, and so on), or
- B3 and B4 count from 00 through 01 over 6 frames and then repeat, or
- B5 and B6 count from 00 through 11 over 16 frames and then repeat the counting process.

Figure 8.9 shows the bit value of byte H4 that corresponds to the V1–V4 phase.

H4 Byte 1 2 3 4 5 6 7 8	V1 - V4
X X X X X X 0 0	V1
X X X X X X 0 1	V2
X X X X X X 1 0	V4
X X X X X X 1 1	V5

Figure 8.9 VT superframe—H4 byte.

8.4   VT PAYLOAD POINTER

The VT payload pointer is analogous to the STS payload pointer. It provides a mechanism for flexible and dynamic alignment of the VT envelope within the VT superframe.

The VT pointer consists of the two consecutive bytes (V1 and V2) that are viewed as one word, although they are obtained in 250 μs. As we look at the

V1 and V2 word, we notice that the first 4 bits are again called N, the next two bits define the VT size and the remaining 10 bits are the I and D.

Figure 8.10 illustrates the bit definition of the two bytes, V1 and V2.

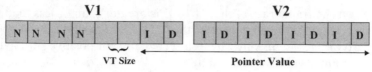

Figure 8.10 VT payload pointer.

The N-bits indicate whether a new data flag occurred or not. The next 2 bits indicate the VT size, as in Figure 8.11.

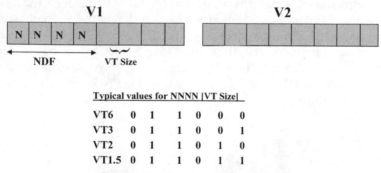

Typical values for NNNN [VT Size]

VT6	0	1	1	0	0	0
VT3	0	1	1	0	0	1
VT2	0	1	1	0	1	0
VT1.5	0	1	1	0	1	1

Figure 8.11 VT payload pointer—NDF.

The five I- and five D-bits point to the beginning of the user frame in the VT superframe and whether a positive, negative, or no frequency justification should be made (Figure 8.12).

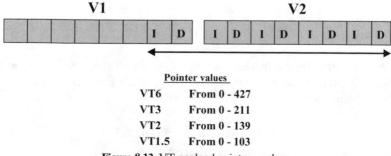

Pointer values

VT6	From 0 - 427
VT3	From 0 - 211
VT2	From 0 - 139
VT1.5	From 0 - 103

Figure 8.12 VT payload pointer—values.

Slipping by a byte forward or back in time the VT envelope, similar to the STS SPE, makes the frequency adjustment.

The pointer increment or decrement is indicated by inverting the I- or D-bits, respectively:

- When the frame rate of the VT SPE is greater than or less than that of the STS SPE, the alignment of the VT SPE is periodically slipped forward or back in time by 1 byte shift (negative or positive stuff byte) and the pointer value is adjusted by 1.
- A pointer increment is indicated by inverting the I-bits.
- A pointer decrement is indicated by inverting the D-bits.

8.5   VT OVERHEAD

Having defined the VT superframe, its pointer, the VT overhead, the envelope capacity, and frequency justification, we further define the VT path overhead (POH) byte as the first byte in the envelope. This byte has a different meaning in each frame of a superframe. Over a period of 500 μs, or four frames, the four overhead bytes are V5, J2, Z6, and Z7 (Figure 8.13). The remaining bytes in a VT are user payload. For a VT1.5 the user payload is 25 bytes, whereas for a VT6 it is 106, see Table 8.1.

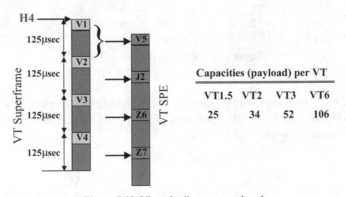

Figure 8.13 Virtual tributary overhead.

Each VT envelope contains four bytes of VT POH (V5, J2, Z6, and Z7); see Figure 8.14. The remaining bytes constitute the VT payload capacity, which is different for each VT type.

	BIP-2	REI-V	RFI-V	Signal Label			RDI-V
V5:	1	2	3	4	5	6	7	8

Figure 8.14 Virtual tributary path overhead.

The first POH byte in the VT superframe, the V5, is used for error checking as a signal label and to indicate the signal status. The meaning of each bit is defined as follows:

- BIP-2 (1): Set if parity of all odd-numbered bits of previous VT SPE is even.
- BIP-2 (2): Set if parity of all even-numbered bits of previous VT SPE is even.
- REI-V: VT remote error indication back to originating VT PTE (old FEBE).
- RFI-V: VT path remote failure indication in byte-synchronous DS1 mapping.
- Signal label: Indicates content of the VT SPE.
- RDI-V: VT path remote defect indication.

8.6 APPLICATION: DS0 BYTE-SYNCHRONOUS MAPPING FOR DS1

As described, in a DS1 frame there are 24 time slots (bytes). Consider the case of mapping these 24 bytes in a VT1.5 (Figure 8.15). Since the user payload in a VT1.5 consists of 25 bytes, the first byte of the 25 is used to indicate (see above):

- The phase of the signaling and the frame bits (bits P0 and P1)
- Signaling for the 24 DS0 channels (bits S1–S4)
- The framing bit (bit F)
- A bit not used (or fixed stuff)

The remaining 24 bytes map the 24 bytes of the DS1 frame.

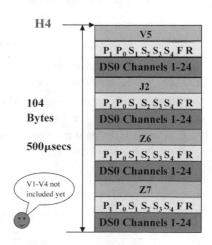

Figure 8.15 VT1.5 DS0 byte-synchronous mapping in DS1.

8.7   APPLICATION: DS0 BYTE-ASYNCHRONOUS MAPPING FOR DS1

As in the byte-synchronous case, a DS1 frame consists of 24 time slots (bytes). Consider the case of mapping them in a VT1.5 (Figure 8.16). Since the user payload in a VT1.5 consists of 25 bytes, the first byte of the 25 is used to indicate (see above):

- Fixed stuff (bits R)
- Information bit (bit I)
- Stuff control bits (bits C1 and C2)
- Overhead bit (bit O)
- Stuff opportunity (bit S)

The remaining 24 bytes in the VT1.5 map the 24 bytes of the DS1 frame.

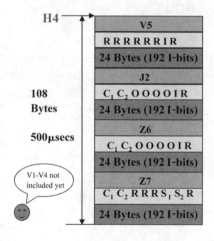

Figure 8.16 VT1.5 DS0 byte-synchronous mapping in DS1.

EXERCISES

1. Calculate the effective bit rate of a VT1.5 in a SONET STS-1 signal.
2. Calculate the effective bit rate of a VT2 in a SONET STS-3 signal.
3. Calculate the rate of a simple group in an STS-3 signal.
4. Calculate the rate of a TU-12 in an STM-1 signal.
5. Can an STM-1 signal transport Ethernet signals and voice signals simultaneously? If yes, how is this accomplished?

Answers

1. $27 \times 8 \times 8000 = 1.728$ Mbps
2. $36 \times 8 \times 8000 = 2.304$ Mbps

3. A simple group repeats every 125 μs. Hence, its rate is 8000 per second.

4. $36 \times 8 \times 8000 = 2.304$ Mbps

5. Ethernet signals and voice signals can be mapped in separate VTs or TUs, which are mapped in groups and then in the STM-1 payload.

CHAPTER 9

STS-N/STM-N FRAMES

9.1 SINGLE-STEP MULTIPLEXER

So far we have discussed the STS-1 SONET frame in some detail. We have also alluded to an STS-N frame. The letter N in the STS-N stands for a number greater than 1, e.g., 3, and hence STS-3. An STS-1 is a subcase of STS-N, where $N = 1$. In actuality, the number N indicates how many STS-1 SPEs are multiplexed into a frame that we call STS-N. Multiplexing is on the byte level.

In general, multiplexing may take place in various stages. A multiplexer may receive N STS-1 SPEs within a time window and then in one single stage to multiplex them to produce an STS-N. This is a *single-step multiplexer* (Figure 9.1).

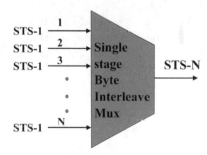

Figure 9.1 STS-N single-stage interleaving.

9.2 TWO-STEP MULTIPLEXER

Alternatively, K STS-1 SPEs may be received and multiplexed in an STS-K and then N/K STS-Ks multiplexed to produce an STS-N. This is a *two-step multiplexer*. Multiplexing is again on the byte level.

In the example illustrated in Figure 9.2, $K = 3$ and $N = 12$, and hence three STS-1's are multiplexed to produce an STS-3 first, and then four STS-3's are multiplexed to produce an STS-12.

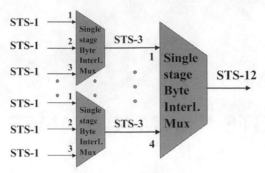

Figure 9.2 STS-N two-stage interleaving.

Two-step multiplexers are more complex compared with single-step multiplexers. Each multiplexing stage produces a certain amount of delay, and therefore, the more steps there are the more the delay and thus the more undesirable it is.

9.3 STS-N FRAME STRUCTURE

An STS-N frame looks like an STS-1 frame where the number of columns is multiplied by N (but not the number of rows); see Figure 9.3. As such, the overhead space is N times the number of columns and similarly the SPE space. Similarly, since each STS-1 SPE has its own path overhead columns, the STS-N SPE will have N path overhead columns.

As an example, an STS-3 frame has a total of $3 \times 90 = 270$ columns by 9 rows, its (line and section) overhead space is $3 \times 3 = 9$ columns by 9 rows, and its SPE is $3 \times 87 = 261$ columns by 9 rows. Its path overhead is 3 columns.

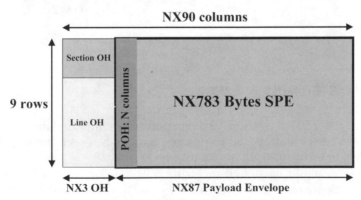

Figure 9.3 STS-N frame structure.

9.4   STS-N FLOATING FRAME

Similar to the STS-1 frame, the component STS-1 SPE in an STS-N frame may be floating. In fact, each component STS-1 SPE may start from a different location in the STS-N SPE (Figure 9.4).

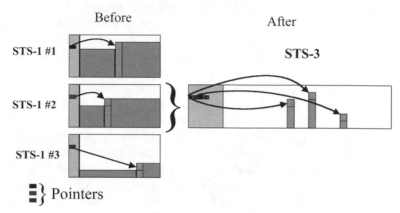

Figure 9.4 STS-N example, $N = 3$.

Q: How are STS-1 SPEs with different offsets mapped in an STS-N?

A: Pointers (H1, H2, H3) for each STS-1 in the STS-N OH locate each STS-1.

This does not present any difficulty because the pointers H1, H2, and H3 for each component STS-1 SPE are still in the STS-N section overhead and each pointer identifies the starting location of its corresponding STS-1 SPE. In fact, each individual H1–H3 is used not only to identify the starting locations of its STS-1 SPE but also to make frequency adjustments, positive, negative, or none.

Q: Is it possible that one or more, but not all, STS-1's (in an STS-N) need frequency justification?

A: Yes. One STS-1 may need positive justification, another negative, and another no justification. The H1–H3 for each STS-1 is used to accomplish individual justifications.

9.5   CONCATENATION OR SUPERRATE

9.5.1   SONET

In the multiplexing scheme previously described, each component STS-1 SPE was arriving from a different source. For example, three STS-1 SPEs from different sources would be multiplexed to fill the SPE space of an STS-3. In particular, because these three SPEs arrive from different sources and because each one may be in different phases with each other and with the node, each requiring its own pointer H1–H3 and frequency justification. One may easily extend this from 3 to N.

Assume that the three received SPEs belong to the same signal (or to the same source) and they arrive in a specific order and in synchronism, which must be maintained throughout the end-to-end path. Therefore, it is important that we distinguish this case and that we handle it carefully so that, as we process the SPEs and pass them through switching elements from node to node, they are not rearranged due to uneven delays and thus change their order. We term these *concatenated SPEs*. Clearly, because concatenated SPEs belong to the same source/signal, there is some redundancy of overhead information (pointers, path overhead, etc). To understand this, consider that three SPEs contain the information of a complete picture (that is, the picture has been split in three segments). The three SPEs are mapped in a known sequence and thus only one overhead pointer is required to point to the first SPE; the remaining pointers contain a fixed code set to a value that means *concatenation indication* (*CI*). In addition, since all three SPEs belong to the same source, only one path overhead column is needed. At the receiving end, in order to reconstruct the picture correctly, all three SPEs must be received in the same order they were transmitted. The STS that transports concatenated SPEs is known as *concatenated STS* and is denoted by the letter c, e.g., STS-Nc.

In the STS-Nc case, since the signal comes from the same source and has the same destination, then instead of N pointers in the section overhead, one needs only one, and instead of N path overhead columns, one needs only one. The easiest way to look at this is if we assume N SPEs but only the first SPE of the N will carry the needed overhead information, whereas the remaining $N - 1$ SPEs will have no useful overhead information in them. Hence, in an STS-3c, three bytes (H1–H3) will have the pointer information and the remaining six will not. Moreover, one column in the SPE will have path overhead information and the remaining two will not, and so on (Figure 9.5). Since not all path overhead columns are needed (but one), it should be possible to utilize the remaining columns and fit more signal bandwidth in the payload. Indeed, this is the case for STS-N, where $N > 3$.

9.5.2   SDH

As in SONET, in SDH we have *contiguous concatenation,* which also allows bit rates in excess of the capacity of the C-4 container. In SDH, too, concatenation implies that the payload should not be split up, and this is accomplished by defining a virtually contiguous container within, for example, an STM-4. Then, the payloads of several consecutive AU-4's are mapped in a fixed order; the first pointer is set to its value and the remaining pointers are set to a fixed CI value. In this case, the VC-4 is identified as a VC-4-4c.

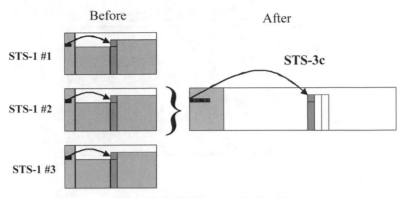

Figure 9.5 STS-Nc example, $N = 3$.

9.5.3 Virtual Concatenation

The above cases assume that the network consists of switching nodes that are able to switch complete STS-3c or VC-4-4c with contiguously concatenated payloads in them. However, depending on the network, some nodes may not be able to do that. For example, the STS-3c may be passed through a node that switches lower order STS-1's. In this case, the STS-3c may be split up in three STS-1's, and each STS-1 will be switched independently. Due to buffering and queuing issues, there is no warranty that the three STS-1 components will be switched in the proper order. Therefore, in this case, it is the responsibility of the network element to reconstruct the three STS-1's back to the original STS-3c. Clearly, the same argument holds for the SDH case.

9.6 STM-N FRAME STRUCTURE

In SDH, an STM-N frame looks like an STS-N frame where the number of columns is multiplied by N (but not the number of rows); see Figure 9.6. As such, the section overhead (SOH) is N times 9 columns, and similarly the payload space is N times 261 columns. Remember that the smallest STM (STM-1) has 270 columns (9 overhead + 261 payload).

In SDH, the first three rows of the first three columns of the SOH are the regenerator section overhead (RSOH), the fourth row is the administrative unit pointer (AUP), and the remaining five rows are the multiplex section overhead (MSOH); see Figure 9.6.

Comparing SDH with SONET overhead, we have SOH versus section overhead, AU pointer versus SPE pointer, and MSOH versus line overhead. In other words, besides nomenclature, the functionality is very similar, with small variations to make them different enough.

In SDH, the construction of an STM-N may be more involved than the SONET case. For a more detailed description, the reader is recommended to

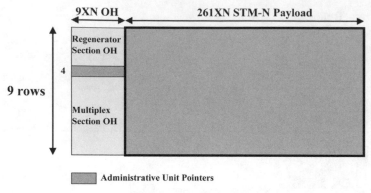

Figure 9.6 STM-N frame structure.

consult the latest version of ITU-T Recommendation G.707. In general, to construct an STM-N frame, one may start with three VC-12's to construct one VC-2, then seven VC-2's to construct one VC-3, three VC-3's to construct one VC-4, and finally, *N* VC-4's to construct one STM-N frame, with appropriate overhead attached.

9.7   STS-NC FRAME STRUCTURE

One item that significantly differs in an STS-Nc payload, as compared with the STS-N case, is the number of path overhead columns in the SPE (in the STS-Nc case only one is needed) and the number of *fixed-stuff* columns. In the STS-Nc case, the number of fixed-stuff columns are calculated by $N/3 - 1$. Thus, an STS-3c contains $3/3 - 1 = 0$, or *no* fixed-stuff columns, whereas an STS-12c contains $12/3 - 1 = 3$ fixed-stuff columns (Figure 9.7). That is, the STS-Nc case frees otherwise dedicated columns and hence allocates more bandwidth for user payload (by reducing the path overhead bandwidth) and thus is more ef-

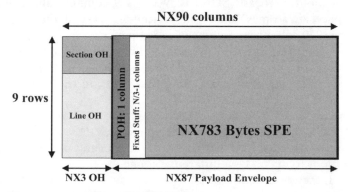

Figure 9.7 STS-Nc frame structure.

ficient. The location of the fixed-stuffed columns (if any) is right after the path overhead in the SPE.

9.8 POINTER PROCESSING

In an STS-Nc, the pointer (H1–H3) of the first STS-1 in the STS-Nc shall perform all pointer processing, the new data flag, and frequency justifications and identify the starting location of the STS-Nc SPE. The pointer bytes of the remaining STS-1's will contain a concatenation indicator value to indicate that the payload is concatenated, that is, it is an STS-Nc case. The concatenation indicator is H1 = 1001XX11 and H2 = 11111111, where XX is undefined.

9.9 TRANSPORT OVERHEAD

In SONET, and in the STS-Nc case, many overhead bytes are redundant. Figure 9.8a illustrates the STS-3c transport overhead bytes (section and line overhead), where X indicates an undefined value. The definition of the valid overhead bytes is as in the STS-1 case. Figure 9.8b depicts the SOH in the SDH case.

The definition of the SOH bytes for the SDH case is as follows:

- A1 and A2 are for frame alignment. They contain the fixed framing pattern set at the hexadecimal value 0xF628 {1111 0110 0010 1000}. A1 and A2 are NOT scrambled.
- B1 and B2 are parity bytes used for quality monitoring (or error monitoring in SONET). The parity is calculated over all bytes of the previous frame *before scrambling* and is placed in the current frame *before scrambling.*
- D1 to D3 are used for network management for the regenerator section. They constitute an 192-Kbps communication channel for alarms, maintenance, control, monitoring, administration, and other needs.
- D4 to D12 are also used for network management as the D1–D3 but for the multiplex section.
- E1 and E2 are a 64-Kbps voice communication channel for craft personnel.
- F1 is a maintenance byte.
- J0 (C1) is known as the trace identifier.
- K1 and K2 are used for automatic protection switching (APS) control.
- S1 is the clock quality indicator.
- M1 is used for transmission error acknowledgment.

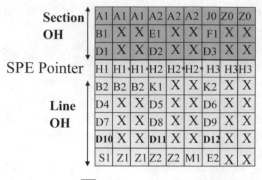

| X | Undefined OH Bytes (all zeroes) |

Figure 9.8a STS-3c transport overhead.

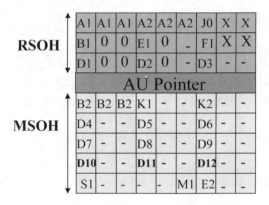

‾ Undefined OH Bytes (all zeroes)

X Reserved for national use

0 Media dependant use (e.g., satellite, radio)

Figure 9.8b STM-1 section overhead.

9.10   SCRAMBLING

When the complete frame has been assembled, the bytes in it are scrambled. Scrambling is performed to assure the receiver that a density of 1's is maintained in the signal. However, the A1, A2, and C1 bytes are not scrambled and the scrambling process begins with the byte right after C1 (Figure 9.9). This applies to both SONET and SDH.

Q: Why are the A1 and A2 bytes not scrambled?

A: The A1 and A2 bytes are not scrambled because as soon as the serial signal is received, A1 and A2 are used to locate the beginning of the frame.

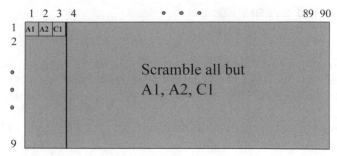

Figure 9.9 Frame scrambled.

9.11   STS-N SCRAMBLER

With respect to the scrambler, the following rules apply:

- The scrambling code is generated by the polynomial $1 + x^6 + x^7$ (SONET and SDH).
- The scrambler is frame synchronous at the line rate (STS-N), and it has a sequence length of 127 bits; that is, its "random" pattern repeats every 127 bits.
- The scrambler is set to 1111111 on the most significant bit (MSB) of the byte following the Nth STS-1 C1 byte (of an STS-N).
- The framing bytes A1, A2 and the C1 from the first STS-1 through the Nth STS-1 are NOT scrambled.
- The scrambler runs continuously throughout the complete STS-N frame.

The above definition and rules for the scrambler applies to both SONET and SDH (see ITU-T Recommendation G.707).

Figure 9.10 illustrates the line rate synchronous scrambler. The clock is at the line rate and the scrambler runs continuously with a pattern periodicity of 127 bits. However, the rules identified earlier should be observed.

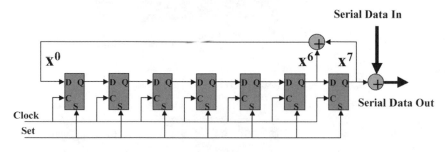

$$\text{Polynomial} = 1 \ + x^6 + x^7$$

$\oplus$ **Exclusive OR**

Figure 9.10 STS-N scrambler.

9.12   LAYERED OVERHEAD
AND TRANSPORT FUNCTIONS

Traditional services and legacy systems are already part of the overall communications network. A basic question addressed in this section is how traditional signals, such as DS1, E1, etc., can be transported with a SONET signal.

The functional sequence that takes place, for example, from a DS1 signal to a SONET signal, can be summarized as follows:

- The incoming DS1 signal at the path layer is mapped onto a VT.
- The VT is mapped onto the SPE, and the SPE path overhead is also constructed.
- The SPE is mapped onto the SONET signal, and the line overhead information is added.
- The signal is mapped onto the STS-N signal, and the section overhead information is added. At this point the complete STS SONET signal is formed, and the signal is scrambled.
- The signal passes through the electrical-to-optical transducer (the transmitter), and the optical signal, with a nonreturn to zero (NRZ) optical coding, is coupled into the optical fiber, in which it travels at the speed of light.

The above process is captured in Figures 9.11a and b.

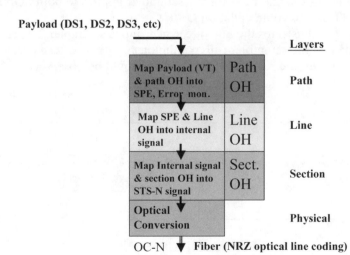

Figure 9.11a Conversion of a legacy signal to a SONET, layered overhead and transport functions.

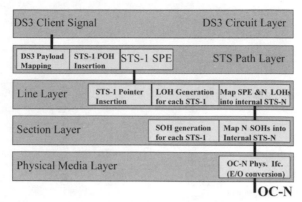

Figure 9.11b Example—from DS3 on OC-N, layered overhead and transport functions.

9.13   INTERACTION BETWEEN LAYERS

When the SONET signal has been constructed, transmitted by an NE, and received by another NE, then similar layers of the SONET signal, as viewed between the transmitting and receiving NEs, interact at the corresponding layers. For example, the section layer interacts with the next section layer, and so on. Figure 9.12 illustrates the conversion of the payload (DS1, etc.) into a SONET OC-N, the various stages where overhead is added and extracted, and the interacting layers between two terminals and a regenerator.

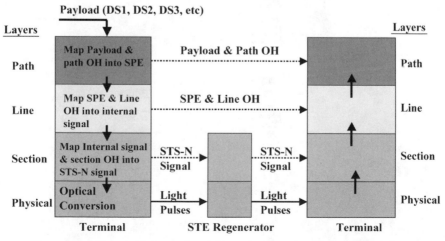

Figure 9.12 Interaction between layers, layered overhead and transport functions.

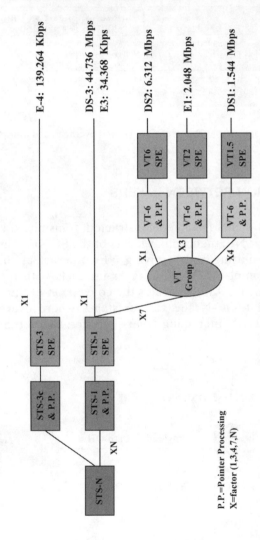

Figure 9.13a SONET multiplexing scheme.

E-4: 139.264 Kbps

DS-3: 44.736 Mbps
E3: 34.368 Kbps

DS2: 6.312 Mbps

E1: 2.048 Mbps

DS1: 1.544 Mbps

P.P.=Pointer Processing
X=factor (1,3,4,7,N)

84

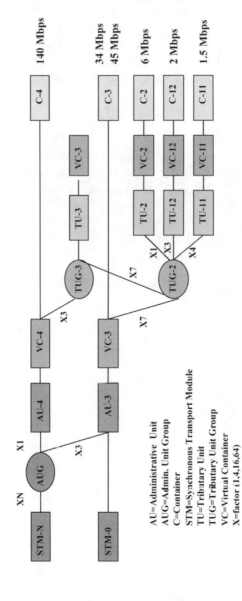

Figure 9.13b SDH multiplexing scheme.

AU=Administrative Unit
AUG=Admin. Unit Group
C=Container
STM=Synchronous Transport Module
TU=Tributary Unit
TUG=Tributary Unit Group
VC=Virtual Container
X=factor (1,4,16,64)

9.14   SDH MULTIPLEXING

In this chapter, we have focused on the hierarchical multiplexing scheme of the SONET payload. The SDH follows a very similar hierarchical multiplexing scheme. In SDH, traditional signals are mapped onto containers, the containers are multiplexed into groups, and overhead is added to construct an STM-N signal (per CCITT Recommendation G.907). The SONET and the SDH hierarchical multiplexing schemes are recaptured in Figures 9.13a and b.

EXERCISES

1. Calculate how many TUG-2's fit in an STM-1 signal.
2. Calculate how many C11 containers fit in an STM-1 signal.
3. If the bit rate of an STM-1 signal is 155.52 Mbps, calculate the bit rate of an AUG.
4. Calculate how many VT2's fit in an STS-1 signal.

Answers

1. 21
2. 84
3. 150.912 Mbps
4. 21

CHAPTER 10

SYNCHRONIZATION AND TIMING

10.1 NETWORK SYNCHRONIZATION

Consider a network that consists of nodes interconnected with fiber. Then, a node receives a variety of signals from nodes in its vicinity and from distant nodes. Moreover, some nodes may be from the same network and some from a different network. As such, the received signals are out of phase. From the receiving node point of reference, all signals are received at different phases with its clock and frame synchronization. This phase difference could be easily engineered if it would remain fixed or bounded; a fixed delay at the signal input would align all received signals. A fixed phase, however, implies that all nodes operate at exactly the same frequency. Although in theory this may sound good, it is not practical. The reason is that NEs have built-in clocks (frequency generators) that, although very accurate, are not EXACTLY at the same frequency. Thus, a small difference between the clocks from node to node may result in a substantial frequency variation as the signal passes through many nodes. In addition to phase and frequency differences, jitter issues further complicate the signal synchronization of nodes in the network.

The above potential problem is addressed by establishing a common timing source. The network receives a frequency of extremely high accuracy from a timing service known as *Building Information Timing Supply* (*BITS*); in Europe, the equivalent of BITS is the *Primary Reference Source* (*PRS*).

Figure 10.1 illustrates a model of an add-drop multiplexer (ADM) node with input-output SONET (SDH) signals and a BITS frequency reference (8 kHz) input, to which every function in the node is synchronized.

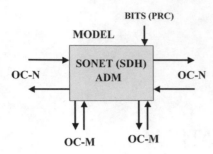

Figure 10.1 Network synchronization—a model.

10.2   TIMING ACCURACY: STRATA

The timing architecture in the communications network is hierarchical. Each node in the network is required to maintain a frequency accuracy that depends on its major function in the network, that is, if other nodes in the network depend on it for timing accuracy.

The highest possible frequency accuracy is 10×10^{-11}, and this is achieved with highly accurate atomic clocks. This clock is the PRS and the accuracy is referred to as *stratum 1*. Nodes that comply with stratum 1 accuracy are allowed to slip up to 2.523 periods per year. Clearly, not many systems (in the United States) are stratum 1 systems. After stratum 1, stratum 2 has an accuracy of 1.6×10^{-8}, stratum 3 has an accuracy of 4.6×10^{-6}, and stratum 4 has an accuracy 3.2×10^{-5}. As an example, systems with stratum 4 are digital PBXs, central office terminals, and digital channel banks.

In SDH networks, the clock also follows a hierarchical structure. In this case, the PRS is called a *primary reference clock (PRC)*, with an accuracy of 10×10^{-11}. This clock is distributed throughout the entire network, which is regenerated at the network element by a synchronization supply unit (SSU), and this is also regenerated by a *synchronous equipment clock (SEC)*. ITU-T Recommendations G.811, G.812, and G.813 define the accuracy of the three clocks, respectively.

Table 10.1 lists the accuracy of each stratum, the permitted slip rate, and some system examples.

Table 10.1 Timing Accuracy

Stratum	Minimum Accuracy	Skip Rate	Notes
1	10×10^{-11}	2.523/yr	Primary reference source (PRS)
2	1.6×10^{-8}	11.06/day	e.g., 4ESS/5ESS
3	4.6×10^{-6}	132.48/h	e.g., 5ESS/DCS
4	3.2×10^{-5}	15.36/min	DCB/COT/DPBX

Abbreviations: 4ESS, 5ESS, No. 4 and No. 5 electronic switch system; COT, central office terminal; DCB, digital channel bank; DPBX, digital PBX.

10.3   TIMING STABILITY

The path that connects user A with user B may pass through several networks that are maintained, provisioned, and owned by more than one provider. Therefore, it is important that the reference frequency of various providers meets certain quality, accuracy, and stability requirements for all NEs in the synchronization hierarchy. SONET NEs must be synchronized with a stratum 3 or better quality clock. Alternatively, SONET NEs that are not synchronized with a stratum 3 external clock must be equipped with an internal clock (oscillator) that has a minimum accuracy of ± 20 parts per million (ppm). This accuracy is required to support *operation, administration, maintenance, and provisioning (OAM&P)* functionality of all nodes in the network. Network providers must also supply a timing reference signal that meets the recommended stability requirements. Consequently, any OC-N output signal from any NE in the SONET network must meet certain stability requirements.

Figure 10.2 illustrates (a) the short-term stability required of the OC-N output and (b) the short-term stability of a timing reference signal furnished by a network provider.

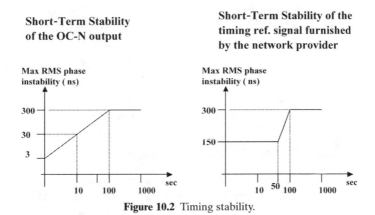

Figure 10.2 Timing stability.

10.4   NE SYNCHRONIZATION

A NE should be synchronized with the network. However, the synchronization strategy may be described by one of several models. For example, a timing signal may be supplied by an external timing source, such as BITS, or it may be derived directly by the SONET NE that terminates an OC-N. In the latter case, timing information may be derived from a DS1 signal that has been embedded in the OC-N.

The general rule is that, where BITS (or its European equivalent SASE) is available, NEs are externally timed from the BITS reference clock. External timing references to a NE are from a BITS clock of stratum 3 or better quality. Where no BITS is available, NEs are timed from a received OC-N.

10.4.1 BITS Timing Model

Where BITS (or SASE) is available, the NEs of a network are externally timed from it. In such cases, BITS supplies the same quality reference clock over two paths, the active and the alternate. The NE receives both, but it operates from the active path. However, if anything goes wrong with the active path (e.g., the transmitter of the BITS, the line between BITS and NE, or the receiver on the NE), then the NE selects the alternate clock. The functional unit responsible for receiving the two clocks from BITS, monitoring the incoming clocks for faults, selecting the correct one, and distributing the clock to all functional units in the NE is the timing unit (TU).

In Figure 10.3, solid lines denote user data paths and broken lines denote clock paths.

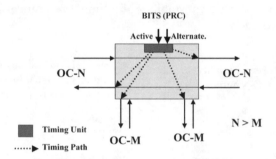

Figure 10.3 BITS network synchronization.

10.4.2 OC-N Single DS1 Line Timing Model

In many cases, the NE extracts the clock from an incoming signal, typically a DS1. In this case, the incoming OC-N is used to extract an 8-kHz reference clock; remember that a DS1 frame occurs 8000 times per second and that DS1 frames are mapped in VT1.5's. The extracted 8 kHz is sent to the TU, which sends it over two separate paths to the BITS, where it is retimed and then is sent back to the NE over the active and alternate paths. The TU distributes the retimed reference clock to all functional units in the NE.

In Figure 10.4, solid lines denote user signals and broken lines denote clock paths.

10.4.3 OC-M Single DS1 Line Timing Model

In this model, the NE extracts an 8-kHz clock from an incoming signal, typically a DS1 that is embedded in an incoming OC-M (where $N > M$) signal similar to the previous model. The extracted 8 kHz is sent to the TU, which sends

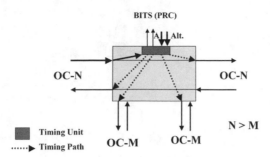

Figure 10.4 OC-N Line (DS1) timing model.

it over two separate paths to the BITS, where it is retimed and then is sent back to the NE over the active and alternate paths. The TU distributes the re-timed reference clock to all functional units in the NE.

In Figure 10.5, solid lines denote user signals and broken lines denote clock paths.

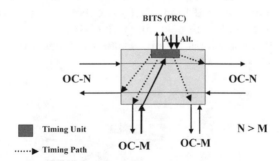

Figure 10.5 OC-M Line (DS1) timing model.

10.4.4   OC-N Dual-DS1 Line Timing Model

In this model, the NE extracts two independent clocks from two OC-N in-coming signals. The two incoming OC-Ns (one from the left and another from the right) are used to extract from DS1's two 8-kHz synchronization signals. The extracted 8-kHz signals are sent to the TU, which sends them over two paths to the BITS, where they are retimed and then sent back to the NE over the active and alternate paths. The TU distributes clock to all functional units in the NE.

In Figure 10.6, solid lines denote user signals and broken lines denote clock paths.

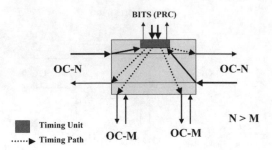

Figure 10.6 OC-N Line (two DS1) timing model.

10.4.5   Loop Timing Model

In this model, the NE is not connected to a BITS. It is connected to only one OC-N and to lower bit rate OC-M ($N > M$) and DS-N.

The NE extracts the clock from incoming signals of the loop, typically a DS1. In this case, an incoming OC-N is used to extract an 8-kHz synchronization signal. The extracted 8-kHz signal is sent to the TU, which retimes it based on an accurate phase-locked loop (PLL) oscillator, located on the TU and then distributes it to all functional units in the NE.

In Figure 10.7, solid lines denote user signals and broken lines denote clock paths.

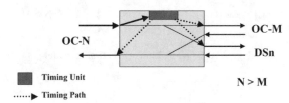

Figure 10.7 Loop timing model.

10.4.6   Through-Timing Model

This model applies to regenerator elements. Each direction has its own TU, and timing is extracted from each direction, indicated by solid lines in Figure 10.8. The through-timing model is not recommended for add-drop multiplexers (ADMs).

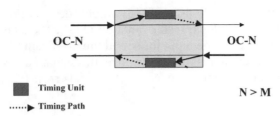

Timing Unit

N > M

⋯⋯▶ Timing Path

Figure 10.8 Through-timing model.

10.5   CLOCK APPLICATIONS

When a reference clock is used to time a system, the following rules apply (see Bellcore GR-1244-CORE for details):

- The minimum free-running accuracy of a SONET minimum clock (SMC) shall be ±20 ppm.
- An ADM could be timed from a clock extracted from a line or from an external clock source, or through-timed. When its reference clock fails, then for a specified limited period of time, it enters a free-running state with a specified tolerance. This is known as a *holdover*.
- A switched digital module in terminal mode (TM) configuration and loop-timed may be required to provide holdover.
- A Digital Cross-connect System with external timing is required with a minimum accuracy of ±4.6 ppm.
- Entry into holdover and restoration from holdover shall be error free.

10.6   JITTER AND WANDER

Jitter and wander are defined by the standards bodies as the *short-term variation* of a signal's significant instants from their ideal position in time. Short-term variation implies some frequency oscillation that is greater or equal to a frequency demarcation. In the North American Hierarchy (DS1 to DS3) the demarcation between *jitter* and *wander* is 10 Hz (GR-253-CORE). That is, below 10 Hz a short-term variation from the center frequency is considered jitter and above 10 Hz it is considered wander.

The optical and electrical transmission inputs and tributary interfaces must be able to tolerate specific jitter levels without loss of signal. Jitter requirements have been developed to limit the levels of jitter, and they are applied at OC-N and at STS-N electrical interfaces. Jitter requirements (ITU-T, ANSI, and Bellcore) apply to interfaces between carriers and users as well as between two carriers.

The maximum tolerable jitter (MTJ) amplitude at various frequencies is defined as well as the jitter transfer function (JTF). The JTF is expressed in terms of the output jitter, the input jitter, and the jitter gain (G) for a given frequency ω. If the jitter gain is too high, and as the signal passes through regenerators, jitter may be accumulated leading to signal errors (signal loss or bit errors).

10.6.1   Jitter and Wander Sources

If there is excessive jitter at the physical interface, that is, rapid phase changes between the incoming signal and the sampling clock, then the position of the sampler is temporally shifted with respect to the center position of a bit. This causes the wrong reading of the bit value and thus bit errors. Alternatively, within the NE, if the signal and the clock both have the same jitter, then the (jittery) sampler tracks the (same jittery) signal and errors do not occur. If, on the other hand, phase changes are slow—the case of wander—the recovered clock can easily track the slow phase changes and thus not cause bit errors.

Jitter or wander is additive, and any sources that cause jitter or wander add to the end result. Such sources are:

Delay variation jitter: Jitter due to delay variations in the transmission path that cause phase variations.

Phase jitter: Jitter due to phase differences between the reference clock and the secondary clocks in a network.

Interference jitter: Jitter due to interference (crosstalk, impulse noise) that cause phase variations.

Pattern jitter: Jitter due to the intersymbol interference on the digital signal.

Stuffing and wait time jitter: Jitter due to stuffing bits in the digital signal and thus waiting to match the system bit rate, an operation that takes place at the multiplexer/demultiplexer level.

Mapping jitter: Jitter due to bit justification or stuffing to match the bit rate of the asynchronous tributary signals to that of the synchronous transport signal during mapping.

Pointer jitter: Jitter due to frequency differences between two networks or between two NEs result in offset in the payload and hence in pointer movements. Depending on mapping, the pointer jumps by 8 or 24 bytes. When the tributary signal is unpacked at the receiver, this pointer jumping results in a signal phase offset. Although a PLL smooths out most of it, there is a residual that is termed pointer jitter.

10.6.2 Jitter Categories

There are two categories of jitter:

Category I: Asynchronous DS-N interfaces to NE

Category II: OC-N, STS-N electrical, and synchronous DS1 interfaces to NE

10.6.3 Jitter Criteria for Network Elements

Jitter criteria for NEs (and per interface categories) are specified in the following areas:

Jitter transfer is defined as the jitter transfer characteristics (limits) of an NE.

Jitter tolerance is defined as the peak-to-peak amplitude of sinusoidal jitter applied on the OC-N input signal that causes a 1-dB power penalty.

Jitter generation defines the limits of jitter generated by an NE without jitter or wander at its inputs. Payload mapping, bit stuffing, and pointer justifications are all operations that cause jitter.

10.6.4 Jitter Measurements

Jitter measurements can be made using sinusoidal jitter applied to the input signal at any level up to the jitter tolerance level for that interface and that specific jitter frequency.

EXAMPLE

Pointer jitter is specified in unit intervals peak to peak (UIpp) for a variety of signals. Thus, the output jitter for DS1 signals is specified at 1.5 UIpp, for an E1 signal at 0.4 UIpp, for a DS3 at 1.3 UIpp, and for a 140-Mbps signal at 0.4 UIpp.   ■

10.6.5 Wander

Frequency wander occurs at the boundary between two networks that have their own primary reference clock (PRC). It may also occur between the reference (master) clock and secondary (slave) clocks within a network. Wander may be accumulated down the synchronization chain, and therefore SONET and SDH systems must avoid low-frequency wander effects. Wander is distinguished from jitter by the above 10-Hz short-term variation from the center frequency.

EXERCISES

1. Comment on stratums and on Primary Reference Source.

2. Review jitter and wander. What is the difference between the two?

3. Review the jitter and wander sources.

CHAPTER 11

MAINTENANCE

The performance of a network element is continuously monitored to assure that its functions perform acceptably error free, as expected. In general, an erratic performance of a function may be classified as an anomaly, a defect, or a failure:

- An anomaly is a discrepancy between the actual and desired characteristics of an item [e.g., bit-interleaved parity-8 field (BIP-8) error].
- A *defect* is a limited interruption in the ability of an item to perform a required function.
- A *failure* is a persistent defect. A network element enters a failure state when a failure condition has been detected, and it exits a failure state when the condition has been corrected.

Maintenance of a system defines the functions to be monitored, the requirements, and the criteria and their parameters. According to these criteria and their parameters, the performance of a function is classified as *acceptable, unacceptable* (failed), or *degraded*. Based on the classification of performance, the system or the network may have to take some action.

The main objective of maintenance is to perform the following tasks:

- Trouble detection
- Trouble sectionalization
- Trouble or repair verification
- Trouble isolation
- Restoration

Maintenance requirements are divided into *alarm surveillance, performance monitoring (PM), testing,* and *control.*

97

Details of maintenance requirements and criteria are described in standards documents (see Bellcore GR-253-CORE and GR-820-CORE and ITU-T Recommendation G.774 for details).

11.1   ALARM SURVEILLANCE

Alarm surveillance deals with the detection and reporting of certain failures and degraded conditions in the network.

Network Element Alarm Surveillance.   Network element alarm surveillance takes place on different levels. These levels are at the section-terminating equipment (STE), at the line-terminating equipment (LTE), at the STS path-terminating equipment (STS PTE), and at the VT path-terminating equipment (VT PTE). The complexity of surveillance is in accenting order. Thus, a VT PTE contains all the functionality of an STE, LTE, and STS PTE; an STS PTE has all the functionality of an LTE and STE, and so on. See Figure 11.1.

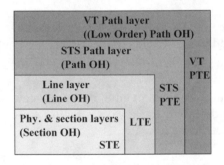

Figure 11.1 Maintenance: layered alarm surveillance.

11.1.1   Alarm Indications

A change of state may cause an *alarm indication* immediately as it occurs or after some period of time, as recommended in SONET/SDH specifications.

When a failure state is detected, an *alarm indication signal* (*AIS*) is constructed and it is transmitted to the next NE on the downstream path (see Section 11.1.3). The purpose of an AIS is to alert downstream equipment of an upstream failure. The response to a received AIS is a *remote defect indication* (*RDI*) signal in the upstream direction (see below, RDI).

The AIS and RDI status signals are communicated to the far end over overhead bytes in the SONET/SDH signal.

11.1.2   Alarm States, Declarations, and Indications

Here, we provide a list of alarm states, when an alarm is declared and how it is indicated; see Table 11.1a for SONET and Table 11.1b for SDH:

Table 11.1a SONET Alarms

	Line AIS	STS Path AIS	VT Path AIS	DS-N AIS
Loss of signal (LOS)	✓	✓	✓	✓[a]
Loss of frame (LOF)	✓	✓	✓	✓[a]
Loss of pointer (LOP)		✓[b]	✓[b]	✓[a]

[a] Depends on the composition of the STS SPE (i.e., DS1, DS3, etc.).
[b] No RDI is generated.

- *Loss of signal* (*LOS*) is declared when no light pulses persist for 100 μs. If light pulses are lost for less than 2.3 μs, then no LOS is declared. However, if they persist for a period longer than 2.5 s, then an alarm message is sent to the operating system (OS).
- *Loss of frame* (*LOF*) is declared when a severely errored frame (SEF) persists for a period longer than 3 ms. If at least four consecutive frames

Table 11.1b SDH Anomalies and Defects (in hierarchical order)

LOS	Loss of signal
TSE	Test sequence error (bit error)
LSS	Loss of sequence synchronization
AIS	Alarm indication signal
OOF	Out of frame (errors in A1, A2)
LOF	Loss of frame (persistent error in A1, A2)
B1	Regenerator error (i.e., calculated B1 mismatch)
RS-TIM	RS trace identifier mismatch (error in J0)
MS-AIS	Multiplex section AIS
MS-RDI	Multiplex section remote defect indicator
MS-REI	Multiplex section remote error indication
B2	Multiplex section error monitoring (i.e., B2 mismatch)
AU-LOP	Administrative unit loss of pointer (error in H1, H2)
AU-NDF	Administrative unit new data found flag
AU-AIS	Administrative unit AIS
AU-PJE	Administrative unit pointer justification event
HP-UNEQ	High-order path unequipped
HP-RDI HP-REI, HP-TIM	High-order RDI, REI, TIM, and PLM
HP-PLM	High-order payload label mismatch
B3	High-order path error monitoring
TU-LOP, TU-NDF, TU-AIS	Tributary unit lOP, NDF, and AIS
TU-LOM	Tributary unit loss of multiframe
LO-UEQ, LO-RDI, LO-REI, LO-TIM, LO-PLM	Low-order UEQ, RDI, REI, TIM, and PLM
Lo-FRI	Low-order remote failure indication

have incorrect framing patterns, then an alarm message is sent to the OS.

- *Loss of pointer* (*LOP*) is declared when pointer failures occur, such as out of range, wrong NDF, or any other failures related to the pointer-processing mechanism. An alarm message is sent to the OS

- There are two types of *equipment failures: service affecting* (*SA*) and *non–service affecting* (*NSA*). Equipment failures are classified as *critical, major,* and *minor.* When equipment failure is detected, a message is sent to the OS.

- *Loss of synchronization* refers to loss of primary or secondary timing reference. A message is sent to the OS stating the reason (LOS, LOF, etc.)

- *Automatic protection switching* (*APS*) *troubles* are related to channel mismatch, K1 with unused code, K2 with APS mode mismatch, etc.

- *DCC failures* are related to any failed hardware or failure to carry a data communications channel (DCC). If this condition occurs, then the switch moves to standby DCC and a report is sent to the OS.

- *Signal label mismatch* is related to signal labels. Two defects are defined: *payload label mismatch* (*PLM*) and *unequipped* (*ENEQ*). Signal label mismatch is performed by monitoring the C2 byte for STS signal labels and for STS payload label mismatch (PLM-P). In addition, it is performed by monitoring the V5 byte (bits b5, b6, and b7) for VT PLM and VT path unequipped.

- The *AIS* alerts the downstream equipment that a defect or a failure has been detected. These signals can be generated for *line* (*AIS-L*), for *path* (*AIS-P*), or for *VT path* (*AIS-V*); see next section.

- *Remote alarm indication* (*RAI*) alerts the upstream equipment of a downstream failure. There are two types: RDI and remote failure indication (RFI); see next section.

- *Payload defect indication* (*PDI*) alerts the downstream equipment that there is a defect in one or more of its embedded payloads.

11.1.3   AIS and RDI

Depending on the type of failure, AISs are generated for line, STS path, or VT path:

AIS-L: An AIS-L is generated when a line LOS and/or LOF is detected. An STE forms an OC-N signal with a valid section overhead and generates a line AIS by sending an all-1's pattern (after scrambling) for the remainder of the OC-N signal. The signal is sent downstream. When the LTE detects AIS-L, an RDI signal is sent upstream.

AIS-P: An AIS-P is generated when a path LOS and/or LOF and/or LOP is detected. An LTE generates a STS path AIS by filling the entire STS

SPE with all 1's, including H1, H2, and H3 bytes (after scrambling). The signal is sent downstream to the STS LTE. An RDI signal is sent upstream if the AIS is for LOS or LOF only (not for LOP).

AIS-V: An AIS-V is generated when a VT LOS and/or LOF and/or LOP is detected. A STS PTE generates a VT path AIS by filling the entire VT with all 1's (after scrambling). The signal is sent downstream to the VT PTE. An RDI signal is sent upstream if the AIS is for LOS or LOF only (not for LOP).

Embedded DS-N with failures (LOS, LOF, or LOP) will cause an AIS depending on the composition (e.g., DS1, DS3).

Similarly, depending on the type of AIS, RDI signals are generated.

RDI alarm signals are sent upstream to alert the network and also to initiate trunk conditioning. There are STS path RDI, VT path RDI, and DS-N RDI signals:

- The *STS path RDI* signal alerts the upstream STS PTE that an AIS has been received in the downstream STS path.
- The *VT path RDI* signal alerts the upstream VT PTE that an AIS has been received in the downstream VT path.
- When a *DS-N RDI* signal is detected, it is converted to a VT Path RDI signal if a DS-N is mapped into its associated VT.

AIS-RDI Summary. The AIS-RDI functions can be summarized as follows:

- When an STE receives an invalid signal, it sends an AIS-L alarm downstream.
- When an LTE receives an invalid signal or an AIS-L and it is unable to protect the line, it sends an STS path AIS downstream.
- When a STS PTE receives either an invalid signal or an STS path AIS, it propagates the appropriate AIS downstream.
- When a VT PTE receives either a VT path AIS or an invalid signal, it generates the appropriate AIS downstream.
- Upon detection at a terminal of a service-affecting failure, a local RED alarm is declared and a RDI signal is returned upstream to the far-end NE that terminates the service.
- Automatic service management processes are initiated at each NE and they are maintained for the duration of the failure.
- Alarm states and RDI are coordinated between source and sink to restore service.

The Bellcore documents GR-499 and GR-253 provide all details for AIS and RDI for SONET.

11.2   PERFORMANCE MONITORING (PM)

Performance Monitoring (PM) is a set of rules for the in-service monitoring of the transmission quality (see Bellcore GR-253-CORE and GR-820-CORE and ITU-T Recommendation G.774.01).

Although there are many commonalties, there is a fundamental difference between SONET and SDH PM philosophy:

SDH: PM is based on counting errored blocks within a period of a second.
SONET: PM is based on counting code violations within a period of a second.

Here, for purpose of simplicity, we focus on the SONET PM case; the reader interested in the details of PM is encouraged to consult the appropriate SONET or SDH standards and recommendations.

The PM function includes:

- Detection of transmission degradation
- Detection of performance parameter deviation
- Communication with OSs

The NE gathers PM information from the value of the following overhead bytes/bits (see SONET overhead byte definition):

- Section BIP (B1)
- Line BIP (B2)
- STS path BIP (B3)
- VT path BIP (bits 1 and 2 of V5: BIP-2)

PM is accomplished by storing information collected over a period of time in specific registers. Such information is related to the *current period,* the *previous period,* the *recent period,* and a *threshold value.*

In general, there are two types of registers:

- The *current-second register (CSR)* contains defects or anomalies that have occurred within a second.
- The *current-period register (CPR)* contains cumulative defects or anomalies detected and stored in the CSR.

11.2.1   PM Requirements

SONET network elements are required to accumulate a variety of PM parameters that are related to section, line, STS path, or a VT path layer entity.

A SONET network element shall provide the following accumulation and storage registers:

- One current 15 min
- One current day
- One previous 15 min
- One previous day
- Thirty-one recent 15 min

11.2.2 Inhibition Registers

Inhibition registers are *positive* and *negative* adjustment registers that are used to add or subtract one of the following to a current period register:

- Coding violation (CV)
- Errored second (ES)
- Severely errored second (SES)
- Unavailable second (UAS)
- Line pointer justification (PJ), STS path PJ, and VT path PJ

All these have a negative adjustment register, a positive adjustment register, or both.

11.2.3 At the Physical Layer

At the (*photonic*) *physical layer* the current-period, previous-period, or recent-period registers are NOT required but only the current value (event). Here, the following performance parameters are required:

- *Laser bias current* (*LBC*) is defined by $LBC_{normal} = LBC/LBC_o$, where LBC_o is the initial/nominal value provided by the network element supplier.
- *Optical power transmitted* (*OPT*) is defined by $OTP_{normal} = OPT/OPT_o$, where OPT_o is the initial/nominal value provided by the network element supplier.
- *Optical power received* (*OPR*) is defined by $OTR_{normal} = OPR/OPR_o$, where OPR_o is the initial/nominal value received by an OC-N at system turnup.

11.2.4 At the Section Layer

Similarly, at the *section layer* the following performance parameters are required:

- *Severely errored framing seconds* (*SEFS-Ss*) is a count of seconds during which an SEF defect was present.

- *Coding violations* (*CV-Ss*) is a count of BIP errors detected at the section layer (using the B1 byte).
- *Errored seconds* (*ES-Ss*) is a count of the number of seconds during which at least one section layer BIP error was detected or an SEF or LOS defect was present.
- *Severely errored seconds* (*SES-Ss*) is a count of the seconds during which *K* or more section layer BIP errors were detected or an SEF or LOS defect was present.

11.2.5   At the Line Layer

The *line layer* performance parameters are divided into *near end* (*NE*) and *far end* (*FE*).

A. The *near-end line layer* performance parameters are:

- *NE line coding violations* (*CV-Ls*) is a count of BIP errors detected at the line layer.
- *NE line errored seconds* (*ES-Ls*) is a count in seconds during which at least one line layer BIP error was detected or an AIS-L defect was present.
- *NE line severely errored seconds* (*SES-Ls*) is a count of the seconds during which *K* or more line layer BIP errors were detected or an AIS-L defect was present.
- *NE line unavailable seconds* (*UAS-Ls*) is a count of the seconds during which the line was considered unavailable.
- *NE line failure counts* (*FC-L*) is a count of the number of near-end line failure events. A failure event begins when an AIS-L is declared and ends when a AIS-L is cleared.
- *Protection switching count* (*PSC*) relates to systems that are equipped with two switching fabrics, the *working* and the *protection*.

For working line: This is a count of the times that service switched from the monitored line to the protection line plus the times it switched back to the working line.

For protection line: This is a count of the times that service switched from any working line to the protection line plus the times it switched back to the working line.

- *Protection switching duration* (*PSD*) is a count in seconds.

For working line: This is a count in seconds that indicates the duration of time service was carried on the protection line.

For protection line: This is a count in seconds that indicates the duration of time the protection line was used to carry service.

- *STS pointer justification (STS-PJ)* is a count of the STS pointer adjustments created or absorbed by an NE due to differences in the frame rates of incoming and outgoing SONET signals. The STS-PJ parameter is accumulated for a nonterminated STS path.

B. The *far-end line layer* performance parameters are:

- *FE line coding violations (CV-LFEs)* is a count of BIP errors detected by the FE LTE, and reported back to the NE LTE using the REI-L in the line OH.
- *FE line errored seconds (ES-LFEs)* is a count in seconds during which at least one line BIP error was reported by the FE LTE using the REI-L or an RDI-L defect was present.
- *FE line severely errored seconds (SES-LFEs)* is a count of the seconds during which K or more line BIP errors were reported by the FE LTE or an RDI-L defect was present.
- *FE line unavailable seconds (UAS-LFE)* is a count of the seconds during which the line was considered unavailable at the FE.
- *FE line failure counts (FC-LFEs)* is a count of the number of FE line failure events. A failure event begins when an RFI-L failure is declared and it ends when an RFI-L is cleared.

11.2.6 STS Path Layer

The SONET *STS path layer* performance parameters are divided into STS and VT. Each is further divided into near end and far end.

A. The *near-end STS path layer* performance parameters are:

- *NE STS path coding violations (CV-Ps)* is a count of BIP errors detected at the STS path layer.
- *NE STS path errored seconds (ES-Ps)* is a count in seconds during which at least one STS path BIP error was detected or an AIS-P defect was present.
- *NE STS path severely errored seconds (SES-Ps)* is a count of the seconds during which K or more STS path BIP errors were detected or an AIS-P or LOP-P defect was present.
- *NE STS path unavailable seconds (UAS-P)* is a count of the seconds during which the STS path was unavailable.
- *NE STS path failure counts (FC-Ps)* is a count of the number of NE STS path failure events. A failure event begins when an AIS-P or LOP-P is declared and it ends when it is cleared.

B. The *far-end STS path layer* performance parameters are:

- *FE STS path coding violations* (*CV-PFEs*) is a count of BIP errors detected by the FE STS PTE and reported back to the NE STS PTE using the REI-P in the STS path OH.
- *FE STS path errored seconds* (*ES-PFEs*) is a count in seconds during which at least one STS path BIP error was reported by the FE STS PTE using the REI-P or a RDI-P defect was present.
- *FE STS path severely errored seconds* (*SES-PFEs*) is a count of the seconds during which K or more STS path BIP errors were reported by the FE STS PTE, or an RDI-P, or an RDI-P server defect was present.
- *FE STS path unavailable seconds* (*UAS-PFE*) is a count of the seconds during which the STS path was considered unavailable at the FE.
- *FE STS path failure counts* (*FC-PFEs*) is a count of the number of FE STS path failure events. A failure event begins when an RFI-P failure is declared and ends when it is cleared.

11.2.7 VT Path Layer

The *VT pointer justification* (*VT-PJ*) is a path layer performance parameter. It is a count of VT pointer adjustments created or absorbed by a network element due to differences in the frame rates of incoming and outgoing STS SPEs. The VT-PJ parameter is accumulated for a nonterminated VT path.

SONET *VT path layer* performance parameters are also divided into near end and far end.

A. The *near-end VT path layer* performance parameters are:

- *NE VT path coding violations* (*CV-Vs*) is a count of BIP errors detected at the VT path layer.
- *NE VT path errored seconds* (*ES-Vs*) is a count in seconds during which at least one VT path BIP error was detected or an AIS-V or LOP-V defect was present.
- *NE VT path severely errored seconds* (*SES-Vs*) is a count of the seconds during which K or more VT path BIP errors were detected or an AIS-V or LOP-V defect was present.
- *NE VT path unavailable seconds* (*UAS-V*) is a count of the seconds during which the VT path was unavailable.
- *NE VT path failure counts* (*FC-V*) is a count of the number of NE VT path failure events. A failure event begins when an AIS-V or LOP-V is declared and it ends when it is cleared.

B. The *far-end VT path layer* performance parameters are:

- *FE VT path coding violations* (*CV-VFEs*) is a count of BIP errors detected by the FE VT PTE and reported back to the NE VT PTE using the REI-V in the VT path OH.
- *FE VT path errored seconds* (*ES-VFEs*) is a count in seconds during which at least one VT path BIP error was reported by the FE VT PTE using the REI-V or a RDI-V server defect was present.
- *FE VT path severely errored seconds* (*SES-VFEs*) is a count of the seconds during which K or more VT path BIP errors were reported by the FE VT PTE or an RDI-V or an RDI-V server defect was present.
- *F-E VT path unavailable seconds* (*UAS-VFE*) is a count of the seconds during which the VT path was considered unavailable at the FE.
- *FE VT path failure count* (*FC-VFE*) is a count of the number of FE VT path failure events. A failure event begins when an RFI-V failure is declared and it ends when it is cleared.

11.2.8 Intermediate-Path PM

Intermediate-path PM is the transparent monitoring of a constituent channel of an incoming signal by a network element that does not terminate that channel. Figure 11.2 illustrates the following cases:

- Facility 1 from PTE 1 is monitored using the incoming signal by PTE 2 for near end and for far end.
- Facility 2 from PTE 2 is monitored using the incoming signal by PTE 1 for far end and for near end.

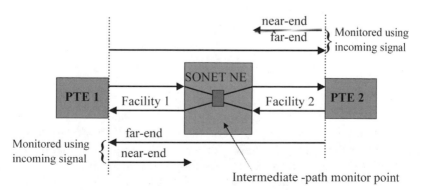

Figure 11.2 Performance monitoring: intermediate path.

Both facilities, although monitored by the network element, are routed transparently (not terminated) through a SONET network element. The network element then acts as an intermediate-path monitor point.

11.3   TESTING

Testing deals with procedures that result in isolation of a failure to a replaceable or repairable entity. Testing may be intrusive or not, service affecting or not. Testing is accomplished by:

- Maintenance tools that are embedded in the SONET signal
- Test access features that perform nonintrusive or intrusive monitoring
- Diagnostic tools that are performed routinely autonomously or on demand with hardware and/or software tools
- Facility loopbacks that are performed routinely autonomously or on demand within the network element and/or at the facility level

Figure 11.3 illustrates the facility loopbacks. The one on the left performs loopbacks toward the far side, and the one on the right toward the near side.

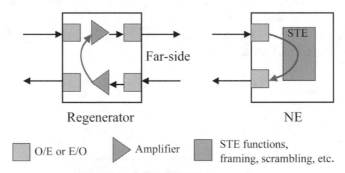

Figure 11.3 Maintenance: facility loopbacks.

Figure 11.4 illustrates loopbacks on the DS-N level. That is, a DS-N signal in the facility is looped back, whereas other DS-Ns in the same facility are not. The one on the left performs loopbacks toward the near end, and the one on the right toward the far end.

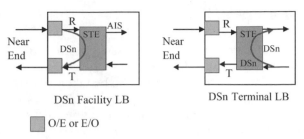

Figure 11.4 Maintenance: DS-N loopbacks.

11.4   OPERATIONS COMMUNICATION INTERFACE

The operations network requires a SONET Operations Communication Interface (SOCI). The requirements of SOCI are described in Bellcore GR-828-CORE. SOCI utilizes a common set of seven-layer OSI protocols: physical, data link, network, transport, session, presentation, and application layer. In the following we describe the requirements for the first two layers.

11.4.1   Physical Layer

OS to NE: Network elements shall support the PHY layer requirements of the TP4/CNLS Protocol Case (GR-828-CORE).

NE to NE-LAN: The PHY layer shall support 10baseT and 10base2 (GR-253-CORE).

NE to NE-DCC: The section DCC is a 192-Kbps channel that is carried in section overhead bytes D1, D2, and D3 of the first STS-1 in an STS-N signal. Section DCC shall be used as the PHY layer of the message-oriented embedded-operations channel (EOC).

11.4.2   Data Link Layer

OS to NE: Network elements shall support data link layer requirements of the TP4/CNLS Protocol Case.

NE to NE-LAN: The media access control (MAC) layer in LANs with carrier sense multiple access/collision detection (CSMA/CD), the logical link control (LLC Class 1, Type 1), and the limit service access point (LSAP); (0xFE) shall be as specified by standards.

NE to NE-DCC: The data link layer protocol shall be based on the link access protocol for the D channel (LAPD) as specified by standards. Both unacknowledged information transfer servers (UITSs) and acknowledged information transfer servers (AITSs) shall be supported. The service access point identifier (SAPI) value shall be preassigned and shall be settable locally or remotely by an OS (see GR-253-CORE for standards).

11.5 SURVIVABILITY

Network survivability addresses two major issues, restoration and protection.

Restoration incorporates traffic-affecting fault detection mechanisms, fault localization testing strategy, and the actions to be taken, per standard requirements, that provide restored service. Restoration addresses self-healing features of a network and the reconfiguration features networks. *Self-healing* of a network refers to the autonomous actions to be taken, after a faulty node is detected, that restore the fault and service. *Reconfiguration* of a network refers to actions to be taken, after a faulty node is detected, to reroute traffic and bypass the faulty node.

Protection incorporates traffic-affecting fault detection mechanisms and the actions to be taken, per standard requirements, that provide uninterrupted service. Protection refers to actions taken to switch traffic flow from one facility (e.g., fiber) to another. Thus protection is also known as *protection switching*. In general, protection in SONET/SDH is referred to as $K:N$, meaning K protection (or spare) fibers for any N active fibers. When any of the N active fibers fails, the traffic from the failing fiber is rerouted to one of the K protection fibers. Typical cases are $1:N$, that is, one protection for each N, or $1:1$, that is, a protection fiber for each active one. In addition to fiber protection, there are protection mechanisms at different levels. For instance, there are protection mechanisms that protect VTs only, known as *low-order* (LO) protection. There are also protection mechanisms that protect SPEs, known as *high order* (HO). In general, in a SONET/SDH system, all protection mechanisms exist; for the physical interface (fibers), the HO payload and the LO payload.

Clearly, restoration and protection for the physical interface depend on network topology, i.e., ring, tree, and so on. In general, SONET and SDH networks use the same protection mechanisms. Such networks consist of rings with dual fibers, one fiber ring for active traffic and the other ring for protection. When a node on the ring fails, the traffic loops around the protection ring, bypassing the failing node, which is a typical protection and survivability case of bidirectional line-switching ring (BLSR).

EXERCISES

1. What is the difference between anomaly and defect?
2. Review AIS and RDI.
3. Performance monitoring is accomplished by storing information in specific registers. What is the stored information related to?
4. Review protection switching.
5. Review the operations communications interface.
6. Review survivability.

CHAPTER 12

IP OVER SONET
AND DWDM

SONET is a mechanism that transports data (voice, data, video) over a fiber medium. In this chapter we briefly explain two very advanced ones that are still being developed: dense wavelength division multiplexing (DWDM) and TCP/IP over SONET or Internet over SONET. The first is not necessarily a SONET mechanism, although some wavelengths may be used to transport SONET payloads. The second is a technique that maps Internet packets in SONET payloads. In a subsequent chapter we will describe the mapping of asynchronous transfer mode in SONET.

12.1 WDM AND DWDM

With advancements in laser and opto-electronic device technology, it has been possible to transmit more than one wavelength in the same fiber. This is known as wavelength division multiplexing (WDM). Adding wavelengths in the same fiber effectively increases the bandwidth capacity of a fiber and thus negates the need for additional fibers. In WDM systems each wavelength is used as a separate channel. Thus, one wavelength may be used to transport an OC-3 traffic and another wavelength to transport OC-12 traffic. WDM is also defined as transporting heterogeneous traffic such as SONET over one wavelength, ATM over another, and perhaps Internet over some other. For example, transporting SONET OC-192 (or SDH STM-64) signals over fiber at 10 Gbps is neither a trivial nor an inexpensive technology. Transporting OC-768 at 40 Gbps is economically not feasible. DWDM enables transporting the equivalent bandwidth over four OC-192 signals.

As opto-electronics technology moves forward, it is possible to have many wavelengths in the same fiber. This high density of wavelengths in the same fiber has coined the term dense wavelength division multiplexing.

WDM systems use wavelengths in the two regions of 1310 and 1550 nm. DWDM systems take advantage of advanced optical technology (e.g., tunable lasers, narrow-band optical filters, etc.) to generate many wavelengths in the range of 1550 nm. The ITU-T recommendation G.692 defines 43 wavelength channels, from 1530 to 1565 nm, with a spacing of 100 GHz. Each channel can carry an OC-192 signal at 10 Gbps. However, systems with wavelength channels more than 40 wavelengths, such as 80 and 128, have been announced, and systems with many more wavelengths are on the experimenter's workbench.

Presently, DWDM systems can transmit over a single fiber an aggregate bandwidth 400 Gbps, and terabits per second (1000 Gbps = 1Tbps) have been demonstrated on an experimental basis. To appreciate the magnitude of 400 Gbps, it is estimated that a single fiber could be able to transport the contents of more than 11,000 volumes of an encyclopedia in a second! The recently announced LUCENT WaveStar system can be configured to handle up to *eight fibers,* or an aggregate of *3.2 Tbps.* At 3.2 Tbps, the contents of 90,000 volumes of an encyclopedia can be transmitted in one second.

Current DWDM systems utilize up to 128 wavelengths (or channels) in a single fiber. If each channel transmits at 10 Gbps, then in a single fiber, a 1.28-Tbps aggregate bandwidth can be transmitted. In the future, these numbers will increase as technology evolves, based on experimental demonstrations with 206 channels.

Presently, commercial systems with 40, 80, and 128 channels (wavelengths) per fiber have been designed. Eighty-channel systems are spaced at 50 GHz and 40-channel systems at 100 GHz. This frequency spacing determines the width of the spectral (wavelength) narrowness of each channel, or how close (in terms of wavelength) the channels are.

The number of channels depends also on the type of fiber used as a medium. A single strand of single-mode fiber can transmit over 80 km without amplification. Placing up to eight optical fiber amplifiers in series, the distance may be extended to 640 km.

Although DWDM is in the making and many issues are being addressed, it is reasonable to assume that in the near future we will see DWDM systems with several hundreds of wavelengths in one single fiber. At about 10 Gbps per wavelength (or higher) and 500 wavelengths per fiber (a presently hypothetical but not unrealistic number), a bandwidth of 5 Tbps per fiber is feasible. Five terabits per second per single fiber is truly a bandwidth that today exceeds all needs and expectations. However, if we look into the data traffic explosion that is taking place, this bandwidth may become tomorrow's norm.

12.2   IP OVER SONET

In this section we briefly describe current activities on mapping Internet Protocol (IP) over SONET. At the writing of this book, mapping IP in SONET SPEs was in the definition stage. In subsequent chapters we describe IP over asynchronous transfer mode (ATM) and also the more mature subject of mapping ATM in SONET.

IP over SONET takes place in four steps.

- First, the IP packet consists of a *header* and a variable-length data field, known as a *datagram.*
- Second, there is a protocol known as *point-to-point protocol* (*PPP*). The IP datagram is encapsulated in a PPP packet; that is, a header is attached to it.
- Third, the PPP-encapsulated IP datagram is framed using *high-level data link control* (*HDLC*).
- The end result is mapped rowwise and bytewise in the SPE. That is, VTs and byte multiplexing is not applicable in this case.

The PPP provides multiprotocol encapsulation, error control, and link initialization control features. HDLC is primarily used for frame delineation, that is, to identify the start and the end of the IP/PPP/HDLC frame. Each HDLC frame starts and ends with the hexadecimal byte 7E or 0x7E (binary 0111 1110). However, the same pattern 0x7E may occur elsewhere in the frame. To avoid misdelineation, during the HDLC step whenever 0x7E is encountered, other than the start and the end of the frame, it is replaced by the escape sequence 0x7D followed by 0x5E. Similarly, the escape sequence 0x7D is replaced by 0x7D 0x5D.

EXERCISES

1. Show that the payload rates for VT1.5 and VT3 are 1.728 and 2.304 Mbps, respectively.
2. A group consists of 12 columns. Is it true that only two VT1.5's and one VT3 can be mapped in this group?
3. In an STS-1 SPE only seven groups may fit. In these groups we need to map the following VTs: 5 VT1.5's, 5 VT2's, and 4 VT6's.
   a. Do they all fit in the STS-1 SPE?
   b. Comment on the mapping efficiency.
4. Explain, from a user's point of view, if there is a bandwidth benefit (or not) in STS-3c as compared with STS-3.
5. Assume the $1 + x^6 + x^7$ scrambler cycles itself every 127 bits.
   a. Calculate the number of full cycles in an STS-3 and in an STS-12 frame.
   b. Is there any difference in the number of cycles in an STS-3c or in an STS-12c?

Answers

1. VT1.5: A VT1.5 consists of 27 bytes, or $27 \times 8 = 216$ bits. The 216 bits transported in 125 μs results in a bit rate of 216×8000 bps = 1.728 Mbps.

VT3: Similarly, a VT3 consists of 54 cytes, which results in a bit rate of 54 × 8 × 8000 bps = 2.304 Mbps

2. A group is allowed to have the same VT type. Thus, a group can have either four VT1.5's or two VT3's but not two VT1.5's and one VT3.

3. a. No.
   b. Four VT6's will occupy four out of seven groups. The remaining three groups can either hit five VT2's (into two groups) and four VT1.5's (into one group) or five VT1.5's (into two groups) and three VT2's (into one group).

4. Yes. There is a bandwidth benefit since the "stuff columns" are used for user's bandwidth.

5. a. 152.5 (153) in an STS-3 and 610.01 (611) in an STS-12.
   b. No.

SECTION II

REFERENCES

[1] G. P. Agrawal, *Fiber-Optic Communication Systems,* John Wiley & Sons, New York, 1997.

[2] L. Boivin, M. C. Nuss, W. H. Knox, and J. B. Stark, "206-Channel Chirped-Pulse Wavelength-Division Multiplexed Transmitter," *Electron. Lett.,* vol. 33, no. 10, 1997, pp. 827–828.

[3] C. A. Brackett, "Dense Wavelength Division Multiplexing Networks: Principles and Applications," *IEEE JSAC,* vol. 8, no. 6, 1990, pp. 948–964.

[4] E. B. Carne, *Telecommunications Primer,* Prentice-Hall, Englewood Cliffs, NJ, 1995.

[5] Ming-Chwan Chow, *Understanding SONET/SDH: Standards and Applications,* Andan Publishers, 1995.

[6] M. Cvijetic, *Coherent and Nonlinear Lightwave Communications,* Artec House, Boston, 1996.

[7] W. Goralski, *SONET: A Guide to Synchronous Optical Networks,* McGraw-Hill, New York, 1997.

[8] S. V. Kartalopoulos, Understanding SONET/SDH and ATM, Tutorial Notes, International Communication Conference, Atlanta, June 1998.

[9] L. Kazovsky, S. Benedotto, and A. Willmer, *Optical Fiber Communication Systems,* Artec House, Boston, 1996.

[10] J. G. Nellist, *Understanding Telecommunications and Lightwave Systems,* IEEE Press, New York, 1996.

[11] K. Nosu, *Optical FDM Network Technologies,* Artec House, Boston, 1997.

[12] S. D. Personick, *Optical Fiber Transmission Systems,* Plenum, New York, 1983.

[13] T. G. Robertazzi, *Performance Evaluation of High Speed Switching Fabrics and Networks,* IEEE Press, New York, 1993.

[14] C. Siller and M. Shafi, eds., *SONET/SDH,* IEEE Press, New York, 1996.

[15] J. M. Simmons, A. A. M. Saleh, E. L. Goldstein, and L. Y. Lin, "Optical Crosscon-nects of Reduced Complexity for WDM Networks with Bidirectional Symmetry," *IEEE Photonics Technol. Lett.,* vol. 10, no. 6, 1998, pp. 819–821.

[16] W. Simpson, "PPP over SONET/SDH," Internet Engineering Task Force RFC 1619, May 1994.

[17] W. Simpson, "The Point-to-Point Protocol (PPP)," Internet Engineering Task Force RFC 1661, July 1994.

[18] B. Thomas, *The Internet for Scientists and Engineers,* SPIE Press and IEEE Press, New York, 1996.

STANDARDS

[1] ANSI/IEEE 812-1984, "Definitions of Terms Relating to Fiber Optics,"

[2] ANSI T1.105, "Synchronous Optical Network (SONET)—Basic Description Including Multiplex Structures, Rates and Formats,"

[3] ANSI T1.105.01, "Synchronous Optical Network (SONET)—Automatic Protection Switching,"

[4] ANSI T1.105.02, "Synchronous Optical Network (SONET)—Payload Mappings,"

[5] ANSI T1.105.03, "Synchronous Optical Network (SONET)—Jitter at Network Interface,"

[6] ANSI T1.105.04, "Synchronous Optical Network (SONET)—DCC Protocols and Architectures,"

[7] ANSI T1.105.05, "Synchronous Optical Network (SONET)—Tandem Connection and Maintenance,"

[8] ANSI T1.105.06, "Synchronous Optical Network (SONET)—Physical Layer Specification,"

[9] ANSI T1.105.07, "Synchronous Optical Network (SONET)—Sub STS-1 Interface Standard Working Document,"

[10] ANSI T1.105.08, "Synchronous Optical Network (SONET)—Directory Services and SONET Draft Standard,"

[11] ANSI T1.105.09, "Synchronous Optical Network (SONET)—Network Element Timing and Synchronization,"

[12] ANSI T1.119, "Synchronous Optical Network (SONET)—Operations, Administration, Maintenance and Provisioning,"

[13] ANSI T1.204-19xy, "Synchronous Optical Network (SONET)—OA&MP Lower Layer Protocols for Interfaces between Operation Systems and Network Elements,"

[14] ANSI T1.208-19xy, "Synchronous Optical Network (SONET)—OA&MP Upper Layer Protocols for Interfaces between Operation Systems and Network Elements,"

[15] ANSI T1.210-19xy, "Synchronous Optical Network (SONET)—OA&MP Principles of Functions, Architectures and Protocols for the Interfaces between Operation Systems and Network Elements,"

[16] ANSI T1.214-1990, "Synchronous Optical Network (SONET)—OA&MP Generic Model for Interfaces between Operating Systems and Network Elements,"

[17] ANSI T1.215-1990, "Synchronous Optical Network (SONET)—OA&MP Fault Management Messages for Interfaces between Operating Systems and Network Elements,"

[18] Bellcore, GR-253-CORE, "Synchronous Optical Network (SONET) Transport Systems, Common Generic Criteria,"

[19] Bellcore GR-499-CORE, "Transport System Generic Requirements," 1995.

[20] Bellcore, GR-820-CORE, OTGR Sec. 5.1, "Network Maintenance: Transport Surveillance," 1994.

[21] Bellcore, GR-828-CORE, OTGR Sec. 11.2, "Generic Operations Interface," 1994.

[22] Bellcore, GR-1244-CORE, "Clocks for the Synchronized Network: Common Generic Criteria," 1995.

[23] Bellcore, TA-NWT-418, "Generic Reliability Requirements,"

[24] Bellcore, TA-NWT-1042, "Ring Information Model," 1992.

[25] Bellcore, TA-NWT-1250, "File Transfer," 1992.

[26] Bellcore, TA-TSY-496-1, "SONET VT Add-Drop Multiplex Equipment Generic Requirements and Objectives," May 1992.

[27] Bellcore, TA-TSY-496-2, "SONET Add-Drop Multiplex Equipment Generic Criteria for a Unidirectional, Path Protection Switched Self-Healing Ring Implementation," 1992.

[28] Bellcore, TA-TSY-496-3, "SONET Add-Drop Multiplex Equipment Generic Criteria for a Self-Healing Ring Implementation," 1992.

[29] Bellcore, TA-TSY-755, "SONET Fiber Optic Transmission Systems Requirements and Objeectives," 1992.

[30] Bellcore, TA-TSY-842, "Generic Requirements for SONET Compatible Digital Radio," 1988.

[31] Bellcore, TA-TSY-917-1, "SONET Regenerator Generic Criteria," 1988.

[32] Bellcore, TA-TSY-917-2, "SONET Regenerator (RGTR) Equipment," 1990.

[33] Bellcore, TA-TSY-1040, "SONET Test Sets for Acceptance and Maintenance Testing Generic Criteria," 1990.

[34] Bellcore, TA-TSY-1042, "Generic Requirements for Operations Interfaces Using OSI Tools: SONET Transport," 1990.

[35] Bellcore, TR-NWT-233, "Digital Cross Connect System," Nov. 1992.

[36] Bellcore, TR-NWT-253, "SONET Common Criteria," 1991.

[37] Bellcore, TR-NWT-782, "Switch Trunk Interface," Oct. 1992.

[38] Bellcore, TR-NWT-917, "Regenerator," Oct. 1990.

[39] Bellcore, TR-NWT-1042, "Ring Information Model," 1992.

[40] Bellcore, TR-TSY-303, "Digital Loop Carrier System," Oct. 1989.

[41] Bellcore, TR-TSY-440, "SONET Digital Switch Interface Criteria," 1992.

[42] CCITT G.652, "Characteristics of a Single-Mode Optical Fiber Cable."

[43] ISO 7498, "Information Processing Systems—Open Systems Interconnection—Basic Reference Model."

[44] ISO 8073, "Information Processing Systems—Open Systems Interconnection—Connection Oriented Transport Protocol Specification."

[45] ISO 8473:1988, "Information Processing Systems—Data Communications—Protocol for Providing the Connectionless Node Network Service."

[46] ISO 9542, "Information Processing Systems—End System to Intermediate System Routing Exchange Protocol for Use in Conjunction with ISO 8473."

[47] ITU-T Recommendation G.651, "Characteristics of A 50/125 μm Graded Index Optical Fiber Cable," 1998.

[48] ITU-T Recommendation G.692 and ITU-T Revised Rec. G.692, "Optical Interfaces for Multichannel Systems with Optical Amplifiers," 1998.

[49] ITU-T Recommendation G.702, "Digital Hierarchy Bit Rates," 1988.

[50] ITU-T Recommendation G.703, "Physical/Electrical Characteristics of Hierarchical Digital Interfaces," 1991.

[51] ITU-T Recommendation G.707, "Network Node Interface for the Synchronous Digital Hierarchy [SDH)," 1996.

[52] ITU-T Recommendation G.708, "Synchronous Node Interface for the Synchronous Digital Hierarchy," 1988.

[53] ITU-T Recommendation G.709, "Synchronous Multiplexing Structure for the Synchronous Digital Hierarchy," 1988.

[54] ITU-T Recommendation G.772, "Protected Monitoring Points Provided on Digital Transmission Systems," 1998.

[55] ITU-T Recommendation G.774, "Synchronous Digital Hierarchy Information Model from the Network Element View," 1992.

[56] ITU-T Recommendation G.774.01, "Synchronous Digital Hierarchy (SDH) Performance Monitoring from the Network Element View," 1994.

[57] ITU-T Recommendation G.774.02, "Synchronous Digital Hierarchy (SDH) Configuration of the Payload Structure from the Network Element View," 1994.

[58] ITU-T Recommendation G.774.03, "Synchronous Digital Hierarchy (SDH) Management of Multiplex Section Protection from the Network Element View," 1994.

[59] ITU-T Recommendation G.774.04, "Synchronous Digital Hierarchy (SDH) Management of Sub-Network Connection Protection from the Network Element View," 1995.

[60] ITU-T Recommendation G.774.05, "Synchronous Digital Hierarchy (SDH) Management of the Connection Supervision Functionality (HCS/LCS) from the Network Element View," 1995.

[61] ITU-T Recommendation G.774.06, "Synchronous Digital Hierarchy (SDH) Unidirectional Performance Monitoring from the Network Element View," 1997.

[62] ITU-T Recommendation G.774.07, "Synchronous Digital Hierarchy (SDH) Management of Lower Order Path Trace and Interface Labeling from the Network Element View," 1996.

[63] ITU-T Recommendation G.774.08, "Synchronous Digital Hierarchy (SDH) Management of Radio-Relay Systems from the Network Element View," 1996.

[64] ITU-T Recommendation G.774.09, "Synchronous Digital Hierarchy (SDH) Configuration of Linear Multiplex Section Protection from the Network Element View," 1996.

[65] ITU-T Recommendation G.775, "Loss of Signal (LOS) and Alarm Indication Signal (AIS) Defect Detection and Clearance Criteria," 1994.

[66] ITU-T Recommendation G.780, "Vocabulary of Terms for SDH Networks and Equipment," 1998.

[67] ITU-T Recommendation G.781, "Structure of Recommendations on Equipment for the Synchronous Digital Hierarchy (SDH) Equipment," 1994.

[68] ITU-T Recommendation G.782, "Types and General Characteristics of Synchronous Digital Hierarchy Multiplexing Equipment," 1994.

[69] ITU-T Recommendation G.783, "Characteristics of Synchronous Digital Hierarchy Multiplexing Equipment Functional Blocks," 1997.

[70] ITU-T Recommendation G.784, "Synchronous Digital Hierarchy (SDH) Management," 1994.

[71] ITU-T Recommendation G.803, "Architecture of Transport Networks Based on the Synchronous Digital Hierarchy (SDH)," 1997.

[72] ITU-T Recommendation G.810, "Definitions and Terminology for Synchronous Networks," 1996.

[73] ITU-T Recommendation G.811, "Timing Requirements at the Output of Primary Reference Clocks Suitable for Plesiochronous Operation of International Digital Links," 1997.

[74] ITU-T Recommendation G.812, "Timing Requirements at the Output of Slave Clocks," 1998.

[75] ITU-T Recommendation G.813, "Timing Characteristics of SDH Equipment Slave Clocks (SEC)," 1998.

[76] ITU-T Recommendation G.825, "Error Performance Parameters and Objectives for International, Constant Bit Rate Digital Paths at or Above the Primary Rate," 1993.

[77] ITU-T Recommendation G.831, "Management Capabilities of Transport Network Protection Architectures," 1998.

[78] ITU-T Recommendation G.832, "Transport of SDH Elements on PDH Networks," 1998.

[79] ITU-T Recommendation G.841, "Types and Characteristics of SDH Network Protection Architectures," 1998.

[80] ITU-T Recommendation G.842, "Interworking of SDH Network Protection Architectures," 1998.

[81] ITU-T Recommendation G.957, "Optical Interfaces for Equipments and Systems Relating to the SDH," 1998.

[82] ITU-T Recommendation G.958, "Digital Line Systems Based on the SDH for Use on Optical Fibre Cables," 1998.

[83] ITU-T Recommendation I.150, "B-ISDN ATM Functional Characteristics," 1995.

[84] ITU-T Recommendation I.432, "B-ISDN User-Network Interface—Physical Network Specification,"

[85] ITU-T Recommendation I.361, "B-ISDN ATM Layer Specification," 1995.

[86] ITU-T Recommendation I.362, "B-ISDN ATM Adaptation Layer (AAL) Functional Description," 1993.

[87] ITU-T Recommendation I.363, "B-ISDN ATM Adaptation Layer (AAL) Specification," 1993.

[88] ITU-T Recommendation I.371, "Traffic Control and Congestion Control in B-ISDN," 1996.

[89] ITU-T Recommendation I.580, "General Arrangements for Interworking between B-ISDN and 64 Kb/s based ISDN," Dec. 1994.

[90] ITU-T Recommendation M.2101, "Performance Limit for Bringing into Service and Maintenance of International SDH Paths, and Multiplex Sections," 1997.

[91] ITU-T Recommendation M.2110, "Bringing into Service International Paths, Sections and Transmission Systems," 1997.

[92] ITU-T Recommendation M.2120, "PDH Path, Section, and Transmission System and SDH Path and Multiplex Section Fault Detection and Localization," 1997.

[93] ITU-T Recommendation O.1700 series, Various documents on SDH/SONET jitter generators and analyzers.

[94] ITU-T Recommendation Q.931, "ISDN UNI Layer 3 Specification for Basic Call Control" 1993.

[95] ITU-T Blue Book X.200 series, Various subjects on OAM&P.

SECTION III
ASYNCHRONOUS TRANSFER
MODE

Part III discusses the asynchronous transfer mode (ATM). Chapter 13 provides an introduction to ATM and how it differs from SONET and SDH. Chapter 14 reviews the ATM cell, the types of cells, the ATM reference model, quality of service (QoS), ATM service classes (e.g., variable bit rate), and generic flow control (including leaky buckets). Chapter 15 reviews ATM connectivity, connection admission control and routing, ATM addressing, and NSAPs. Chapter 16 describes the basics of ATM cell switching. This includes virtual-channel switching and virtual-path switching. Chapter 17 reviews the ATM adaptation layer, as well as how a non-ATM packet or a signal from a legacy communications network is converted to ATM cells, an operation known as segmentation and reassembly (SAR). Chapter 18 reviews circuit emulation with practical examples, such as frame relay on ATM and Internet (IP) on ATM. Chapter 19 addresses the issue of congestion control, traffic policing, congestion management, and traffic shaping. Chapter 20 reviews the performance management of ATM systems, as well as the operations, administration, and management (OAM) cells, for both virtual paths and virtual circuits, and also loopbacks and fault location. Chapter 21 reviews ATM tandem connections and wireless ATM. Chapter 22 describes ATM cell mapping onto SONET or SDH frames, and Chapter 23 reviews the management of ATM over SONET or SDH. Finally, Chapter 24 provides an epilogue to legacy systems, SONET or SDH, and ATM systems and introduces convergence and what is expected of the network of the future.

CHAPTER 13

INTRODUCTION

We have described what SONET/SDH is and how it works. As we pointed out, S in SONET and SDH stands for *synchronous,* and this is one of the most fundamental differences, as well as a host of others, between it and what we are about to describe, namely the asynchronous transfer mode, or ATM.

ATM is a standardized technology that enables the convergence of a variety of services, low bandwidth and very high bandwidth, synchronous and asynchronous, voice and data, real time and non–real time, slotted and packetized, and switched and nonswitched. In addition, ATM is independent of the transmission medium, wire, wireless, or fiber. Hence, ATM is considered an enabler of the information superhighway of the future.

Legacy transport systems, as well as SONET/SDH, are most efficiently utilized when the DS1's, E1's, DS3's, STSs, and STMs are fully (or almost fully) occupied by data; that is, all or most time slots in DSx or all VTs/TUs in the SPE/TUG signals are full of data. Conversely, ATM technology allows a variety of bit rates to be transported, which with sophisticated bandwidth management enables the network to be more efficient where SONET/SDH is not, and at the same time maintain a QoS that is custom suited to each user.

To understand the significance of the word asynchronous in communication systems and networks, we briefly contrast synchronous communications systems with the asynchronous one.

As already described, the synchronicity of communication systems stems from traditional services that by nature were synchronous, such as real-time voice. The term real-time voice here is a differentiation from the term stored and forward. In the former case, real-time voice signifies that spoken words are transmitted as they are generated, and they are received with only a negligible delay that perceptually it is either not detected by the human ear or not annoying. In the latter case, a sentence may be stored, and then each word may be transmitted at a later time one word at a time; that is, time is not of the essence. Then, at the receiving end, when all words are put together in the correct sequence, the complete sentence is reconstructed and played back. A similar operation takes place with stored and forwarded images, as is currently the case in Internet applications, although real-time transmission of voice and image has also been demonstrated; this will become more common in the near future.

Figure 13.1 illustrates an analog signal (voice) that is sampled 8000 times per second to yield a 64-Kbps (DS0) rate. Notice that each sample is encoded to an 8-bit PCM code. This figure also illustrates the DS0 channels, all being synchronous with a switching system. The point made here is that between slots there is no time wasted and where one slot ends another one begins, before and after the switching function.

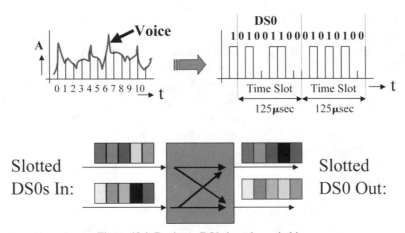

Figure 13.1 Review—DS0 time slot switching.

In a different case, consider that the analog signal does not represent (amplitude) voice as in Figure 13.1, but it represents information rate, or bits per second, as in Figure 13.2. That is, an analog graph with a higher value means a high rate of bits per second as compared to fewer bits per second when the graph has a lower value. Such a graph indicates that the rate (number of bits per unit of time) is not constant, as opposed to a 64-Kbps rate which is constant (such a graph would be a straight horizontal line at 64 Kbps). When the rate is not constant but varies between two extremes, we say that data are bursty. Now, in the case of bursty data, as bytes are formed (or fixed-length packets), they are spaced in irregular time intervals. Exactly this irregularity is what makes a system asynchronous. Figure 13.2 illustrates the case of bursty data and the need for buffers at the switching function to compensate for their time irregularity. The latter case is particularly necessary if bursty data should be transported over a synchronous network.

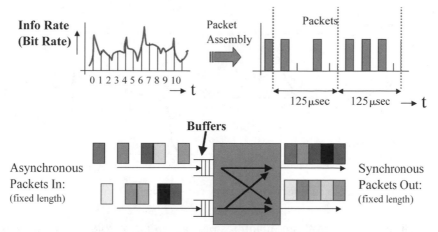

Figure 13.2 Review—fixed-length packet switching.

Although several sources generate bursty data, a communications system that offers both synchronous and asynchronous services must internally synchronize both types of data for simplicity of design, lower cost, and thus lower tariff. This internal synchronization is easily accomplished by employing buffers at the switch.

If the average flow of bytes (or fixed-length packets) is equal to the rate of the switch, then the switch switches them in synchronism.

If the average flow is less, then the buffer inserts some "idle" bytes (or packets) to maintain synchronicity.

If the average flow is momentarily higher, then a limited-size buffer averages out the flow.

However, if the incoming rate is such that the switch is not able to cope with the incoming flow, then some bytes (or packets) will be periodically lost due to buffer overflow. These concepts will be discussed in more detail.

13.1 NATURAL BIT RATE

A plot of the natural bit rate of information versus time would have three levels of interest: maximum natural information rate, minimum natural information rate, and average natural information rate.

The maximum natural information rate sets an upper limit of rate above which information could be lost, due to the inability of the switch to cope with it. The minimum natural information rate sets a low limit of rate below which the service may be uneconomical. The average natural information rate sets an average rate that must be maintained by the information source (Figure 13.3).

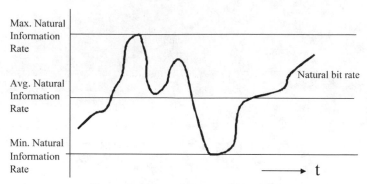

Figure 13.3 Natural bit rate—definition.

We will see that these three quantities play a significant role in providing an efficient asynchronous service.

The burstiness of a service is illustrated by plotting the peak rate versus the peak over the average rate. The graph in Figure 13.4 maps the burstiness of various services. Based on the correlation of burstiness and efficient services, the space of Figure 13.4 is divided into two; the heavy line separates the space, the circuit switch services (e.g., DS0, DS1, etc.), and packet-switching services (e.g., frame relay, ATM).

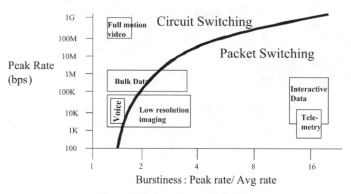

Figure 13.4 Burstiness—definition.

Here we consider an asynchronous system with many asynchronous inputs with bursty data at each input. Clearly, burstiness at each input is not organized or synchronized. Consider the sum of flow at all inputs. If we think of a total natural bit rate that arrives at the system, then the graph in Figure 13.5 may be plotted. In addition, consider that a *transfer rate* or a total bandwidth characterizes the system (or the switching function). For a given system, the transfer rate is constant and is represented as a horizontal line in Figure 13.5. In a typical case, the transfer rate crosses the plot of the aggregate natural bit

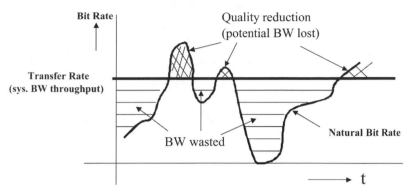

Figure 13.5 Bandwidth utilization—definition.

rate. In such a case, there are instances when the natural bit rate exceeds the transfer rate, instances when it is below it, and instances when it is the same.

When the aggregate natural bit rate is higher than the transfer rate, we run into the danger of losing bandwidth. When the aggregate natural bit rate is lower than the transfer rate, the system is underutilized and potential revenue from the unused bandwidth is lost. When the average of the natural bit rate is equal to the transfer rate (perfect balance), as soon as the balance is disturbed, we may run into the danger of losing bandwidth. Typically, one wants the average natural bit rate to be close and a little under the transfer rate. In addition, the maximums should not be above the transfer rate for prolonged times, since this implies long buffers and undesirable delays, or below the transfer rate for prolonged times, since this implies wasted bandwidth.

EXERCISES

1. Consider an ATM system with a maximum transfer rate of 11 Gbps. Assume that at its input there is an incoming natural bit rate with a profile of 7 Gbps for 10 s, ramping up to 12 Gbps within 5 s and ramping down to 8 Gbps in 4 s. Comment on the bandwidth utilization.
2. Consider the system of exercise 1, except the system has at its inputs a 2-gigabit buffer. Comment on the bandwidth utilization.
3. A data rate has a peak rate of 500 Mbps and an average rate of 50 Mbps.
   a. What type of service would you recommend: circuit switched or packet?
   b. Give examples of the data rate.

Answers

1. The natural bit rate will exceed the maximum transfer rate for about 2 s.
2. The system will buffer the excess bandwidth that occurs for 2 s.
3. The burstiness is 500/50 = 10.
   a. Packet-switched service is recommended.
   b. The data rate may be Internet data or banking data, for example.

CHAPTER 14

ATM SYSTEMS

We have described the asynchronicity and burstiness of information and the implications in passing through a switching system. In general, information generated asynchronously and burstly is not formed and sent one byte at a time; this would be very inefficient due to the nature of data. Instead, information is collected over several octets (8-bit bytes), some overhead information is attached to it and then it is sent. The complete construct is called a *packet*.

Depending on the system, this packet may be many thousand octets long; it may have a fixed length or it may have a variable length. In ATM systems, the packet is fixed to 53 octets, known as a *cell*. The following logical question arises: If ATM systems are designed to handle 53-octet cells, then how can they handle a packet arriving from another system that is designed to handle several thousand-octet-long packets? The answer is simple: Not a problem!

We will see that any type of traffic—voice, data, video, synchronous or asynchronous, short or long packets—can be converted into ATM cells by a process known as *emulation*.

14.1 THE ATM CELL

The 53-octet ATM cell consists of two fields (Figure 14.1). The overhead field consists of 5 octets and the information field of 48 octets. In the following we take a closer look at both fields.

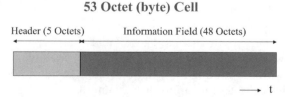

53 Octet (byte) Cell

Header (5 Octets)   Information Field (48 Octets)

Figure 14.1 ATM cell—definition.

14.1.1 ATM Cell: Overhead

The overhead field of all ATM cells consists of 5 octets. The content of the overhead, which is attached to the information field to construct a cell, does not remain intact as it is transferred from one network element to another throughout the ATM network; it changes. We will see more on that. In addition, the definition of the overhead is different at different places in the ATM network. Here, we distinguish two cases: the user-to-network interface (UNI) and the network-to-network interface (NNI); see Figure 14.2.

UNI case: The ATM cell overhead in the UNI case is partitioned into six subfields. The first 4 bits are designated for generic flow control (GFC), the next 8 bits are designated for the virtual-path identifier (VPI), the next 16 bits for the virtual-channel identifier (VCI), the next 3 bits for the payload-type identifier (PTI), 1 bit for the cell loss priority (CLP), and the last octet for header error control (HEC).

NNI case: The ATM cell overhead in the NNI case is partitioned into five subfields. The first 12 bits are designated for the VPI, the next 16 bits for the VCI, the next 3 bits for the PTI, 1 bit for the CLP, and the last octet for HEC.

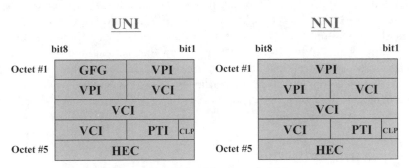

Figure 14.2 ATM cell header—definition.

The definition of each subfield is as follows:

1. GFG consists of 4 bits. It is used at the UNI to assist the customer network in the cell flow control but NOT in traffic flow control. GFG is not carried through the network

2. VPI/VCI consists of 24 bits. These labels identify a particular *virtual path* (*VP*) and *virtual channel* (*VC*) on a link. The switching node uses this information and with the routing information (tables) established at connection setup routes the cells to the appropriate output port. The switching node changes the input value of the VPI/VCI fields to new output values.

Although to this point we have not defined the VC or VP, it suffices to say that 12 VPI bits provide $2^{12} = 4096$ binary combinations and 16 VCI bits provide $2^{16} = 65{,}536$ binary combinations. If each combination corresponds to an addressed destination, then each cell may address one of many destinations.

Certain VCI values are reserved and are not to be used by the customer or the end user. Such VCI values are reserved by ITU-T (e.g., VCI = 0–15) and by the ATM Forum (e.g., VCI = 16–31). Reserved cells may indicate that a cell is idle, or it is for operations, administration, and maintenance (OA&M), or it is an unassigned cell, and so on.

3. CLP consists of 1 bit, having one of two values, 0 or 1. The CLP indicates the priority of a cell when the network element has to make the decision to drop cells when its throughput bandwidth exceeds its transfer rate. In congestion situations, cells with CLP = 1 may be dropped and not transferred at all. The end user or the service provider sets the priority.

4. PTI consists of 3 bits. The PTI identifies the payload type, that is, whether the cell payload contains user data or network information, and also provides a congestion indication.

The three PTI bits identify whether congestion is experienced on the path and in which direction (source to destination, or vice versa). They also identify if the payload is a resource management cell, an OA&M cell, or a reserved (for the future) type cell. Table 14.1 lists all PTI codes and their meaning.

5. HEC consists of 8 bits. The HEC code detects and corrects a single error or detects multiple errors in the header field (previous 4 bytes). It is based on the $x^8 + x^2 + x + 1$ cyclic redundant code (CRC). The HEC algorithm serves a dual purpose:

(a) *Error control:* Error control of the header field only is based on the generating polynomial $g(x) = x^8 + x^2 + x + 1$ and the coset polynomial $c(x) = x^6 + x^4 + x^2 + 1$.

Table 14.1 ATM Cell Header: Payload Types

Code	Meaning
000	User data cell; congestion not experienced, SDU = 0
001	User data cell; congestion not experienced, SDU = 1
010	User data cell; congestion experienced, SDU = 0
011	User data cell; congestion experienced, SDU = 1
100	OAM F5 segment associated cell
101	OAM F5 end-to-end associated cell
110	Resource management cell
111	Reserved for future

Abbreviation: SDU, service data unit.

The source divides the header-protected bits (first 32 bits) by the generating polynomial $g(x)$. The remainder is EX-ORed (mod-2) with the coset polynomial $c(x)$, a fixed pattern 01010101, and the binary result (8 bits) is placed in the HEC field. At the destination the received header is correlated with the same generating polynomial to detect errors in the header-protected bits and the HEC field.

Equipment supporting the UNI shall implement error detection (ITU-T Recommendation I.432). This method is also capable of correcting a single error (per ITU-T Recommendation I.432).

(b) *Cell delineation:* When the destination correlates the received header with the generating polynomial, the result should be the pattern 01010101. This pattern provides the identification of cell boundaries in the payload (ITU-T Recommendation I.432). A state machine may also be followed to define transition-timing requirements (per ATM Forum).

Figure 14.3 illustrates the transition state diagram for HEC. The state machine has two modes, the *correction state* and the *detection state.*

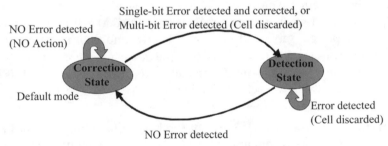

Figure 14.3 Header error control—state machine.

When the machine is at the correction state and no errors are detected, there is no action. This is the default state. When a single error is detected, then it is corrected and the machine moves to the detection state. When a multiple error is detected, then the cell is discarded and the machine moves to the detection state.

When the machine is at the detection state and an error is received, the cell is discarded. When no error is detected, the machine moves to the correction state.

Figure 14.4 illustrates the transition state diagram for delineation. In this case, the state machine has three modes, the *hunt state,* the *presync state,* and the *sync state.* The machine starts in the hunt state, calculating bit after bit.

When at the hunt state and a wrong HEC is detected, the machine remains at the hunt state. When a correct HEC is detected, the machine moves to the presync state.

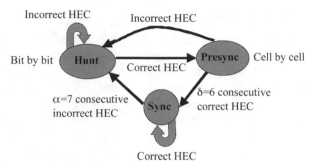

Figure 14.4 ATM cell delineation—state machine.

When at the presync state and the machine detects six consecutive correct HECs (in six consecutive cells), it moves to the sync state; else one incorrect HEC will move it back to the hunt state.

When at the sync state and the machine detects correct HECs, it stays there; else, when it receives seven consecutive wrong HECs (in seven consecutive cells), it moves to the hunt state.

14.1.2   ATM Cell: Information Field

The information field does not contain 48 octets (or bytes) of user data, as one might think. One or 2 octets (the one following the header) are dedicated for administration and cell sequence purposes. Thus, the first octet (after the overhead) consists of three subfields (Figure 14.5):

The first bit is known as the *convergence sublayer indicator* (*CSI*); it is used to indicate whether a pointer is used or not.

The next 3 bits are a *sequence number* (*SN*), from 000 to 111, used to detect lost cells or erroneously inserted cells.

The next 4 bits are the *sequence number protection* (*SNP*); it performs error detection on the CSI and SN subfields.

The second octet is *optional* and is used (if it is) as a *pointer* to mark the start of a long *encapsulated* message (we will elaborate on this later).

53 Octet (byte) Cell

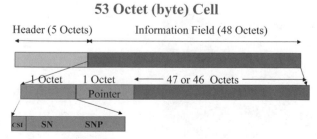

Figure 14.5 ATM cell—information field.

14.1.3 The Scrambler

In ATM, only the cell payload, i.e., the 48-octet information field, is scrambled. The *cell payload scrambler* is self-synchronizing and is defined by the generating polynomial $1 + x^{43}$. This polynomial is implemented with a 43-bit shift register, the output of which is fed back to its input. The shift register is clocked at the data rate and every bit of the data is exclusively ORed with its output. This scrambler operates continuously through the stream of ATM cells, scrambling only the 48-octet information field of ATM cells. The cell header is NOT scrambled.

The scrambler's state at the beginning of the cell payload is at the state it was at the end of the previous cell payload. That is, the scrambler is *not* running or advancing its states during the header. The scrambler operates when the cell delineation state machine is at the presync and sync states (Figure 14.4). At the ATM cell-receiving end, descrambling is disabled when the cell delineation state machine is at the hunt state.

14.2 THE ATM REFERENCE MODEL

The ATM functionality is organized in a stack of layers, each layer assigned a specific function:

The layer that deals with issues related to physical connectivity of the transmission medium and transmission of the ATM cells is the physical layer.

Above the physical layer, the *ATM layer* deals with flow issues of the ATM cells.

Above the ATM layer, the *ATM adaptation layer* (AAL) deals with the assembly of a continuous data bit stream in ATM cells.

Above the first three layers there are higher layers and the application layers.

All layers in this model deal with control and management issues.

The model in Figure 14.6, known as the *ATM reference model*, illustrates the layers and their relationship.

The functions performed at the first two layers are discussed next.

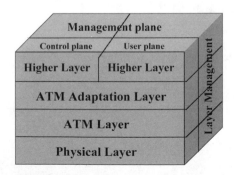

Figure 14.6 ATM cell—reference model.

14.2.1 Physical Layer Functions

At this layer the following are defined:

- The physical medium connectivity and bit timing
- Bit error control: includes the HEC (overhead byte) generation and verification
- Cell delineation
- Transmission frame adaptation
- Transmission frame generation and recovery
- Cell scrambling and descrambling
- Cell mapping (e.g., in STS-3c SONET payload)
- ATM payload construction indication

14.2.2 ATM Layer Functions

ATM cells from different ATM channels arrive with different quality-of-service (QoS) requirements (see paragraph 14.5). At this layer, the corresponding QoS for ATM cells from different channels are verified and monitored.

When the cell stream at the sending entity is not continuous (see natural bit rate, Section 13.1), the cell rate *decoupling function* inserts unassigned cells to convert the cell stream to a continuous stream of cells.

There are user cells and nonuser cells. This function recognizes and discriminates cells based on the payload-type (PT) value.

There are predefined header field values that distinguish among a variety of ATM cells. Such cells are unassigned, meta-signaling, point-to-point signaling, invalid pattern, segment OAM F4 flow cell, and end-to-end OAM F4 flow cell (see ATM Forum document for details). At this layer, these cells based on the predefined header values are discriminated.

14.3 TYPES OF CELLS

Besides customer data cells, there are cells used by the ATM network and its nodes. For example:

- The *idle cell* is inserted or extracted by the physical layer in order to adapt the cell rate to the available rate of the transmission system.
- The *valid cell* is a cell with no header errors or with a corrected error.
- The *invalid cell* is a cell with a noncorrectable header error.
- The *assigned cell* is a valid cell that provides a service to an application using the ATM layer service.
- The *unassigned cell* is an ATM layer cell, which is not an assigned cell.
- The *meta-signaling cell* is used for establishing or releasing a switched

virtual-channel connection. Permanent virtual-channel connections need no meta-signaling.

- *OAM cells* are used for operations, administration, and maintenance of the ATM node and the network.

These cells and their meaning are listed in Table 14.2.

Table 14.2 ATM Cell Types

Idle cell	Inserted/extracted by the physical layer in order to adapt the cell rate to the available rate of the transmission system
Valid cell	A cell with no header errors or with a corrected error
Invalid cell	A cell with a noncorrectable header error
Assigned cell	A valid cell that provides a service to an application using the ATM layer service
Unassigned cell	An ATM cell layer cell that is not an assigned cell
Meta-signaling cell	Used for establishing/releasing a VCC. VCs in permanent virtual connections need no meta-signaling.

Figure 14.7 illustrates certain types of cells that are recognized, terminated, and generated at the physical layer and at the ATM layer of an ATM network element.

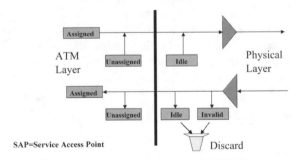

Figure 14.7 ATM cell in physical and ATM layer.

14.4   ATM SERVICE CLASSES

ATM services fall in several classes. The *constant bit rate (CBR)*, the *variable bit rate (VBR)*, the *real-time VBR,* the *non-real-time VBR,* the *available bit rate (ABR)*, and the *undefined bit rate (UBR)*.

The CBR defines cells that arrive at a negotiated constant bit (or cell) rate. This service requires low cell loss rate ($<10 \times 10^{-9}$) and tightly constrained cell delay variations. Services with CBR are real-time voice and video.

The VBR defines cells that arrive at a negotiated variable bit (or cell) rate, characterized by a *minimum* (*MCR*) and *maximum* (*PCR*) rate, *sustained cell rate* (*SCR*), and *maximum burst size* (*MBS*).

The rt-VBR defines cells that arrive at a negotiated variable bit (or cell) rate, characterized by a minimum and maximum rate and burstiness. It requires low cell loss rate ($<10 \times 10^{-9}$) and stringent cell delay variation. This service is intended for applications that require tightly constrained cell delay and cell delay variations, such as real-time variable-rate video.

The nrt-VBR defines cells that arrive at a negotiated variable bit (or cell) rate, characterized by a minimum and maximum rate and burstiness. It requires low cell loss rate but has no requirements for cell delay variation. This service is intended for applications that are bursty and require low CLRs, such as high-speed file transfers.

The ABR service class defines cells that arrive at a cell rate determined by the node, based on bandwidth availability. No explicit CLR ($<10 \times 10^{-5}$) is expected. It is intended for applications that can adapt their cell rate to the available bandwidth; they can tolerate long delays but require low cell loss rate. When an ABR connection is set up, the network guarantees an MCR. In addition, a flow control loop is established between source and destination and through all transit switching nodes on the path. Based on feedback about congestion states and network resource availability along the path, the source receives information about the rate that should transmit and adapts its cell rate.

The UBR service class defines no specific QoS requirements. It is intended for non-real-time applications, such as file transfer protocol, electronic mail, and low-cost *transmission control protocol/Internet Protocol* (*TCP/IP*) with non-real-time requirements.

14.5 QUALITY OF SERVICE

The QoS of a connection pertains to a set of parameters that have been negotiated and agreed upon between the end user and the service provider. The QoS of a connection in the ATM network relates to cell integrity and cell flow parameters, such as *cell loss, cell delay,* and *cell delay variation.* From a node point of view, the QoS is also closely related to the bandwidth (BW) used as compared with the BW available.

When an ATM connection is established, both the user and the service provider warranty that the agreed QoS parameter values for that connection are honored. However, since ATM services vary, different connections may have different QoS parameter values. For example, a connection may require high priority and higher cell rate throughput across the network than a connection that requires low priority and low cell rate as defined by the node (available bit rate).

Semantic transparency determines the capability of the network to transport information from source to destination with an acceptable error rate. The

QoS parameters are closely linked to the potential transmission and network errors. Therefore, it is logical that the "standard" negotiable QoS parameters for a connection are expressed in terms of errors.

14.5.1   Error Definitions and QoS Parameters

Errors Pertaining to Transmission

The *bit error rate* (BER) is defined as the number of erroneous bits over the total number of bits sent.

The *packet error rate* (PER) is defined as the number of erroneous packets over the total number of packets sent.

Errors Pertaining to Accuracy

The *cell mis-insertion rate* (CMR) is defined as the number of mis-inserted cells over a time interval.

The *cell error ratio* (CER) is defined as the number of errored cells over the total cells sent.

Error Pertaining to Dependability

The *cell loss rate* (CLR) is defined as the number of lost cells over the total cells sent.

Errors Pertaining to Speed

The *cell transfer delay* (CTD) is defined as the elapsed time between an exit and an entry measuring point for a cell.

The *cell delay variation* (CDV) is defined as the variability of cell arrival for a given connection.

14.5.2   Rate Parameters

The following rate parameters are defined for each UNI connection:

The *peak cell rate* (PCR) is the permitted maximum cell rate in the burst profile of ATM traffic associated with that connection.

The *sustainable cell rate* (SCR) is the permitted upper bound on the average rate for each UNI connection, i.e., a maximum average throughput.

14.5.3   Services and Requirements

A cell with an erroneous header is discarded. In addition, the node may discard good cells when it is severely congested. Therefore, it is logical that the cell rate reduction and the number of discarded cells be monitored.

Traffic shaping (TS) is an important function that is performed at the endpoints to achieve the desired QoS (see also Chapter 18). This function is ac-

complished taking into account the traffic parameters that have been negotiated and agreed upon between the end user and the service provider; these parameters are known as *traffic descriptors*.

Traffic shaping is defined as the altering of the flow (rate) of cells in a VC
or VP connection (see also Chapter 18) to comply with agreed-upon QoS requirements (rate reduction, cell discarding). Cell loss priority (CLP) indication
and selective cell discarding are used, based on the network congestion state,
to shape traffic.

Rate reduction establishes the negotiated low limit to which an initial rate
may be reduced when the network experiences congestion.

Cell discarding establishes the negotiated limits of discarding cells per cell
successfully transmitted when the network experiences congestion.

Tables 14.3 and 14.4 list ATM services and data rates.

Table 14.3 Services and Requirements

Service	BER	Cell Loss Ratio	Delay (ns)
Telephony	10×10^{-3}	10×10^{-3}	<25
Data transmission	10×10^{-7}	10×10^{-6}	1000
Hi-fi sound	10×10^{-5}	10×10^{-7}	1000

Table 14.4 Services and Requirements

Application	Delay (ms)	Jitter (ms)
64-Kbps video conference	300	130
1.5 Mbps MPEG, NTSC	5	6.5
20 Mbps	0.8	1
160 Kbps	30	130
256 Kbps	7	9.1

14.6 GENERIC FLOW CONTROL

Generic flow control (GFC) is exercised to warranty the agreed-upon QoS for
each connection. GFC consists of *traffic management* and *congestion control*.
Both are part of the ATM layer functionality. GFC is implemented at the UNI.

Traffic management assures that the allocated bandwidth and QoS negotiated at connection admission control (CAC) procedures is maintained for
both old and new connections. This is accomplished by utilizing at the UNI the
usage parameter controls (*UPCs*), the CLP, and TS mechanisms. *Traffic control*
specifies the actions needed to avoid congestion control.

Congestion control assures that the accepted traffic by a node does not exceed the maximum traffic that the node can pass through its switching fabric. TS is also used as a flow control mechanism (see above).

14.6.1   Traffic Management

ATM networks and nodes are designed for optimum usage of bandwidth. As such, the network allows traffic at an assortment of bit rates, e.g., constant bit rates, variable bit rates, and bit rates based on available bandwidth. Moreover, a different QoS parameters characterize each service. Consequently, for the network to be able to sustain the agreed-upon traffic and QoS of each connection and at the same time utilize its bandwidth optimally, that is, introduce the minimum possible delay and be at near full capacity but never exceed capacity, the traffic must be continuously managed.

Managing traffic means monitoring and managing traffic and service parameters. The ATM Forum and ITU-T have defined parameters that can be managed to maintain the agreed-upon QoS. They also have defined algorithms for policing the traffic parameters at the UNI for both the CBR and the VBR; see above. This assortment of bit rates implies that the network may receive large bursts, which require deep buffers that introduce delays. To ameliorate this, cells are spaced by applying a *generic cell rate algorithm* (*GCRA*) that schedules cell transmission on a per-VC or per-flow basis.

The GCRA provides the format definition of conforming cells to the traffic contract. The traffic contract is defined by source traffic descriptors that consist of PCR, SCR, MBS, and CDV. The GCRA is implemented with the continuous-state *leaky bucket,* and it is based on two parameters, the *increment* (I) and the *limit* (L). The I parameter affects the cell rate and the L parameter affects the cell burst.

The parameters utilized for traffic management are:

PCR for CBR connections and for VBR connections.

SCR and MBS for VBR connections are provided by the user during CAC at the UNI.

The CDV determines how much delay between cells can be introduced as a result of queuing. CDV also determines the amount of jitter introduced in intermediate nodes.

In addition, there is a *burst tolerance* (*BT*) parameter that puts a restriction on the additional traffic above the SCR, before it is tagged as excessive traffic. The burst tolerance is defined by the relationship

$$BT = (1/SCR) - (1/PCR) \, MBS - 1$$

14.6.2   Leaky Buckets

The *fast leaky bucket* is an approach to assure that the average number of cells per unit of time complies with the agreed-upon cell rate so that the agreed-upon QoS is sustained.

The fast leaky bucket employs a *periodic token credit* that is added to a customer's bucket (or credit) for as long as NO cells arrive from this customer, whereas a token is subtracted for each cell arrived.

When the bucket has enough tokens in it, arriving cells with CLP = 0 remain set to 0 (that is, the cell rate conforms to the agreed-upon traffic rate). When the bucket becomes empty, the CLP is set to 1 (that is, the cell rate does not conform to the agreed-upon traffic rate). This mechanism implies that for each connection there is a separate bucket. In reality, a bucket is a buffer or a counter.

Figure 14.8 illustrates the principle of the leaky bucket. Here, a timer generates a periodic token credit that is deposited in the bucket. At start, the bucket is partially full with tokens. When a valid cell with CLP bit set to logic 0 arrives, a token is removed from the bucket.

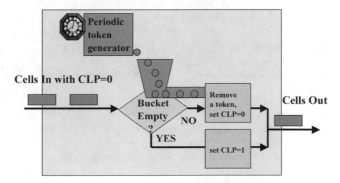

Figure 14.8 Traffic management—fast leaky bucket.

If the cell rate is slower than expected, the timer adds tokens faster than removing them and the bucket eventually will overflow, indicating that the agreed-upon minimum rate is not sustained. The VBR services define a maximum and a minimum bit (and a cell) rate.

If the cell rate is faster than expected, tokens are removed faster than added and the bucket becomes empty, thus indicating that the maximum cell rate has been exceeded. Then the cell is passed but its CLP is changed to 1.

The above leaky-bucket process is a requirement for all nodes at the UNI and may also be repeated at every node on the path source-destination. Cells with CLP = 1 do not contribute to this process, and if they are passed through the node, there is no warranty that they will pass all subsequent nodes down the path. Cells with CLP = 1 pass through a node only when there is bandwidth available.

The *overflow leaky bucket* is another approach to assure that the average number of cells per unit of time complies with the agreed-upon cell rate so that the agreed-upon QoS is sustained.

The overflow leaky bucket employs a *periodic token penalty*. That is, a token is subtracted from a customer's bucket for as long as NO cells arrive, and a token or more (as agreed) is added for each cell arrived.

When the in-flow of cells is faster than the leak, the bucket overflows, and subsequent cells are *nonconforming*.

When the flow is within the agreed limits, the bucket is either empty or partially full and the cells are conforming.

Figure 14.9 illustrates another periodic token-penalty leaky-bucket principle. At start, the bucket is partially full with tokens. A timer periodically removes a token from a bucket, hence the term periodic token penalty. When a valid cell with CLP = 0 arrives, a token is added in the bucket.

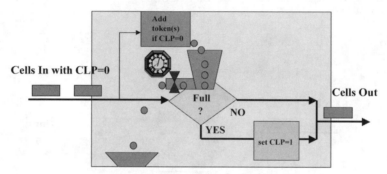

Figure 14.9 Traffic management—overflow leaky bucket.

If the bucket overflows, it indicates that the rate is higher than agreed. Then, the cell is passed but its CLP is changed to 1.

If the bucket becomes empty, it indicates that the cell rate is lower than the agreed-upon minimum.

The *dual leaky bucket* employs two leaky buckets (Figure 14.10), one that measures the *sustainable rate* and the other that measures the *peak rate*. Thus, arriving cells (with CLP = 0) are checked for these two parameters, and if both conform, then the cells depart with CLP = 0; else their CLP is set to 1.

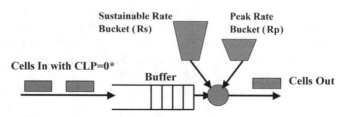

Figure 14.10 Traffic management—buffered dual leaky bucket.

EXERCISES

1. An ATM node is connected to 100 channels and has a throughput of 100,000,000 cells per second. The 100 channels have the following traffic parameters: 40% of them have a constant cell rate of 1,000,000 cells/s; 30% of them have a variable cell rate with a minimum cell rate of 300,000 cells/s and a maximum of 600,000 cells/s; 20% of them have a variable minimum cell rate of 1,000,000 cells/s and a maximum of 1,300,000 cells/s; and 10% of the channels are not active. A new customer requests all bandwidth available. Calculate the best- and worst-case bandwidth that can be given to the new customer if the node should operate up to 85% capacity (assume all cells at high priority, CLP = 0).

2. An ATM service contract defines a high cell priority (CLP = 0), maximum cell rate of 120,000 cells/s and a minimum of 60,000 cells/s. A traffic manager using a leaky-bucket mechanism monitors the incoming cell rate. The leaky bucket has a capacity of 1000 tokens and adds a token every 10 μs. Comment on the traffic management for the service provided if the actual cell rate on this channel varies between 60,000 and 120,000 cells/s linearly.

Answers

1. The following bandwidth utilization table is constructed:

$$40 \times 1 \text{ M cells/s} \quad = 40 \text{ M cells/s}$$
$$30 \times 300 \text{ K cells/s} = \quad 9 \text{ M cells/s} \quad \text{min}$$
$$30 \times 600 \text{ K cells/s} = 18 \text{ M cells/s} \quad \text{max}$$
$$20 \times 1 \text{ M cells/s} \quad = 20 \text{ M cells/s} \quad \text{min}$$
$$20 \times 1.3 \text{ M cells/s} = 26 \text{ M cells/s} \quad \text{max}$$

$$\text{Total} \quad 69 \text{ M cells/s} \quad \text{min}$$
$$84 \text{ M cells/s} \quad \text{max}$$

Thus, the new customer can be granted a VBR service between 1 M cells/s and 16 M cells/s.

2. The average cell rate is 80,000 cells/s. In 1 s there are 10,000 tokens added but only 80,000 removed. Since the bucket capacity is only 1000 tokens, the bucket will quickly overflow in 50 ms, on the average.

CHAPTER 15

ATM CONNECTIVITY

15.1 CONNECTIVITY TYPES

ATM networks are capable of establishing point-to-point, multicasting, and multipoint-to-multipoint connectivity:

Point to point establishes connectivity between two users (one source and one destination) and may be unidirectional or bidirectional.

Multicasting establishes connectivity between one user with many (one source and many destinations) and predominantly is unidirectional (e.g., e-mail).

Multipoint to multipoint establishes connectivity between many users (many sources and many destinations).

The first case has been standardized whereas the second is in near completion and the third in draft form. Clearly, multicasting and multipoint add an additional degree of complexity to the system, network congestion, and call processing. Here, we address the point-to-point connectivity case.

15.2 CONNECTION ADMISSION CONTROL (CAC)

Consider that an ATM terminal originates a request to the network to establish a connecting path between it and a *destination terminal.* Consider that the *originating terminal* requests a service that should conform to certain QoS parameters as they are defined by a contract of service. Such parameters may be cell transfer rate, cell error rate, cell delay, etc. In addition, consider that the destination terminal also has a contract of service, not necessarily the same as the originator and not necessarily with the same service provider. When a

145

connection is requested, the service provider takes action to assure first that the requested service is within the contract parameters and second that the network can support the requested connection with the QoS parameters, that is, that *all participating* network elements (NEs) on the path have sufficient resources to honor the service requested and so do all carriers on the path. The set of actions taken by a NE to determine whether a new connection can be established, denied, or released is called *connection admission control* (*CAC*).

A connection or release request is made with specialized ATM cells. When a NE receives a connection request and determines that it can be granted, it sends a connection request to the next NE, and so on. The information presented next is sent from originator to destination during the CAC process.

15.2.1   Source Traffic Descriptors

The source traffic descriptors are the *peak cell rate* (*PCR*), the required *quality of service* (*QoS*), the acceptable *cell delay variation* (*CDV*) tolerance, and the *conformance definition*.

The CAC function of the carrier receiving a connection request determines the traffic parameters needed by this carrier's *network parameter control* (*NPC*) functions, *routing* and *allocation* of network resources within the carrier's network, and whether this new ATM connection is accepted at its required QoS class by the carrier's network.

15.2.2   CAC Capabilities

The algorithm of CAC has the following capabilities:

- Connection on demand
- Point-to-point connection
- Point-to-multipoint connection
- Multicasting operations
- QoS parameter negotiations
- VPI/VCI range specification
- Error recovery mechanisms
- Client registration procedures
- End-to-end parameter identification

15.2.3   CAC Functions

Table 15.1 lists the functions performed at each step of the Call Admission Control (CAC) process.

Table 15.1 Connection Control Messages (Q.2931)

Message	Function
Call establishment	
• Call setup	• Initate call
• Call processing	• Begin call establishment
• Connect	• Call (connection) accepted
• Connect acknowledge	• Call acceptance acknowledged
Point to multipoint	
• Add party	• Add party to existing connection
• Add party acknowledge	• Add party acknowledged
• Drop party	• Drops party from existing connection
• Drop party acknowledge	• Dropped party acknowledged
Call clearing	
• Connection release	• Initiate call clearing
• Connection release complete	• Call has been cleared
Global call reference	
• Restart connection	• Restart all VCs
• Restart acknowledge	• Restart acknowledged
Miscellaneous	
• Status Inquiry	• Send for status
• Status (S)	• Send inquired status or report error

Note: Q.931 5 protocol for ISDN UNI; Q.2931 5 protocol for ATM/B-ISDN UNI.

15.3   CAC CALL PROCESSING

15.3.1   Connect Case

Consider that user terminal A wants to establish connectivity with user terminal B. User terminal A is connected with a (network edge A) NE, and user terminal B is connected with another (network edge B) NE. Between NE A and NE B, there may be more intermediate NEs (transit NE).

The call establishment begins with user terminal A issuing a SETUP message to NE A (Figure 15.1). The SETUP message contains the addresses (source-destination), source traffic descriptors, and QoS, as described earlier. Upon receiving the SETUP message, NE A examines the source traffic descriptors, and if it can satisfy them (based on the contract and traffic parameters), it replies with a call-in-process (CALL_PROC). In addition, NE A allocates resources, determines the route (based on the destination address), and sends a SETUP message to the next NE. The receiving NE examines the SETUP message, and if it can grant the requested connectivity, it repeats the process of NE A.

This process continues from NE to NE until NE B is reached. Then, NE B determines the destination of the called party (user terminal B), and if it allows the connection, it sends a SETUP message to terminal B. Terminal B

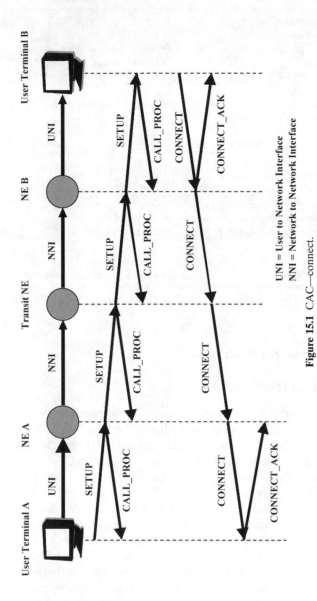

Figure 15.1 CAC—connect.

UNI = User to Network Interface
NNI = Network to Network Interface

responds with a CALL_PROC message, and if it accepts the call, then it sends back a CONNECT message to NE B. This CONNECT message is replied with a CONNECT_ACK message to terminal B and it is also transmitted, in the reverse direction, from NE to NE, while each NE establishes connectivity and updates its VC tables. When the CONNECT message reaches the source, user terminal A replies with a CONNECT_ACK. After this, the connectivity has been established and user data transfer begins.

15.3.2 Release Case

Assume that connectivity between user terminal A and user terminal B has been established. Assume also that user terminal A would like to disconnect. Then user terminal A issues a RELEASE message (Figure 15.2). NE A recognizes this and replies with RELEASE COMPLETE, disconnects connectivity, updates its VC table, frees the allocated resources, and sends to the next NE in the path (transit NE) a RELEASE message. This process is repeated from NE to NE on the path until it reaches NE B. NE B then sends a RELEASE to user terminal B, which replies with a RELEASE COMPLETE and the connectivity is fully released across the complete path.

15.3.3 Signaling Path

When a call is initiated, ATM cells assigned by the UNI CAC protocol (with $VPI = 0, VCI = 5$) will be sent for this protocol. As these cells pass from node to node down the path (the red path in Figure 15.3), a sequential agreement is made by all nodes involved on the path, and this agreement is returned to the initiating UNI node. If the returned agreement is within the parameters for the requested service, then the path is established and user data (formatted as ATM cells) are routed on the established path (blue line).

15.3.4 Calls per Second

In actual systems, it may happen that more than one ATM terminals simultaneously request connectivity. Today's telephone exchanges can handle some 500 calls per seconds, whereas ATM systems can handle approximately 200. As technology matures, the expected number of calls per second is expected to greatly surpass telephone exchanges. The protocol is individually processed for each connectivity. Therefore, CAC protocol processing for a large number of (simultaneous) calls may become a potential bottleneck. The efficiency of call processing per NE depends on the efficiency the protocol is executed by it. Consequently, large-bandwidth NE architects and designers should take this into account.

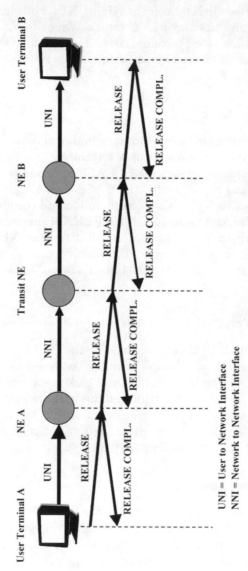

User Terminal A NE A Transit NE NE B User Terminal B

UNI = User to Network Interface
NNI = Network to Network Interface

Figure 15.2 CAC—release.

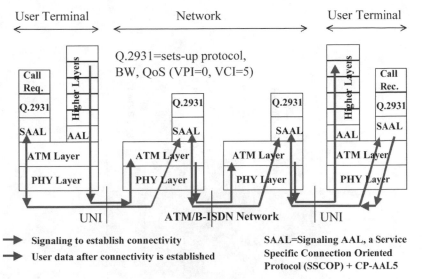

Figure 15.3 CAC—signaling.

15.4 ROUTING

When a connection is requested via the CAC process, the node must find an optimum path across the network that can support the required service. This is accomplished with three functions: the topology exchange, the topology database, and route determination:

Topology exchange: Each node advertises to the others information about the NNI links attached to it. That is, reachability and desirability for additional connections (based on bandwidth capacity and utilization). This information is exchanged according to a link state routing protocol.

Topology database: This is based on the link state information that has been exchanged at the NNI. Based on this information, a logical topology database is constructed by each node.

Route determination: This is based on an algorithm that selects an optimum route that satisfies the performance parameters of the requested service.

15.4.1 Routing Summary

When connectivity is requested with SETUP signaling, the UNI node replies to the requesting user terminal with a call-in-process (CALL_PROC) and sends the connectivity request to its Connection and Traffic Management (Call Control) function (Figure 15.4).

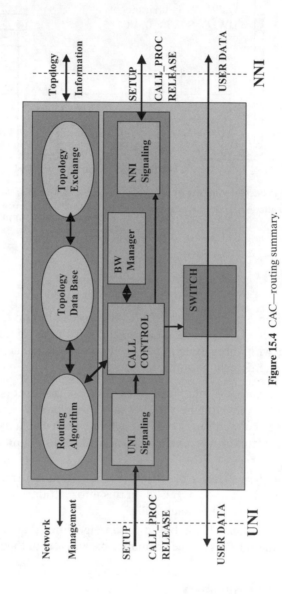

Figure 15.4 CAC—routing summary.

The Call Control function sends a message to the Route Determination function. The latter, based on information from the topology database, returns to the Call Control the best route available. The Call Control, based on already established links, bandwidth utilization, QoS, and bandwidth availability (from the Bandwidth Management function), negotiates the service parameters with the user terminal.

When the requested service and its parameters have been agreed upon, it passes a message to the NNI signaling function, which sends a SETUP signal to the next node (NNI).

When, eventually, end-to-end connectivity has been established, the UNI node sends topology information to all nodes connected with it to update their topology database and information about the connection (connectivity data and billing) to network management.

When connectivity is released, again the node sends topology information to all nodes connected with it to update their topology database and also information about the released connection (connectivity data and billing) to network management.

15.5   THE ATM ADDRESS

The CAC process implies that a *switched virtual channel* (*SVC*) is established and released dynamically at the user's request (similar to traditional telephony). Thus, for each SVC connection, each destination may be different, and so also may be the VCI/VPI values. When an SVC connection has been established, the VCI/VPI values (between adjacent nodes) should remain only for the duration of the call. Hence, for SVC, a standardized coding convention for the destination and source address is necessary.

In *permanent virtual channels* (*PVCs*), the source and destination are a priori known and the VCI/VPIs are preallocated.

15.5.1   NSAP Fields

In ATM, the address is modeled after the OSI *Network Service Access Point* (*NSAP*), defined by ITU-T X.213.

The NSAP format consists of two fields, the *initial-domain part* (*IDP*) and the *domain-specific part* (*DSP*) (Figures 15.5 and 15.6).

The IDP is further subdivided into two subfields, the *authority format identifier* (*AFI*) and the *initial-domain identifier* (*IDI*).

The AFI identifies the meaning of the IDI and of the DSP:

If AFI = 39, then IDI identifies the data country code (DCC)
      = 47, then IDI identifies the international code designator (ICD)
      = 45, then IDI identifies a format known as the E.164 Format

The IDI specifies the addressing domain and authority for the DSP values:

A. DCC

B. ICD

C. E.164 address

The DSP contains the address determined by the network authority and is subdivided into three subfields, the high-order DSP (HO-DSP), the end-system identifier (ESI), and the selector (SEL). In ATM, the contents of the DSP depend on the AFI value:

The *HO-DSP* contains a hierarchical address such as a routing domain and areas within the domain and the authority identified by the IDP establishes it.

The *ESI* identifies an end system within the area.

The *SEL* is not used in ATM; it could contain upper layer service access points (SAPs).

ATM public networks must support the E.164 address, and private networks must support all formats.

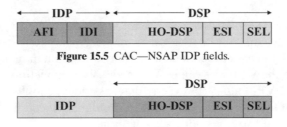

Figure 15.5 CAC—NSAP IDP fields.

Figure 15.6 CAC—NSAP DSP fields.

15.5.2   ATM Address Registration

The ATM Forum UNI signaling specification provides a procedure for the user and the network (at UNI) to register the ATM address(es).

This procedure begins with the network (UNI) initializing its address table; then it continues by asking the user for address(es), the user returns the address(es), the UNI returns a network prefix and address(es), and the user registers the address(es) and replies with an acceptance.

15.5.3   Broadband Inter-Communications Interface

Figure 15.7 illustrates the case of connection where the source subscribes to one ATM service provider and the destination may subscribe to another ATM service provider. In such a case, data cross a boundary between two service

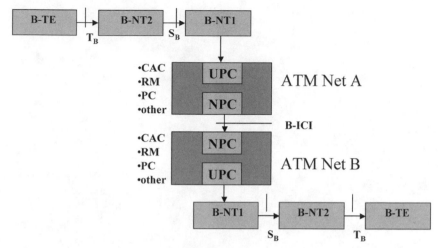

Figure 15.7 UPC/NPC reference configuration.

providers known as the *Broadband Inter-Carrier Interface* (B-ICI). At this interface, clearly there may be several issues with regard to standards compatibility. In reality, more than two service providers may be involved along the path source-destination and thus there are more than one B-ICI. Typically, regardless of how many B-ICIs in the path, both end users and all service providers are required to maintain the QoS agreed upon.

EXERCISES

1. List the CAC descriptors.
2. List the CAC functions.
3. Assume that an ATM system can process 200 connectivity calls per second. The system maximum bandwidth is 5 Gbps. The system provides nonpermanent connectivity service to 10,000 users, all with a variable rate from 50 to 150 Mbps and permanent connectivity to 20,000 users with 100 Mbps. If 5% of the users request connectivity calls simultaneously, comment on the CAC processing efficiency of this system.

Answers

1. Peak cell rate (PCR), quality of service (QoS), cell delay variation (CDV) tolerance, and the conformance definition.
2. See Table 15.1.
3. Five percent of 10,000 users is 500 call requests. Since the system can handle only 200 calls per second, the first 200 calls will be processed within the first second. The remaining 300 calls will be dropped, unless the system stores the remaining 300 requests, to be processed in the next 2 s.

CHAPTER 16

ATM CELL SWITCHING

16.1 MULTIPLEXERS

We have seen that cells arrive at a random rate but within rate limits. Consider that cells from several sources must be rearranged (i.e., multiplexed) in a continuous cell stream. Figure 16.1 illustrates an ATM cell multiplexer that polls in a round-robin fashion all input sources for cells; here, for simplicity, five sources are shown. A *round robin* is an expression of a mechanism (borrowed from the old days), which starts polling cell source 1, then cell source 2, and so on, and when it polls the last source, it starts with cell source 1 again, and so on. In Figure 16.1, five potential input sources are shown. Each rectangle at the input represents a buffer where the arriving cell is temporarily stored. As the multiplexer polls each buffer, it takes a cell from each buffer and puts it at its output in an orderly serial manner. However, if an input buffer has no cell in it, as for example source buffer 4, then the multiplexer generates an idle cell. During the next polling cycle, the source buffer 4 may have a cell but some other buffer may not, for which the multiplexer generates an idle cell.

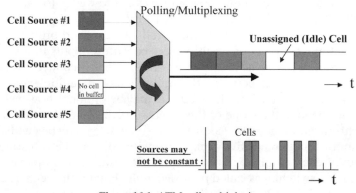

Figure 16.1 ATM cell multiplexing.

In the reverse direction, the cell stream is received, the poller is synchronized with the cell stream, and cells extracted from the stream and are delivered to their corresponding destination buffers (Figure 16.2). If a received cell is recognized as idle, it is discarded, the corresponding destination buffer is skipped (no data is entered), and the polling is continued with the next destination buffer.

This type of multiplexer is deterministic. Such multiplexers are simple, they are synchronized with the system, and they introduce very little overhead on the cell. Multiplexers (at the receiving port) of a NE that multiplex cells without maintaining cell order should add a tag on each cell. Such a tag should contain necessary information (e.g., a source number and a time stamp) so that cells are switched to the proper destination buffer (transmitting port) in the right order. This tag is for NE cell routing management and should be removed prior to transmitting the cell onto the network.

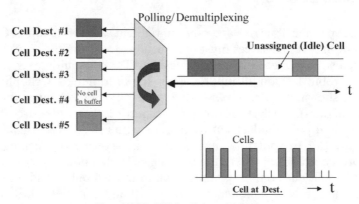

Figure 16.2 ATM cell demultiplexing.

16.2   CELL SWITCHING: A MODEL

Having explained the cell multiplexing process, here we try to capture in one figure cells from their individual sources to their destinations (Figure 16.3). Consider that many sources are multiplexed, as described previously. Moreover, the outputs from several multiplexers constitute inputs to a switch. The switch will route each input to one of its outputs that is connected with a demultiplexer. Notice that between the multiplexers, demultiplexers, and the switch there are some buffers. These buffers may be optional; however, for reasons that are beyond the scope of this discussion, they indicate that some further synchronization may be needed and/or some delay may be needed. Based on the input-output connectivity map, the switch directs the cell stream from the output of each multiplexer to an input of another demultiplexer. We will see that such a switching is called *path switching*. Finally, the cell stream is demultiplexed and the cells are distributed to their destinations.

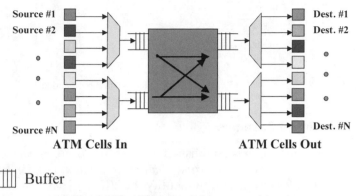

Figure 16.3 ATM cell switching—a model.

Consider many multiplexed sources, as described previously. Assume that each cell from each source is individually switched and directed dynamically to a different destination. That is, a cell from source 1 is dynamically routed to destination N. This switching is not based on a preexisting input-output connectivity map but on a channel request to be connected with a destination. We will see that such a switching is called *channel switching*.

16.3   VIRTUAL PATHS AND VIRTUAL CHANNELS

Previously, we discussed the notion of path and channel connectivity. To further illustrate this connectivity, consider traffic from various sources (channels) that converges at some point in the network. In addition, consider that all traffic is "bundled" (multiplexed) in a "pipe" (serial stream or path) and, from there, the network directs the pipe as a whole until it reaches its destination. Although a path in the network may not remain fixed but be redirected through the network, all bundled channels arrive at their destination. The latter is called a *virtual path* (*VP*) and the action of switching a whole VP is called *virtual-path switching* (*VPS*).

Similarly, various sources or channels are requesting connectivity with specific destinations. However, these channels are not fixed throughout the network (they are not in the same pipe throughout a single path), but at some nodes, they may "jump" from a VP to another until they reach their destination. These are called *virtual channels* (*VCs*) and the action of switching VCs is called *virtual-channel switching* (*VCS*).

Figure 16.4 illustrates the bundling of VCs and also VPs in larger "pipes" that constitute the physical layer. This implies that the physical layer is able to handle many VPs and in each VP many VCs.

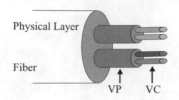

Physical Layer

Fiber

VP VC   **Figure 16.4** Virtual path and virtual channel.

16.3.1 Virtual Channels

An end-to-end connection is established with a series of VC links from source to destination. This is known as *virtual-channel connection* (*VCC*). Each ATM cell has in its header field a VCI to identify the VC.

Each switching node has routing translation tables that, upon receiving a cell, translates the incoming VCI into an outgoing VCI. Thus, the VCI value is different from node to node.

The translation values at each node are determined during the setup of the connection.

16.3.1.1 Virtual-Channel Connections. The following VCCs can be established:

User to user: VCC from user's equipment extends to S or T reference point per ISDN specific action (CCITT Recommendation I.361). Information is carried in ATM cells from one customer's equipment to the other's.

User to network: The VCC is between the customer's equipment and a network node and provides access to an NE.

Network to network: The VCC extends between two network nodes. This also includes network traffic management and routing information.

16.3.1.2 Properties of VCCs. The general properties of VCCs are:

(Semi)-permanent connections: VCCs may be established on a semipermanent or permanent basis.

Cell sequence integrity: It is preserved within a VCC.

Quality of service (*QoS*): Specified by parameters such as cell loss ratio and cell delay variation.

Traffic parameters: Negotiated between the user and a network for each VCC (at call setup or permanently, for the length of a contract).

16.3.1.3 Virtual-Channel Connectivity

(Semi)-permanent: Without using signaling procedures established by the network (by subscription).

Temporary: A special VCC is used (known as meta-signaling VCC) for signaling to establish or release a VCC connection.

Temporary: Following user-to-network signaling procedures (call admission control) to establish or release a VCC connection (for the duration of the connection).

Temporary: Following user-to-user signaling procedures using a VCC within a preestablished VPC between two UNIs to establish or release a VCC.

16.3.2 Virtual Paths

A *virtual-path connection* (*VPC*) is a concatenation of virtual-path links (VPLs). VPLs can be used on a B-ICI link to aggregate VCCs carrying like services so that optional network parameter control (NPC) can be applied to aggregate traffic flow. This can only be done for VPCs that do not terminate at the B-ICI. For VPCs terminating at the B-ICI, individual VCCs need to be enforced by the NPC function, if supported. That is, a VPC that contains a set of VCCs with similar services that do not terminate at the NE may be switched and routed together like a "bundle" by the NE.

16.3.2.1   Virtual-Path Connections.   VPCs can be established as follows:

User to user: The customer can use the channels in the path (bundle) for a mix of applications, provided that the parameters of the path permit it, similar to leased lines.

User to network: Allows a customer to have separate VPIs for groups of connections (bundles) that are to be routed to different networks or service providers.

Network to network: Provides a dedicated route to a path (bundle of channels) between two exchanges using a permanent path (i.e., without the need for switching at an intermediate exchange).

16.3.2.2   Virtual-Path Connectivity

Permanent VPC: Without using signaling procedures a permanent connection is established by the network (by permanent provisioning).

VPC on demand: Following signaling procedures. VPCs may be set up and released by the network or by the customer.

16.3.2.3   Virtual-Path Properties.   The properties of VPCs are:

Usage parameter control: Provided on a VP and on a VC basis. However, some VCs may be reserved for network purposes and may not be available to the user.

Traffic parameters: Negotiated between the user and a network for each VPC.

16.3.3 Virtual-Path and Virtual-Channel Switching

Figure 16.5 illustrates VPS in a simplified way. Notice that the VPI and VCI do not remain constant throughout the switch, and this is what is meant by the word *virtual*.

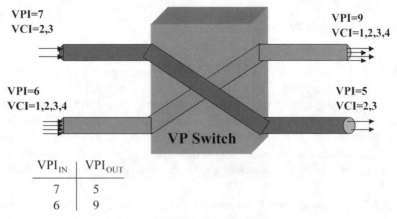

VPI$_{IN}$	VPI$_{OUT}$
7	5
6	9

Figure 16.5 Virtual path switching.

Clearly such a switch that performs VPS is the simplest in ATM. VPS takes advantages of high-rate traffic that connects a source with a destination. VPS provides a cost-effective solution to the applications that require high data rates between two points or between a limited number of points. Examples are the stock and banking industry and transfer of corporate voice/data to a small set of destinations.

Figure 16.6 illustrates VCS in a simplified way. Notice that the VPI and VCI do not remain constant throughout the switch, and again the word virtual. In addition, notice that this switch will remove cells (channels) from one "path pipe" (VP) and place it in another. Clearly a switch with such capability must have been designed accordingly to be able to support such action.

VCS is most likely to happen when connection admission control is established.

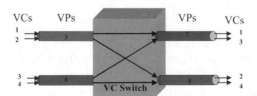

Figure 16.6 Virtual channel switching.

Figure 16.7 illustrates VCS and VPS in a simplified way, or a *hybrid switch*. Notice that VPI and VCI do not remain constant throughout the switch, and again this is the meaning of the word virtual. In addition, notice that this switch may have some "pipes" allocated for VPS only and some others for VCS or both. How many pipes should be allocated for each type of switching depends on the system application and forecasted type of traffic.

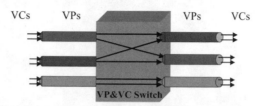

Figure 16.7 Virtual path and virtual channel switching.

EXERCISES

1. Could a VC be connected:
   a. Permanently?
   b. Dynamically on a per-call basis?
2. Is a VPC used for dynamic switching? Rationalize your answer.
3. What is VC temporal connectivity?
4. Could the same switching node switch both VCs and VPs or only one?

Answers

1. a. yes, b. yes
2. Typically no, if the path is committed to one user with the same point-to-point destination, unless the user has requested VPC on demand, or semi-permanent connectivity.
3. VCs connected on a temporal basis upon customer initiation and termination of a call.
4. Yes. This is the case of the hybrid switch.

CHAPTER 17

SEGMENTATION AND REASSEMBLY

17.1 ATM ADAPTATION LAYER

We have described the ATM reference model. The ATM adaptation layer (AAL) has a primary function known as *segmentation and reassembly (SAR)*. At AAL, this function takes a continuous bit stream of information from a service, splits it into segments, and packetizes it in ATM cells. At the receiver, the AAL receives ATM cells and follows a reverse process to restore back to the original continuous bit stream of information. In addition to the SAR function, the AAL performs more functions such as *rate adaptation, cell jitter,* and *error control.*

Figure 17.1 illustrates that, although the user data at the source may be a long stream, the stream is partitioned in smaller chunks, an operation known as *segmentation,* and each segment is converted to an ATM cell by attaching to it the cell header, an operation known as *encapsulation.*

At the destination, the received cells are stripped of their header and the original data stream is reconstructed, an operation known as *reassembly.* The complete operation from source to destination is known as segmentation and reassembly.

Notice that, at the destination, the received cells *must* be positioned in the same order they were transmitted. This implies that the source must

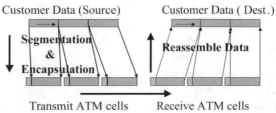

Figure 17.1 AAL—segmentation and reassembly (SAR).

165

incorporate a sequence number in the cell stream so that the receiver can de-tect any dislocated cells and reposition them. In subsequent sections we will encounter the mechanisms that help restore the integrity of the data stream.

17.2   AAL TYPES

Depending on the class of application (A, B, C, and D), the connection mode (connectionless vs. connection oriented), and the type of bit rate (VBR or CBR), the AAL may be defined differently. AALs are classified as *types,* such as AAL type 1, AAL type 2, and so on. Table 17.1 lists various AAL types and their applications.

In addition to VBR and CBR, there is another type known as available bit rate (ABR). This is defined for very low priority data to take advantage of un-used bandwidth in the network. This means that data may depart the source, pass a few nodes, and be dropped at some intermediate node before it reaches its destination because the node has no available bandwidth. Clearly, this service is successful only if all nodes in the path have available bandwidth to offer.

Such service finds application of data transfers that can wait to be trans-mitted during off-peak hours, e.g., file updates and back-ups, data store and forward, and so on.

Table 17.1 AAL Types by Class

	Class A	Class B	Class C	Class D
AAl Type	1	2	5, 3/4	5, 3/4
Tuning relation between source and destination	Required	Required	Not required	Not required
Bit rate	Constant	Variable	Variable	Variable
Connection mode	Connection oriented	Connection oriented	Connection oriented	Connectionless
Examples	CBR, voice/video	VBR, voice/video	CBR, voice/video	TCP/IP, SMDS

17.2.1   AAL-1

AAL-1 is used in synchronous bit stream transport (SONET/SDH) over ATM networks (Figure 17.2). AAL-1 has mis-sequencing protection (via a 3-bit counter) and allows for regeneration of the original clock of the data received at the far end of the link.

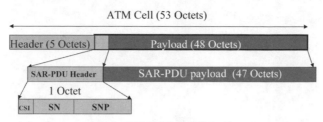

Figure 17.2 AAL-1 ATM cell.

Clock recovery is performed with the *synchronous residual time stamp* (*SRTS*) if both transmitter and receiver are on the same reference clock. SRTS is a 4-bit residual *time stamp,* the value of which is transmitted over eight cells (over the CSI bit) or with an adaptive clock.

The time stamp represents $y = N \times \text{fnx/fs} \times e$, where N is the period of RTS in cycles of fs, e is the service clock tolerance $\pm e$, and fnx is the derived clock frequency from a common reference clock fn.

We have indicated that the source must include a mechanism in the SAR operation so that the reassembly function reconstructs the original data stream faithfully. In AAL-1 this mechanism is provided by the first byte in the payload (the first byte of the 48 bytes).

The first byte of the payload path overhead is defined as the *convergence sublayer indicator* (1 bit), the *sequence number* SN (3 bits), and the *sequence number protection* (4 bits). When the CSI is set, the SN is a 3-bit counter and the 4 bits of the SNP is the complement of the first 4 bits to provide error detection over this byte. The remaining 47 bytes in the payload are known as the *SAR-PDU* (*SAR Payload Data Unit*).

17.2.2 AAL-2

AAL-2 is used in variable-bit-rate (VBR) services, or class B traffic (e.g., compressed video); see Figure 17.3.

Video information, once segmented, requires a sequence number and error control.

In addition, since AAL-2 ATM cells may transport different types of information, an indication should be included in the PDU, as well as an indication of the length of information, in octets, within the PDU.

Figure 17.3 AAL-2 ATM cell.

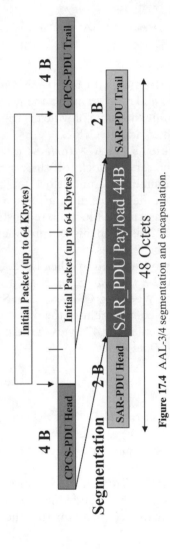

Figure 17.4 AAL-3/4 segmentation and encapsulation.

We have indicated that the source must include a mechanism in the SAR operation so that the reassembly reconstructs the original data stream faithfully. In AAL-2 this mechanism is provided a prefix and postfix information to the SAR-PDU. The prefix contains the sequence number and the information type (IT), and the subfix contains the length indicator (LI) and the cyclic redundancy code (CRC); details of their definition were not available at the time of writing. The total number of bytes SN+IT+SAR-PDU+LI+CRC must be equal to 48.

AAL-2 is used in VBR services, or class B traffic (e.g., compressed video). Clearly, video information, once segmented, requires a sequence number and error control. In addition, since AAL-2 ATM cells may transport different types of information, an indication should be included in the PDU, as well as an indication of the length of information, in octets, within the PDU.

17.2.3 AAL-3/4

AAL-3/4 applies to variable-length packets (up to 64 Kbytes); see Figure 17.4. Encapsulation takes place at two different levels, at the packet level and at the segment level, as follows:

Packet encapsulation and segmentation: Variable-length packets, such as switched multimegabit digital services (SMDSs), are encapsulated with a header and a trailer to form a *convergence sublayer PDU* (CS-PDU). The CS-PDU then is segmented into 44 octet lengths.

ATM cell encapsulation: Each of the CS-PDU segments (44 octets) is further encapsulated with another header (2-B) and a trailer (2-B) to become a SAR-PDU that constitutes the payload of ATM cells. To the payload, a cell header is attached and the cell is formed.

Figure 17.5 identifies all parts of the AAL-3/4 ATM cell.

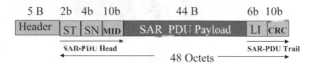

Figure 17.5 AAL-3/4 segmentation and encapsulation—last cell.

17.2.4 AAL-5

AAL-5 is straightforward and more efficient for point-to-point ATM links (Figure 17.6). At this level, all SAR level encapsulation is removed so that 48 class B common part conversion sublayer (CPCS) PDUs can be carried within a cell. There is no mis-sequencing protection. All AAL-5 CPCS-PDUs are sent

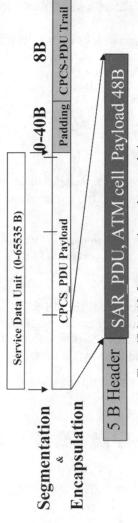

Figure 17.6 AAL-5 segmentation and encapsulation.

sequentially. A payload-type identifier (PTI) bit in the ATM header marks the last cell in the PDU. The CPCS-PDU has only a payload and a trailer. The trailer contains padding, a length field, and a CRC-32 for error control. It is in the last SAR-PDU (in the last ATM cell).

AAL-5 applies to variable-length packets (up to 64 Kbytes). Encapsulation takes place at two different levels, at the packet level and at the segment level, as follows (Figure 17.6):

Packet encapsulation and segmentation: Variable-length packets are encapsulated with a trailer to form CPCS-PDU. The CPCS-PDU then is segmented into 48-octet lengths.

ATM cell encapsulation: Each of the CPCS-PDU segments (48 octets) are further encapsulated with the ATM cell header.

AAL-5 is much simpler and with less payload overhead than AAL-3/4 and thus is preferred by many types of data.

Figure 17.7 identifies all parts of the AAL-5 ATM cell.

Figure 17.7 AAL-5 segmentation and encapsulation—last cell.

EXERCISES

1. A digitized image is contained in a long packet and is to be transmitted through an ATM network. At the network interface, the SAR function segments the long packet into cells. As the cells are transported through the network, there is no assurance that all cells will follow the same path. Comment on the order of arrival of the cells and identify a reliable mechanism that will reconstruct the image correctly at the receiver.

2. A digitized image is contained in a long packet. The SAR function adds a sequence number in each cell. In which field should the sequence number be included and why?

3. Comment on the main differences between the various AAL types and their applicability.

Answers

1. The ATM cells, due to different path delays, arrive out of order. Therefore, a time stamp or a sequence number should be included in the cells so that, as they arrive out of order at the receiver, they may be reordered.

2. Since the header changes at each node, the sequence number should be included in the first bytes of the information field.

3. The main differences lie in the segmentation and assembly of an information signal into ATM cells. Figures 17.1–17.7 illustrate these differences. Each AAL performs the SAR function differently as they map payloads into ATM cells from various applications, per Table 17.1.

CHAPTER 18

CIRCUIT EMULATION

An ATM system should be able to receive and transport any type of payload. This means that at the network interface there should be a function able to translate the incoming payload type to ATM cells. Indeed, ATM offers functions that translate traditional rates such as DS1, E1, DS3, LAN, etc., into ATM cells, and vice versa. This is done with AAL-1. Figure 18.1 illustrates the various SAR steps in the DS1 data stream.

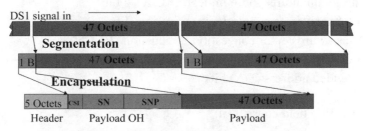

Figure 18.1 Circuit emulation. Example: DS1 to ATM.

Many Questions Need Answers

What are the major issues if the emulated DS1 transports:

- Voice?—delay, cell sequencing
- Non-real-time data?—none, cell sequencing
- Real-time image?—delay, cell sequencing

18.1 FRAME RELAY ON ATM

Frame relay (FR) is a data service that transports information embedded in a packet that is up to 8169 octets long. Frame relay has been a cost-effective data service, but not so for time-sensitive services, such as voice, although the

Frame Relay Forum has addressed an interest on transporting voice over frame relay, which has accepted two implementation agreements, FRF-11 IA and FRF-12 IA:

> *FRF-11 IA addresses voice over frame relay:* The basic problem here is that the PDU of a frame relay packet is up to 8000 octets long. This long PDU may congest the network such that packets that may transport voice and enter the same queue may be unacceptably delayed. The end result is poor voice quality.

> *FRF-12 IA addresses frame relay fragmentation:* Long PDUs are now allowed to be fragmented into smaller sizes, up to 30 octets, and thus queue delays have a lesser effect on packets that transport voice.

A typical frame relay packet consists of a flag, a header, the information field, a frame check sequence (FCS) and an end flag.

The flag consists of the fixed code 0x7E (binary 0111 1110).

The FR header consists of:

- The data link connection identifier (DLCI), a 10-bit address
- The command/response indicator (C/R), 2 bits
- A forward error congestion notification (FECN)
- A backwards error congestion notification (BECN)
- A discard eligibility (DE) bit
- Extended address (EA) bits

The information field consists of:

- A control field that has been added on user data during encapsulation of frame relay
- User data

Finally, the FR frame is concluded with the FCS field and the flag.

When an FR frame is mapped onto ATM, the interworking function (IWF) of the ATM adaptation layer (AAL-5) translates the FR header and maps onto the ATM header fields, VCI, VPI, PTI, and CLP. Then the control field in the information field is also translated from one type to the one specified by RFC-1483. RFC-1483 specifies encapsulation in ATM cells. Finally, the long information field is segmented and mapped over many ATM cells. Figure 18.2 illustrates the initial process of translation and segmentation of an FR frame onto ATM.

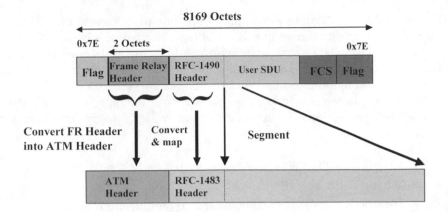

Figure 18.2 Mapping frame relay frames onto ATM.

RFC 1483 uses AAL5 and specifies encapsulation of multiprotocol data over ATM
RFC 1490 specifies encapsulation of multiprotocol data for transmission over Frame Relay
FCS=Frame Check Sequence

18.2 IP ON ATM

Internet is a new packet connectionless service that enables users to access data that are distributed over many interconnected servers that communicate between them using a packet protocol, such as the transmission control protocol/Internet Protocol (TCP/IP). In a nutshell, TCP is responsible for defining end-to-end packet connectivity and IP is responsible for routing data from one node to another throughout the network.

The IP is evolving to accommodate new demands and services such as voice and QoS. Voice over IP (VoIP) is studied by several standards bodies such as the ITU, ETSI, and IETF. The VoIP Forum has ratified an agreement based on H.323. As IP evolves, a version number accompanies the initials IP, such as IPv2 meaning IP version 2, also known as Internet2. Next-generation IP (IPng) protocols IPv4 and IPv6 address more advanced Internet services with real-time requirements and true quality of service.

Internet is a data service that requires high aggregate bit rates but very low cost. High speed and low cost seem to be at opposite ends, and therefore an efficient and very high bandwidth network infrastructure is necessary. The optical network is expected to provide the infrastructure that will, by integrating services, respond to high-speed and low-cost market needs. Internet therefore needs an efficient and low-cost transport mechanism, and among these mechanisms is ATM.

ATM has the flexibility of adding functions that convert TCP/IP traffic into ATM cell traffic and vice versa. As of the writing of this book, IP traffic is estimated to be 3000 terabytes per month and is growing. In contrast, the mature U.S. long-distance (LD) traffic is about 600,000 terabytes per month. However, although the comparison between the two (IP vs. LD traffic) is still in favor of the latter, new services are planned over the rapidly growing IP. The bottom-line prediction is a massive growth in capacity needs that raise many questions:

- How long will it take for IP to catch up with LD traffic?
- What will the new IP services be?
- How does this expansion impact the communications network?
- How does this expansion impact cost and quality of service?
- How will the network be managed?

These and more questions are presently being addressed and solutions are being proposed. IP over ATM transmitted over fiber is one of the solutions.

The IP packet consists of a *header* field and a data field known as the *datagram*. The IP datagram contains up to 65,535 octets of user data, and the header contains many fields (expected to increase with new Internet standards) for routing and packet managing purposes:

- Version field (IP format, version of protocol): 4 bits
- Internet header length field (measured in 32-bit words): 4 bits
- Type-of-service field (QoS): 8 bits
- Total length of datagram field (up to 65,535 octets): 16 bits
- ID field (unique for each datagram, used to reassemble): 16 bits
- Flags: 3 bits
- Fragment offset field (up to 8192 fragments): 12 bits
- Time to live field (or, time to remain on Internet): 8 bits
- Protocol (upper layer protocol): 8 bits
- Header checksum: 16 bits
- Source address: 32 bits (IP version 4)/128 bits in colon hexadecimal (IP version 6)
- Destination address: 32 bits (IP version 4)/128 bits in colon hexadecimal (IP version 6)
- Options and padding: 32 bits

The Internet network consists of simple managed devices. The IP network is a "managed" network (that is, via embedded management messages), not over a separate network, as for example in telephony. However, the Internet network is presently largely managed manually and not automatically as in telephony.

18.2.1   IP Encapsulation and Segmentation

IP on ATM works similar to circuit emulation (Figure 18.2). From an applications layer viewpoint, an IP data packet of less than 9180 bytes is encapsulated by adding an 8-byte header to form the TCP/IP packet. The 8 additional bytes are subdivided in two main fields, the *logical link control* (*LLC*), which consists of 3 bytes, and the *SubNet Access Protocol* (*SNAP*), which consists of 5 bytes. Then, this long packet is undergoing all AAL 5 and ATM layer processes (segmentations and ATM encapsulation), as illustrated in Figure 18.3.

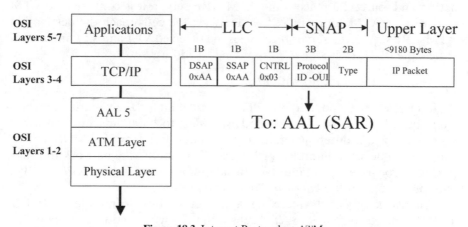

Figure 18.3 Internet Protocol on ATM.

LLC

- The destination service access point (DSAP) is the first byte and is set to the fixed value 0xAA.
- The session service access point (SSAP), as defined by the ISO, or the source SAP (SSAP), as defined by IEEE 802, is the second byte and is set to the fixed value 0xAA.
- The control byte (CNTRL) is the third byte and is set to the fixed value 0x03.

SNAP

- The first 3 bytes in the SNAP are the organization unit identifier (ID-OUI).
- The next 2 bytes indicate the type of data in the Internet data field.

18.2.2   Address Resolution

The obvious question with IP on ATM is: How are IP addresses resolved? Or, how does the network know where to send an Internet packet as it is routed throughout a large network with many nodes? To answer this question, one should consider that each Internet terminal (such as a PC supporting Internet software) is connected via a modem (or a high-speed interface) with a server that provides Internet service, the Internet service provider (ISP). The ISP itself is registered and has its own address that is recognized by the network.

Each ATM network has an address resolution protocol (ARP) server (the document RFC 1577 extends ARP to support ATM subnets). All hosts on the ATM network register with the ARP server. The ARP server maintains an address conversion table (or address resolution protocol) that associates an ATM address to an IP address. Thus, when an IP packet of data with a destination and source ID reaches the ATM ARP server, it is converted to ATM cells with an ATM address (VCI, VPI). When the cells reach the destination ATM ARP server, the server recognizes the received VCI and VPI and reconstructs the IP data with the corresponding IP address.

18.2.3   Interworking with IP

As has already been pointed out, all types of data interface with the network. Consequently, users with ATM UNI will want to communicate with other users that have a different interface. Such interfaces may be SMDS, LANs, some legacy network interface, or Internet. This ability of a network to transport data from one type of interface to another is known as *interworking* (*IW*) and the function as the *interworking function* (*IWF*).

Interworking entails receiving a packet in one format (e.g., SMDS, TCP/IP) and converting it to ATM cells with the SAR function, as already discussed. However, SAR does not address an important issue, i.e., addressing. Addressing in one protocol is not the same with another. The addressing scheme in IP or in SMDS, for example, is different than the VPI/VCI of ATM. Consequently, in addition to the SAR function, when a non-ATM signal enters the UNI interface of an ATM network, address validation, address recognition, address screening, and address translation to/from ATM must take place. Address screening is a function whereby a customer has allowed or not allowed certain addresses to send to or receive from. In addition, there are more issues specific to particular interworkings.

The Internet Engineering Task Force (IETF) has studied the classical IP over ATM. However, the ATM quality of service (QoS) is not fully supported with the current version of IP on ATM as well as other real-time issues.

The ATM Forum has studied the *LAN emulation* (*LANE*) using layer 2 bridging in an ATM network. This emulation uses the media access control (MAC) sublayer of an open-system interconnect (OSI) model so that various network layer protocols (e.g., IP, IPX, NetBIOS, DECNet) will work. However, the ATM QoS is again not fully supported, as well as other real-time issues.

The ATM Forum has also studied a *multiprotocol over ATM* (MPOA) using layer 3 switching in an ATM network. The MPOA model builds on the LANE model; it can route between different IP subnetworks and supports ATM QoS. Layer 3 switching is presently in the proposal phase. However, the goal is to take advantage of powerful router-based networks with fast hardware-based ATM switching networks. This is a reasonable approach if one considers that fast ATM switches (many megabits per second) are designed, and powerful microprocessors and advanced high-speed bus interfaces are used in servers.

ITU-T Recommendation E.164 has also recommended the SMDS addresses, according to which they are structured into two parts, a country code and a nationally significant number.

EXERCISES

1. Assume ATM cells arrive at a constant bit rate of 600 Mbps. Assume that at the port unit of a node there is a function that recognizes the VPI and the VCI of each cell. How fast should this recognition function be?

2. The SAR function is to convert one type of payload in ATM cells. What major additional issues does interworking address?

3. Quality of service is not addressed in some data communications systems. If voice is to be transmitted over them, comment on QoS.

4. The address in ATM is included in the header of each cell and in the connectivity tables in each node. If IP payload is to be transmitted over ATM, comment on the addressing issues that must be resolved.

Answers

1. Twice as fast as the cell rate, i.e., $\dfrac{2 \times 600 \times 10^6}{8 \times 53} = 2.83 \times 10^6$ patterns/s.

2. Among others, QoS, addressing issues, and concatenation.

3. If QoS is not addressed, then the quality of voice, the continuity of speech, and the recognition of the speaker may not be expected.

4. The IP payload far exceeds the length of an ATM cell. Thus, each ATM cell (the union of which makes up the IP packet) must contain at minimum the destination indication of the IP packet.

CHAPTER 19

CONGESTION CONTROL

In Chapter 15, we described CAC and mentioned the parameters UPC and NPC. Here, we examine them closer and also examine what causes congestion in a node and in the network and how it is addressed.

19.1 TRAFFIC POLICING (UPC/NPC)

Traffic policing is a function that monitors whether a connection is in compliance with the traffic parameters. After a connection is granted, the network has reserved resources for that connection. If all things work as agreed upon by both the user and the service provider, in theory there should not be a necessity for policing traffic. However, because things happen, inadvertently or on purpose, the traffic policing function is important. Thus, the network polices the user's session. This assures that user traffic is compliant with the given parameters and the VPI/VCI of each cell is valid. When the node detects noncompliance, it sends a rapid response to the user, who must correct the noncompliance, or cells with noncompliant parameters may be altered, dropped, or changed to low priority (CLP = 1). This is known as usage parameter control (UPC). In addition, the policing function assures that the network is compliant with the given parameters. This is known as network parameter control (NPC).

In addition, the UPC/NPC policing function watches for users that may unintentionally or intentionally violate the connection parameters. It watches for users that intentionally and illegally attempt to penetrate the network and for malfunctioning user equipment.

19.2 CONGESTION MANAGEMENT

Congestion is defined as a state of one or more network elements in a network that do not meet negotiated network performance objectives (traffic descriptors, QoS) for the already established connections.

19.2.1   Congestion Causes

Congestion may be caused by fault conditions within the network (e.g., a faulty node, a broken fiber link, etc.), by unpredictable statistical fluctuations of traffic flow, and perhaps by malicious users.

19.2.2   Reactions to Congestion

When congestion is encountered, the first order of action is to renegotiate lower traffic rates with the variable-bit-rate services. In addition, offending cell sources may be discarded selectively, or even a block of cells (AAL5). If this does not alleviate congestion, cells with lesser priority (CLP = 1) are dropped. If this does not help, then traffic is rerouted, bypassing the faulty node. If the faulty node does not recover, then the network ends the node that has caused congestion notification.

19.2.3   Congestion Management Methods

Congestion management is achieved by two methods. The first method monitors the state of a bit in the ATM cell header known as the CLP. Under no-congestion conditions, the CLP bit is left to the value it was set, logic 0 or logic 1. If congestion is experienced, the NE may set the CLP bit of selective cells to logic 1, even though the initial CLP value was 0. If congestion is severe, then the NE may discard cells with initial CLP value 1.

Figure 19.1 captures the congestion management by *policing the CLP* bit. If the CLP bit is set to 1, even though the cell may pass a congested node, any subsequent congested node in the path may drop the cell. This is one reason that ABR or UBR services may not be successful during peak-traffic hours, when congestion is more probable.

The second method polices the state of the 3-bit code in the ATM cell header known as the PTI.

Under no-congestion conditions, the PTI code is set to logic 000. If congestion is experienced, then the PTI code of selective cells is set to 010, whereas the CLP bit may still remain at logic 0. This is known as congestion

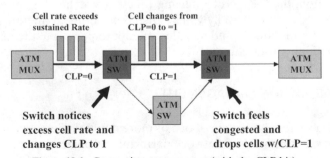

Figure 19.1   Congestion management (with the CLP bit).

management by policing the *explicit forward congestion notification* (*EFCN*) process (Figure 19.2).

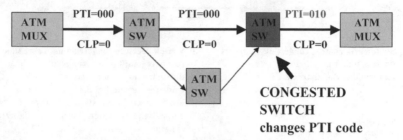

Figure 19.2 Congestion management (with EFCN).

In the EFCN case, as soon as a bandwidth threshold is reached, which is close to the maximum bandwidth of the node, the PTI received code (PTI = 000) is changed to PTI = 010 so that it notifies the destination in advance that congestion is experienced. The destination echoes the PTI received value back to the source, and thus the source, and all nodes in the path, learns of the congestion condition on its path. The source now should "slow down" its cell rate, and if all sources that receive PTI = 010 follow this practice, then congestion and dropping of cells will be avoided. Clearly, EFCN is suitable for services with adaptable bit rates, such as ABR.

19.3 TRAFFIC SHAPING IN ABR/VBR SERVICES

On the path between two end users there are one or more switching nodes. As traffic builds up, one of the switches may be approaching a predefined congestion threshold level. This is monitored via the traffic descriptors (see Chapter 14). When this occurs, the switching node is said to be in the *near-congestion state*. To avoid congestion, it is logical that the near-congestion node tries to renegotiate with sources that support variable cell rates and lower the cell flow. Indeed, the switching node sends via PM cells the near-congestion status in both directions, upstream and downstream (Figure 19.3). Near congestion is indicated by changing the CLP bit of the PM cell to 1. In the upstream direction, this indication reaches the (ATM) end-user terminal, which lowers its rate to the negotiated minimum. In the downstream direction, the switching nodes receive the indication from the near-congestion switch, and they pass the near-congestion indication down to the destination (ATM) end user. The destination end user receives the near-congestion indication and sends back the received PM cell with CLP = 1 in the upstream direction. When this PM cell reaches the near-congestion switch, the switch changes the CLP bit back to zero. In the meantime, the end user has lowered its cell rate

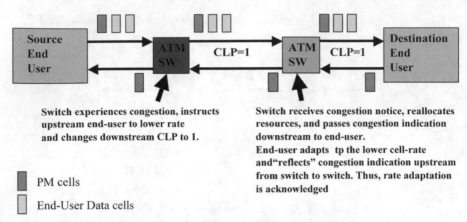

Figure 19.3   Congestion management: traffic shaping.

to its minimum, and all switches in the path, including the far end user, adapt to the new rate and the near-congestion condition may be removed. This is called traffic shaping. However, if the congestion is persistent and *traffic shaping* does not remedy the congestion, then cells may be dropped, as already discussed.

EXERCISES

1. Why is congestion an issue in ATM nodes and networks?
2. How is congestion created in an ATM system?
3. Describe mechanisms to relieve congestion.
4. Assume that a user needs to transport data with certainty. Which is the suggested CLP value?
5. If a node experiences congestion, what may happen to cells with CLP set to 1?
6. What is traffic shaping?

CHAPTER 20

PERFORMANCE MANAGEMENT

20.1 PERFORMANCE SURVEILLANCE

The behavior of a network is monitored regularly for performance and is evaluated based on defined statistical parameters. This function is known as *performance surveillance*. Based on this, an NE collects performance data from the various functions on a continuous basis and logs these data typically every 15 min. The collected data are summarized and reported on an hourly, daily, weekly, and monthly basis to the ATM operations system (ATM OS) over an operations communications interface. At the OS, data are analyzed to better predict bandwidth utilization, congestion, better QoS, or some other type of fault.

Traditional networks collect parameters to deduct busy-hour call attempts, block attempts, usage, etc. In ATM systems the performance parameters are related to cell *connectivity* via call admission control, the *throughput* of cells, the *number of cells lost, congestion state, jitter parameters, faults,* etc. The ATM Forum Interim Local Management Interface (ILMI) Management Information Base (MIB) defines performance parameters for the physical layer and for the ATM layer for both VP and for VC connections for public and private interfaces.

In ATM systems, the framework for performance management is based on a hierarchical model. Thus, performance parameters from an ATM switching node are communicated over an SNMP (simple network management protocol) interface to an element management function, which in turn communicates over a CMIP (common management information protocol) or an SNMP interface with the performance surveillance function of the ATM (OS).

20.2 ATM LAYER OAM

According to ATM Forum, a segment in an ATM network is defined, by default, as the link between the customer premises network and the first point of switching in the provider's network.

A segment may also represent a VP link or a group of interconnected VP links within a single provider's network, such as between the provider's network UNI and B-ICI interfaces. Segment and end-to-end management applies to both VP and VC connections. The cells used for this purpose are called *F4 flow cells* and *F5 flow cells*. However, VPC (F4) and VCC (F5) are managed independently.

The operations, administration, and management (OAM) cells should nonintrusively be inserted in the VPC or VCC cell stream. This means that bandwidth must have been allocated for OAM cells. The OAM cells for each case are identified by values in the header fields.

20.3 OAM CELLS

The OAM cell type field (4 bits) identifies three types of OAM cells: *fault management* (0001), *performance management* (0010), and *activation/deactivation* (1000); see Figure 20.1 and Table 20.1.

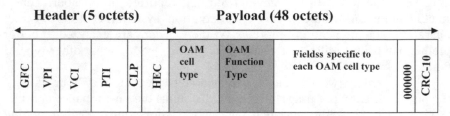

Figure 20.1 ATM layer—OAM information fields.

Table 20.1 OAM Cell Types

OAM Cell Type	Value	OAM Function Type	Value
Fault management	0001	AIS	0000
		RDI	0001
		OAM cell loopback	1000
Performance management	0010	Forward monitoring	0000
		Backward reporting	0001
		Monitoring and reporting	0010
Activation/deactivation	1000	Performance monitoring	0000

If the OAM cell is fault management, then the OAM function type (4 bits) may be an *alarm indication signal* (AIS = 0000), a remote defect indication (RDI = 0001), or an OAM cell *loopback* (1000).

If the OAM cell is performance management, then the OAM function type (4 bits) may indicate *forward monitoring* (0000), *backward reporting* (0001), or *monitoring and reporting* (0010).

If the OAM cell is activation/deactivation, then the OAM function type (4 bits) indicates *performance monitoring* (0000).

VP/VC performance monitoring consists of counting the number of user data cells between consecutive OAM cells and determining the number of lost or mis-inserted cells in the block, recalculating the error detection code, and comparing to the code in the incoming cell. In addition, it keeps records of all findings and reports findings to the near-end terminal.

Performance monitoring, activation/deactivation, alarm surveillance, and loopback testing may be performed on the segment and end-to-end level in both VPCs and VCCs.

The CRC-10 polynomial $g(x) = x^{10} + x^9 + x^5 + x^4 + 1$ is stored in the last 10 bits of the last two octets (6 bits are filled with zeros, 000000).

20.4 VP MANAGEMENT

The ATM layer VP management is accomplished using a specific ATM cell with a code in the VCI field that indicates segment or end-to-end management (Figure 20.2). A VCI code set to 011 identifies a segment management cell, whereas a value set to 100 identifies an end-to-end connection management cell. This is known as *F4 flow.* In this case, the VPI code remains the same as the user's cell.

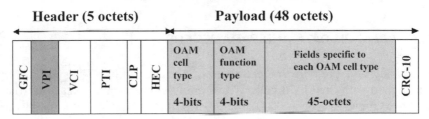

Figure 20.2 ATM layer—VP management.

20.5 VC MANAGEMENT

ATM Layer VC Management is accomplished using a specific ATM cell that has a code in the PTI field that identifies segment or end-to-end management (Figure 20.3). A PTI code set to 100 identifies a segment management cell, whereas a value set to 101 identifies an end-to-end connection management cell. This is *F5 flow.* In this case, the VPI and the VCI codes remain the same as the user's cell.

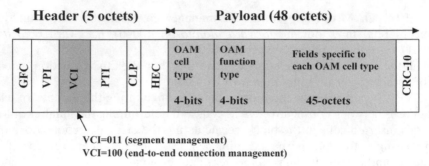

Figure 20.3 ATM layer—VC management.

The PTI field in VC management is depicted in Figure 20.4.

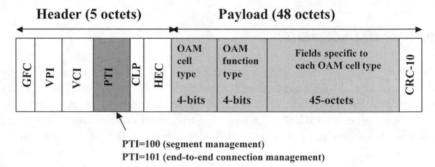

Figure 20.4 ATM layer—VC management.

20.6 VP/VC PM DATA AND PARAMETERS

As already said, the performance monitoring function in ATM systems is accomplished with the OAM cells. When the OAM cell type is set at 0010 and the OAM function type at 0000 or 0001 or 0010, the next 45-octet field is used for performance management functions.

The first octet in this field contains a (binary) sequence number of monitoring cells. The next 2 octets contain the total number of user cells. The next 2 octets contain the error-control code BIP-16. This is the even parity computed over the information field of the block of user cells transmitted after the last monitoring cell. The 4 octets after the BIP-16 may contain (optionally) a time stamp. The 33 octets are not used and each octet contains the hexadecimal code 6A (01101010). The next octet contains the block error result, which is the number of errored parity bits in the BIP-16 code of the incoming cell. The last 2 octets in this field contain a count of the lost or mis-inserted cells (Figure 20.5).

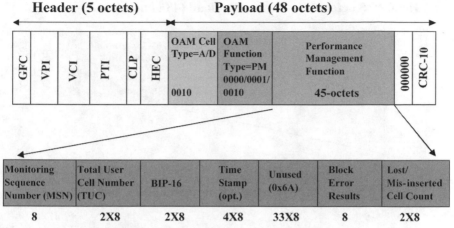

Figure 20.5 ATM layer—performance management field.

Based on the contents of the aforementioned field, the data collected by an ATM NE for each VP or VC are:

- Severely errored cell blocks (SECBs)
- Errored cells
- Lost user information
- Mis-inserted user information cells
- Number of impaired blocks
- Number of transmitted user information cells

The PM parameters are:

- Total user cell difference (TUCD)
- BIP violations

20.7 ACTIVATION/DEACTIVATION OF PM CELLS

Activation is part of the handshaking process between user terminal A and user terminal B in order to synchronize the beginning and end of transmission and reception of PM cells and also to establish agreement on block size and direction of transmission to start or stop monitoring.

The activation/deactivation field (Figure 20.6) consists of the following subfields:

- Message ID (6 bits, a direction of action, 2 bits)
- Correlation tag (8 bits)

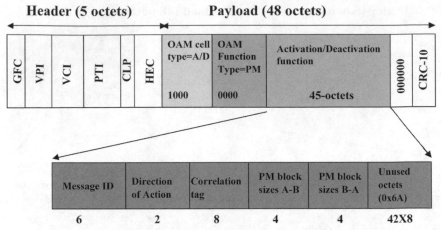

Figure 20.6   ATM layer—activation/deactivation.

- PM block sizes from user A to user B (4 bits)
- PM block sizes from user B to user A (4 bits)
- Forty-two unused octets, each set at 0x6A

Depending on the binary value of the 6-bit code in the message ID, it may indicate:

000001 = Activate

000010 = Activation confirmed

000011 = Activation request denied

000101 = Deactivate

000110 = Deactivate confirmed

000111 = Deactivate request denied

20.8   VP/VC ALARM SURVEILLANCE

We have described that some of the PM parameters are linked to data lost. User data may be lost due to any number of unpredictable faults that may take place on the path between the two user terminals. Specifically, VPC or VCC failures may occur from physical link failures, corrupted VPI/VCI translation tables, or inability to delineate ATM cells.

As in SONET/SDH, so in ATM there are AIS and RDI signals, but here they are distinguished by the VP or VC connection. Thus, when intermediate nodes detect a failure, they generate a VP-AIS or VC-AIS to alert the downstream nodes of the failure.

Similarly, the terminating node generates a VP-RDI and VC-RDI and sends it to the upstream nodes to acknowledge that it has received the VP-AIS or VC-AIS signal and also that the failure has occurred in the downstream direction.

The AIS/RDI field consists of an octet to indicate the fault type, 15 octets to identify the fault location, and 29 octets that are not used (Figure 20.7).

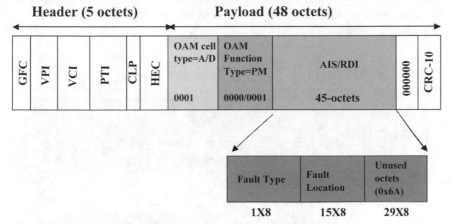

Figure 20.7   ATM layer—VP/VC alarm surveillance.

20.9   FAULT REPORTING

An ATM specific failure is declared only if a defect persists for 2.5 ± 0.5s. In this case, an ATM NE reports the fault to the *network management system* (*NMS*) identifying the faulty location and the time the fault occurred (within an accuracy of ±1s).

20.10   FAULT LOCATION: VCC/VPC LOOPBACKS

A method of locating a fault is to perform loopback of a signal (Figure 20.8). The transmitted signal is looped back, and as it is received, it is monitored for integrity. Loopbacks may be performed around a segment, around several contiguous segments, or even around a complete path between user A and user B and for either VCC or VPC. Thus a fault may be detected and localized.

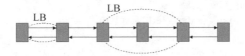

Figure 20.8   VCC/VPC loopbacks.

The loopback function field consists of a loopback indication that contains the binary code 00000001 or 00000000 (Figure 20.9). When the loopback cell is received with the code 00000001, it is reflected back with the code changed to 00000000 and it also initiates a loopback cell in the reverse direction (with code 00000001) containing the same information in the remaining loopback field. When this indication is zero, the loopback cell is not looped back but is discarded by the endpoint. At any time, multiple loopback cells may be inserted in the same connection.

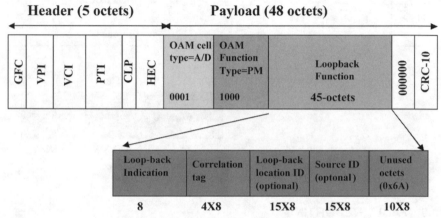

Figure 20.9   ATM layer—VCC/VPC loopback field.

Next to the loopback indication is the correlation tag that consists of 4 octets. This field may contain correlating data between the transmitted loopback cell and the received loopback cell.

Next is the (optional) loopback location ID field, which consists of 15 octets, and next to this the (optional) source ID field that also consists of 15 octets. The remaining 10 octets are not used and contain the code 0x6A in each octet.

EXERCISES

1. Name the three types of OAM cells.
2. In a cell where is the type identified? By how many bits?
3. Does the OAM cell contain customer data in the data field?
4. What is the purpose of the activation/deactivation cell?
5. How long after a malfunction is a fault declared? One second? Two and a half seconds? Five seconds?
6. What happens if a fault is detected? Explain.

CHAPTER 21

ATM MISCELLANY

21.1 ATM TANDEM CONNECTIONS

The ATM signal from a user A to a user B travels through many different nodes. These nodes may not all belong to an all-ATM network, but depending on the network path, some nodes may belong to a synchronous network (e.g., SONET). That is, different types of connections must be established *in tandem* to connect user A with user B (Figure 21.1).

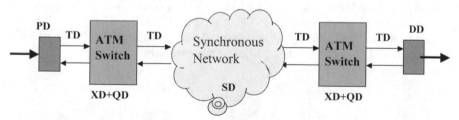

Figure 21.1 Delays in tandem connection.

What is important to evaluate with tandem connections, among other parameters, is the latency of the signal. An ATM signal entering a node buffers and switches the node and then propagates to the next node, where more buffering takes place, and so on. Latency is compounded over the total path, and in certain cases it may exceed the level of acceptance. The various contributing components to latency are:

- *Transmission delays:* Delay at the physical interface that depends on the distance (kilometers) of the medium and the PHY functionality (synchronization, frame alignment, etc.)
- *Switching delays:* Small delays experienced by the switching fabric at each node

- *Queuing delays:* Delays due to cell buffering and cell queuing
- Synchronous network delays: Delays imposed by the synchronous network
- *Packetization delays:* Delays due to mainly the SAR and multiplexing functions
- *Depacketization delays:* Delays due to mainly SAR and demultiplexing functions

In the above list we have not included additional delays that may be experienced due to congestion and fault conditions.

21.2   WIRELESS ATM

This section addresses the wireless aspects of ATM. ATM is defined as an asynchronous transport mechanism over land networks. In the next section we will see in much detail how ATM is applied over a SONET network (Figure 21.2).

Current wireless services support speech (wireless telephony) and low-speed data (paging, messaging, etc.). However, as the workspace becomes more and more mobile, a need emerges for high-speed TCP/IP data over wireless ATM networks. Figure 21.2 illustrates an end-to-end TCP/IP connection and the protocol conversions necessary. Thus, as described earlier, the TCP/IP data are undergoing the AAL and wireless ATM (WATM) operations and are transmitted over a custom wireless signal. The received custom signal is converted to a standard signal and transmitted through the ATM standard wireless network. The reverse takes places at the receiving end.

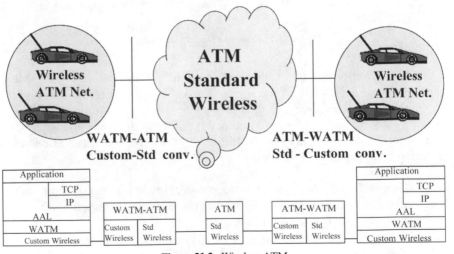

Figure 21.2 Wireless ATM.

In addition to existing wireless communication services, the ITU-T, with the cooperation of other bodies, is defining standards for global voice and data services known as the Global Information Infrastructure (GII). The GII is expected to further enhance person-to-person communications, business transactions, and sociocultural interaction. ATM technology plays an important role in the shaping of the GII.

Low Earth Orbit Satellite (LEOS) and Medium Earth Orbit Satellite (MEOS) systems have also been deployed to support wireless global voice and data services. LEOS and MEOS provide direct-to-satellite communication services. LEOS forms a satellite communications network at about 500–1500 km above Earth's surface and MEOS at 5000–12,000 km [the Geosynchronous Earth Orbit (GEO) satellites are at 35,800 km]. ATM technology plays an important role in the communication links with LEOS and with MEOS.

EXERCISES

1. True or false:
   a. Video and voice cannot be offered on the same VP.
   b. An ATM switch supports both VPC and VCC.
   c. A VC contains a VP.
   d. VPIs are assigned at the originating nodes and stay unchanged across the path; also across the section.
   e. ATM can handle both circuit and packet modes on the same VP.
2. A user terminal sends a data packet that consists of 5000 bytes to an ATM user-to-network interface. At the UNI, an AAL-¾ layer converts the packet to ATM cells. Calculate the number of cells generated.
3. A user terminal sends a data packet that consists of 5000 bytes to an ATM user-to-network interface. Calculate the number of cells generated with an AAL-5 layer.
4. The 5000-byte packet of exercises 2 and 3 is transmitted at 10 Mbps. Calculate the average ATM cell rate for (a) AAL-3/4 and (b) AAL-5.
5. A (hypothetical) NE has the following specifications.

   Total bandwidth capacity: 1 Gbps

   Number of physical (user) inputs: 1000

   Payload of several users may be multiplexed at each input signal.

   Buffer size at each physical input: 5 cells.

   Switching fabric size (inputs): 100X100

   Flow speed per connection (in the switching fabric): 10 Mbps

   Physical media: fiber and wire

   Type of connectivity: permanent and switched

   Expected traffic loading: 90% between 7:00–10:00 AM and 5:00 PM–10:00 PM, 50% otherwise.

Assume that other parameters are not important. The contracts with users are as follows:

> 600 users with permanent connectivity at a cell rate of 20% of users at 1000 cells/s CBR each 50% at 500 cells/s CBR and 30% at 400–800 cells/s VBR
>
> 2000 users with switched connectivity, as follows: 50% of users at 1000 cells/s CBR each, and 50% at 400–1000 cells/s VBR

If switched-service users connect for an average of 1 h per day each, determine the congestion conditions for that NE.

Answers

1. a. T, b. T, c. F, d. F, T, e. T
2. 114
3. 114
4. a. 18.5 Kcells/s, b. 18.5 Kcells/s
5. The total bandwidth switching capacity of the fabric is 1 Gbps. The worst-case scenario is when all users request connectivity, in addition to permanently connected users, which accounts for over 70% of total bandwidth. The remaining 30% of bandwidth can be used for switched services, which on the average last 1 h per day. Thus, allowing a worst-case scenario, the NE will approach near-congestion condition, and it may exceed the 90% traffic loading.

CHAPTER 22

ATM OVER SONET/SDH

22.1 TYPES OF ATM

There are three options to transport ATM traffic over SONET/SDH: *embedded* ATM transport, *hybrid* transport, and *pure* ATM transport.

In embedded ATM transport the ATM cells are mapped in the SONET/SDH payload of an STS/STM frame and the switching SONET/SDH NE route an STS/STM and thus ATM cells are completely transparent. Clearly, such NEs require SONET/SDH traffic management only.

In hybrid transport SDH/SONET (VT) traffic and ATM traffic are combined onto the same SONET/SDH bearer over SONET/SDH tributaries. However, the NEs have visibility of the ATM cells. NEs separate the SONET/SDH traffic from the ATM, and they route the traffic to their corresponding switching fabric. After the two different traffics have been switched, they may be recombined to form a hybrid payload. Clearly, such NEs require both SONET/SDH and ATM traffic management.

In pure ATM transport all STS/STM traffic from a tributary is *circuit emulated* into ATM cells. This is the reverse case of SONET/SDH over ATM. Circuit-emulated and pure ATM cells are all then carried as ATM cells. Clearly, such NEs require ATM traffic management only.

22.2 ATM MAPPED IN SONET

We have studied the structure of the STS-3c and STS-12c SONET frames and also the corresponding SDH frames. We have also studied the structure of the SONET synchronous payload capacity. The ATM Forum defines the mapping of ATM cells in the payload capacity (PC) as follows:

In STS-3c: ATM cells are mapped into the STS-3c PC by aligning the byte structure of every cell with the STS-3c byte structure. The entire PC (260 columns) shall be filled with cells, yielding a transfer capacity for ATM cells at 149.760 Mbps. Cells are mapped in the PC in a contiguous rowwise manner, the starting byte depending on alignment.

In STS-12c: ATM cells are mapped into the STS-12c PC by aligning the byte structure of every cell with the STS-12c byte structure. The entire PC (1040 columns) shall be filled with cells, yielding a transfer capacity for ATM cells at 599.040 Mbps. Cells are mapped in the PC in a contiguous rowwise manner, the starting byte depending on alignment.

For ATM mapping description purposes, consider that ATM cells (5 bytes overhead and 48 bytes payload) arrive in a sequential order and that the first byte of a cell is aligned with the Kth column byte of the Nth row in the SONET PC. Notice that the Kth column byte cannot be in the overhead space of the SONET frame (Figure 22.1).

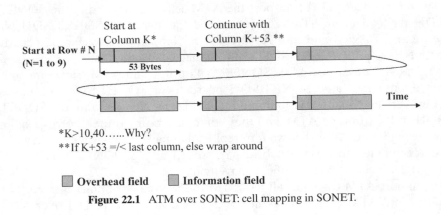

Figure 22.1   ATM over SONET: cell mapping in SONET.

22.2.1   ATM Mapped in STS-3c

In an STS-3c frame the first 9 columns are committed for the SONET overhead. Then, the 10th column is reserved for ATM path overhead information, and the remaining PC is used to map ATM cells. That is, from a total of $270 \times 9 = 2430$ bytes, $260 \times 9 = 2340$ bytes are available to map ATM cells in this case. Then, the total number of ATM cells in the PC is obtained by dividing 2340 by 53. Doing so, one obtains about 44.15094339 cells in a frame (Figure 22.2).

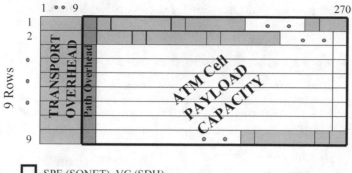

SPE (SONET), VC (SDH)

Figure 22.2 ATM over SONET: cell mapping in STS-3c.

Table 22.1 defines the overhead bytes at the UNI.

Table 22.1 ATM over SONET Overhead Definition

OH Byte	Coding	Definition
A1, A2	11110110,00101000	Framing bytes
C1	000000001-000000010-000000011	STS-1 identifiers
B1	BIP-8	Section error monitoring (previous STS-3c)
B2	BIP-24 (STS-3c)	Line error monitoring
H1 (1–4)	0110 (norm), 1001 (act)	New data found flag (change of pointer indication)
H1–H2 (7–16)	0000000000-1100001110	Pointer value (set to 1a for AIS)
H1*, H2[a]	10010011,11111111	Concatenation indication (set to 1s for AIS)
H3		pointer action (frequency justification)
K2 (6–8)	111,110, any non-110 value	Line AIS, line RDI, removal of line RDI
Third Z2 byte (2–8)	B2 error count	Line FEBE
J1		STS path trace
B3	BIP-8	Path error monitoring (previous SPE)
C2	00010011	Path signal level indicator
G1 (1–4)	B3 error count	Path FEBE
G1 (5)	0 or 1	Path RDI (also used to indicate loss of cell delineation)

[a] Defined at the UNI.

Table 22.2 provides another view of the overhead bytes.

Table 22.2 ATM over SONET Overhead (PHY Layer OAM)

	Functions	SONET OH Bytes		
Performance monitoring	Cell header error monitoring	Error corrected/uncorrectable		
	Line error monitoring	B2, Z2 (18–24)		
	Path error monitoring	B3, G1 (1–4)	SDH or	B-ISDN
	Section error monitoring	B1	SONET	specific
Fault management	STS path AIS	H1, H2, H3 G1 (5)		
	STS path RDI			
	Loss of cell delineation /Path RDI	G1 (5)		
	Line alarm indication Signal AIS and RDI	K2 (6–8)		
Facility testing	Connectivity verification trace (path)	J1		

22.2.2   ATM Mapped in STS-12c

In an STS-12c frame the first 36 columns are committed for the SONET overhead. Then, the 37th column is reserved for ATM path overhead information and the following 3 columns do not contain any information (known as stuff columns). The remaining PC is used to map ATM cells. That is, from a total of $1080 \times 9 = 9720$ bytes, $1040 \times 9 = 9360$ bytes are available to map ATM cells in this case. Then, the total number of ATM cells in the PC is obtained by dividing 9360 by 53. Doing so, one obtains about 176.60377358 cells in a frame.

In general, the number of stuff columns is calculated by the $N/3 - 1$. That is, for STS-3c, $N = 3$, the number of stuff columns is 0. In STS-12c, $N = 12$, and $12/3 - 1 = 3$ (Figure 22.3). Notice that in the case of STS-12c more bandwidth may be contained in the payload capacity. This is useful in cases where incoming signal from a single source is at a rate that requires a larger payload capacity than the STS-12.

22.2.3   Floating ATM in STS-3c and STS-12c

In the previous section, and for simplicity of ATM mapping description, it was shown that the first cell was aligned with the first byte of the payload capacity. However, in practice, this may not be the typical case. To avoid

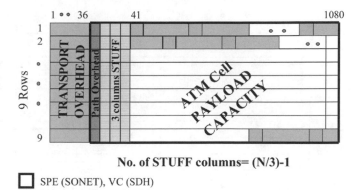

No. of STUFF columns= (N/3)-1

☐ SPE (SONET), VC (SDH)

Figure 22.3 ATM over SONET: cell mapping in STS-12c.

unnecessary delays, cells are mapped within a floating SPE, that is, with an offset. This implies that a pointer is required in the SONET overhead to point to the J1 byte of the payload, as was the case of mapping VTs in the SPE. Figure 22.4 illustrates a floating SPE with ATM cells in an STS-3c frame.

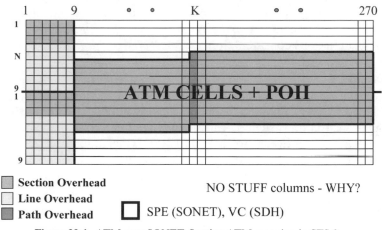

■ **Section Overhead**   NO STUFF columns - WHY?
☐ **Line Overhead**
■ **Path Overhead**   ☐ SPE (SONET), VC (SDH)

Figure 22.4 ATM over SONET: floating ATM mapping in STS-3c.

Similarly, Figure 22.5 illustrates a floating SPE with ATM cells in an STS-12c frame. In this case, notice the position of the stuff columns.

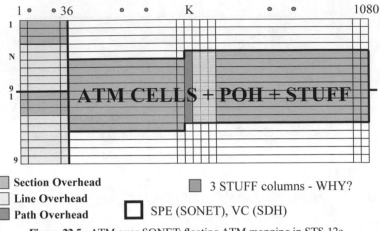

Section Overhead

Line Overhead

Path Overhead

3 STUFF columns - WHY?

SPE (SONET), VC (SDH)

Figure 22.5   ATM over SONET: floating ATM mapping in STS-12c.

22.3   ATM MAPPED IN SDH

In SDH, as in SONET, ATM cells are mapped contiguously rowwise in C11, C12, C3, or C4 containers. Again, the fixed-stuff columns in a STM-4 are only 3, and a pointer is required in the SOH to point to the J1 byte of the floating payload. When the container transport capacity does not meet the ATM bandwidth, for example, because the ATM bit rate is higher than the equivalent bit rate of one of these containers, the ATM bandwidth may be split up and use virtual or continuous concatenation.

EXAMPLE

Mapping a pleisiochronous signal onto STM-1. In this case, the signal is mapped in C4 containers, path overhead is added, and the virtual container VC4 is constructed. The pointer is added and the AU-4 is constructed. Section overhead (MSOH 1 RSOH) is added and the STM-1 is produced.

22.4   LAYERS

As in SONET with VT mappings, the path, line, and section layers in ATM over SONET are defined as follows:

Path layer: Deals with the transport of "services," e.g., DS3, between DS3 path-terminating network elements (PTEs). It maps "services" into the required format by the line layer.

Line layer: Deals with the reliable transport of path layer payload and its overhead across the physical medium. Provides synchronization and multiplexing for the path layer network based on services provided by the section layer.

Section layer: Deals with the transport of an STS-Nc frame across the physical medium and uses the services of the physical layer to form the physical transport. It frames, scrambles, monitors for errors, etc.

ATM is an asynchronous mechanism that transports data from one end user to another. User data may be a long string of binary bits, a long string of bytes, synchronous or asynchronous bytes, or real-time or not-real-time data. How data are encapsulated, segmented, and encapsulated in ATM cells have been already described. Figure 22.6 illustrates the various operations that take place on a DS-N client signal at the various layers (path, line, section, and physical) to eventually convert it to an OC-N signal.

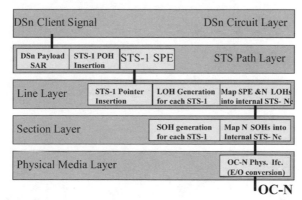

Figure 22.6   ATM over SONET. Example: mapping DS-N on OC-N.

EXERCISES

1. How are ATM cells mapped in SONET SPE?
2. Calculate the number of ATM cells in an STS-12c.
3. Review the layers in ATM over SONET.

Answers

1. In a continuous, rowwise manner
2. 176-6
3. OAM, VP, and VC management, performance management, activation/deactivation, alarm surveillance, and loopbacks

CHAPTER *23*

MANAGEMENT OF ATM OVER SONET

23.1 ATM NETWORK MANAGEMENT

The ATM over SONET/SDH network management encompasses the following functions:

- *Performance management:* performance monitoring
- *Fault management:* failure localization, isolation, testing, and restoration; alarm surveillance
- *Configuration management:* memory update and database query; database backup and database restoration
- *Security management:* data and system integrity; system/resource access control
- *Accounting management:* PVC and/or SVC accounting
- I*nterim local management interface* (ILMI) (ATM Forum: UNI): ILMI protocol (stack and messages) and traffic requirements

23.2 OAM LEVELS AND FLOWS

Operations, administration, and maintenance (OAM) functions in an ATM network are hierarchical and performed at various layers and levels. In order to distinguish the level of network management, such as regenerator section to regenerator section at the physical layer or VP level to VP level at the ATM layer, distinguishable OAM cells are sent by each level. These OAM cells are known as the *OAM flow Fn* level. Based on this, OAM flow F1 cells are used for network management between two regeneration points at the physical layer. Similarly, OAM flow F2 cells are used for network management at the digital section level, and so on. Figure 23.1 illustrates the various OAM flow Fns at the various network management levels.

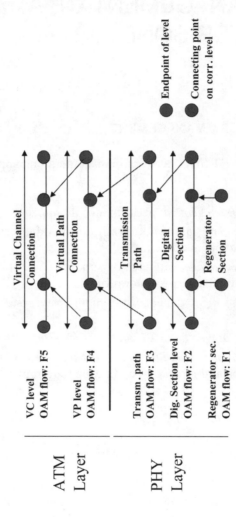

Figure 23.1 ATM over SONET: OAM levels and flows.

23.3 PM AND ALARM SURVEILLANCE

The performance monitoring (PM) function in ATM over SONET/SDH is responsible for monitoring the range of the performance parameters that depend on the transmission system used, i.e., DS1, DS3, E1, E3, SONET, etc. In addition, it gathers and analyzes performance data, such as bit or block errors (BER, HEC), framing errors (out of frame), and pointer errors, for ATM over SONET.

This function also detects signal defects, anomalies, or failures, such as signal degrade and signal fail, which are indicated in corresponding bytes in the overhead space of the SONET frame for ATM over SONET. It also generates alarm signals, such as local (or red) alarm, AIS (blue) alarm downstream, and RDI (yellow) alarm upstream.

When failures are detected and localized, the OAM may perform a nonintrusive test (a test that does not affect service), or depending on the fault, an intrusive test. All fault and performance parameters are recorded in a database and are reported to the network management system (NMS).

Figure 23.2 illustrates the red, blue, and yellow alarms in the upstream and downstream directions.

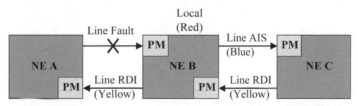

Figure 23.2 ATM over SONET: PM and alarm surveillance.

23.4 PERFORMANCE MONITORING PARAMETERS

PM parameters are associated with the following overhead bytes:

- Path error monitoring (B3: BIP-8), in path overhead
- Line error monitoring (B2: BIP-24), in line overhead
- Section error monitoring (B1: BIP-8), in section overhead
- Cell delineation, in the physical layer
- Cell header error monitoring (HEC), in ATM cell overhead

The failure states that are identified and reported are:

- Loss of signal (LOS)
- Loss of frame (LOF)

- Loss of pointer (LOP)
- Path signal label mismatch
- Loss of cell delineation (LCD)

The alarm signals that are generated and transmitted are:

- Line AIS (all 1's with framed SONET/SDH), blue alarm
- Path AIS (H1, H2 all 1's), in the overhead
- Line RDI (K2 byte), in line overhead, yellow alarm
- Path RDI (G1 byte, bit 5), in path overhead

EXERCISES

1. Calculate the number of ATM cells that fit in the SPE of an STS-3c, an STS-12c, and an STS-48c.
2. ATM traffic arrives at a SONET NE equipped with an input unit that maps ATM cells in SONET payloads. The SONET NE has a switching fabric that can switch at STS-3 rates. ATM cells arrive at a rate 300,000 cells/s. Determine the STS-Nc frame that can fit the cells in the most efficient manner.
3. ATM traffic arrives at a SONET NE equipped with an input unit that maps ATM cells in SONET payloads. The SONET NE has a switching fabric that can switch at STS-3 rates. ATM cells arrive at a rate between 100,000 and 112,000 cells/s. Determine the STS-Nc frame that can fit the cells in the most efficient manner.
4. ATM traffic arrives at a SONET NE equipped with a unit that maps ATM cells in SONET payloads from two sources. The SONET NE has a switching fabric that can switch at STS-3 rates. ATM cells arrive at a rate between 80,000 and 100,000 cells/s from one source and at a rate of 220,000 cells/s from the other source. Determine the most efficient mapping.
5. ATM traffic arrives at a SONET NE equipped with a unit that maps ATM cells in SONET payloads from multiple sources. The SONET NE has a switching fabric that can switch at STS-1 rates. ATM cells from any of the sources arrive at a variable rate between 10,000 and 20,000 cells/s. Comment on an efficient mapping method.
6. ATM traffic arrives at a SONET NE equipped with an input unit that maps ATM cells in SONET payloads. The SONET NE has a switching fabric that can switch at STS-12 rates. ATM cells arrive at a rate approximately 10^6 cells/s. Before mapping the ATM cells in the SONET payload, the VPI and VCI code of each cell must be recognized by a pattern recognizer. How fast should the pattern recognizer be in terms of patterns per second?

Answers

1. 44.1509 for STS-3c, 176.603 for STS-12c, 707.094 for STS-48c
2. STS-3c

3. STS-1

4. STS-3c

5. Assuming buffering and an average 1500 cells/s, ATM cells from about six sources may be mapped onto an STS-1.

6. 2×10^6 patterns/s or 0.5 μs/pattern

CHAPTER 24

EPILOGUE: CONVERGENCE

24.1 INTRODUCTION

Currently, voice plays a dominant role in communications and telephone companies will always consider voice as a key part of the network service. However, this dominance may soon change. While in the 1980s the average telephone traffic per user (i.e., phone calls at 64 Kbps or less) was estimated to be around 6 min/h, in the 1990s the average has been dramatically increased to 180 min/h. This increase is a combination of telephone and data bandwidth. By some estimates, the next millennium will witness a growth in rapid and massive data access, voice, video, high-definition image, and high-speed data (including video data). Bandwidth demands will far surpass the bandwidth that a monochromatic optical signal can carry in a fiber. Advanced techniques, such as DWDM, allow many wavelengths to propagate along a single fiber, thus multiplying the bandwidth per fiber. An infrastructure based on DWDM allow for a mix of pipes, SONET, IP, ATM, etc. However, to make DWDM bandwidth efficient, wavelength pipes should only be used at their maximum bit rate, i.e., 10 Gbps.

Voice services may change from the traditional to non-real-time store and forward and also to real-time over asynchronous services. Among the many asynchronous services, Internet will carry real-time voice and video, and appliances will be remotely voice- or computer-controlled, from the office or when riding a car. Home/office video surveillance will be from any place, doctors will perform surgery from remote places, and educators and students will not have to be in the same room. Such services will affect everyone's life and will redefine education, the law, medicine, government, entertainment, communication, business, life-styles, etc. It is predicted that with this data explosion data traffic will soon be at parity or even surpass voice traffic. As a result, these diverse services will require one global network that consists of programmable nodes capable of routing any type of payload and establishing "unconstrained and instantaneous connectivity." This is known as *convergence*.

Convergence of diverse services over the same network that offers SONET/SDH, ATM, and IP, as many predict, is becoming the direction of the communications industry and is presently in the evolution stage. The first steps in this direction are interoperability, interworking, and simple yet comprehensive network management standards. In addition, wireless voice and data networks are expected to be connected to fiber networks. Although we cannot devote a comprehensive chapter, it is projected that, along with ultra-high transmission speeds and ultra-broadband optical networks, convergence will trigger the next communications revolution.

24.2 CHALLENGES

From an engineering standpoint, this convergence will not be an easy task. The challenge will be a demanding communications network with complex yet miniaturized and cost-effective system components. The challenged will be the scientist and the technologist. Transistors operating on the electron level will be able to offer integrated systems in a single chip. Photonic devices operating on the photon level and devices capable to generate and detect ultra-dense wavelengths will increase the bandwidth capacity and switching speed of systems at levels unprecedented. The challenged will be the communications engineer to develop engineering rules never attempted before. The challenged will be the standards bodies to be able to develop standards for interoperability purposes of high-quality systems. And finally, the challenge will be a communications network with unprecedented speeds, scalable capacities (to beyond terabits per second), flexibility to add new services, backward compatibility with existing networks, reliability, high quality of service, network survivability, efficient network management, low system cost and low-cost competitive services, and interoperable.

24.3 PREDICTIONS

The next millenium will meet us with a voracious appetite for data capacity and robust services. Data traffic needs will be increasing exponentially to the point that data traffic capacity will exceed that of voice. Major advances in microelectronic, opto-electronic, digital signal processing, and software technologies will make this possible.

Traffic capacities over fiber will reach unprecedented levels, primarily due to dense wavelength multiplexing, more inexpensive and faster opto-electronic devices, as well as optical switches.

Mobility will be key and wireless communications (including Low Earth Orbit Satellite technology, or LEOS) will play a major role to bring image ubiquitously, and global positioning systems (GPSs) will offer more advanced services.

Networks will provide the quality (QoS) requested by the user and network management will make all that possible.

Voice and real-time video (synchronous data) and non-real-time data services (asynchronous data) over one network may sound like an oxymoron. Should we expect to see a single network that supports both types (synchronous and asynchronous) of services, or should we expect an overlay of interoperable networks with standard interfaces? Then, what are the underlining characteristics that we should look for in such networks? What will be the fault management and fault detection issues? What will the standard operating systems be?

24.4   NETWORK SHOULDs

Clearly, when a network is designed to support real-time and non-real-time services, the best of *both* worlds should be designed into it. Network delay management, network reliability, and network survivability become of importance where they were not. Quality of service becomes of importance where it was not. High performance, integration with legacy networks, efficient bandwidth utilization, scalability, and low cost of service, all become of importance where they were not. Moreover, one must add ease of media integration, reduced infrastructure complexity, easy and efficient billing, and high network security. Security, end to end and node to node, increases in importance if one considers the cost penalty to service providers if a network is accidentally or maliciously accessed by unauthorized people or if it is crashed by hackers. (Could people do this? What do you think?)

24.5   FROM TODAY TO TOMORROW

Today, new applications that converge voice and data (e.g., one-way video, interactive or two-way video, asynchronous HS data, computation data, Internet) arc in the design phase, and as new applications make headlines, the stock market bounces like a basketball. For example, video over the Internet and voice over the Internet are services that have been recently announced. New intelligent protocols, new network elements with ultra-high bandwidth, and new transport systems at ultra-high speeds are all on the drawing board to offer enhanced services with many features and to meet the voracious bandwidth hunger of users (Figure 24.1).

Some of these applications may have a severe impact on traditional services and systems. For example, it is estimated that a 6–10% shift of telephony services from long distance (LD) to IP would reduce the LD profits to low levels (the LD traffic in United States is about 2000 Tbytes/day). Therefore, a low cost per bit per kilometer has been and still is very critical in communications service providers.

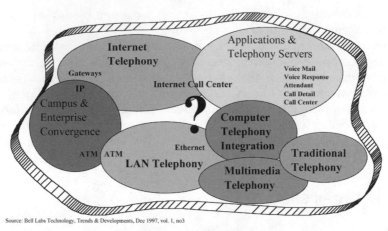

Source: Bell Labs Technology, Trends & Developments, Dec 1997, vol. 1, no3

Figure 24.1   Convergence: a picture is 1000 words!

As convergence of services is taking place, in a single network one should expect to transport all traditional services and new "untraditional" services that challenge our imagination. Just wait and see!

Yet, the most frequently asked questions within the communications community are:

- What will the new killer application(s) be?
- What will the bandwidth allocation for voice, video, and data be in the future?
- Which is the best network strategy to meet customer needs, and what are these needs?
- Which application(s) would generate most of the revenues?
- What will the future network look like?
- One can only guess. It's a jungle out there!

SECTION III

REFERENCES

[1] E. Ayanoglu and R. D. Gitlin, "Broadband Network Restoration," *IEEE Commun. Mag.,* vol. 34, no. 7, 1996, pp. 110–119.

[2] U. Black, *ATM: Foundation for Broadband Networks,* 3 vols. Prentice-Hall Englewood Cliffs, NJ, 1995.

[3] J. C. Collins, J. Dunn, P. Emer, and M. Johnson, "Data Express: Gigabit Junction with the Next-generation Internet," *IEEE Spectrum,* vol. 36, no. 2, 1999, pp. 18–25.

[4] D. C. Cox, "Wireless Personal Communications: What Is It?" *IEEE Pers. Comm.,* vol. 2, no. 2, 1995, pp. 20–35.

[5] J. S. DaSilva, D. Ikonomou, and H. Erben, "European R&D Programs on Third-Generation Mobile Communication Systems," *IEEE Pers. Comm.,* vol. 4, no. 1, 1997, pp. 46–52.

[6] S. Dixit, and S. Elby, "Fram Relay and ATM Interworking," *IEEE Commun. Mag.,* vol. 34, no. 6, 1996, pp. 64–82.

[7] G. H. Bobrowski, "The ATM Forum: Developing Implementation Agreements," *IEEE Commun. Mag.,* Sept. 1998, pp. 121–125.

[8] M. Figueroa and S. Hansen, "Technology Interworking for SMDS: From the DXI/SNI to the ATM UNI," *IEEE Commun. Mag.,* vol. 34, no. 6, 1996, pp. 90–95.

[9] N. Finn and T. Mason, "ATM LAN Emulation," *IEEE Commun. Mag.,* vol. 34, no 6, 1996, pp. 96–100.

[10] M. Gagnaire, "An Overview of Broad-Band Access Technologies," *Proc. IEEE,* vol. 85, no. 12, 1997, pp. 1958–1972.

[11] L. G. Guthbert and J-C Sapanel, *ATM: The Broadband Telecommunications Solution, IEEE,* New York, 1993.

[12] K. Y. Eng and M. J. Karol, "High-Performance Techniques for Gigabit ATM Switching and Networking," International Communications Conference '93, Geneva, Switzerland, May 1993, pp. 1673–1678.

[13] S. V. Kartalopoulos, "Understanding SONET/SDH and ATM," Tutorial Notes, International Communications Conference '98, Atlanta, June 1998.

[14] S. V. Kartalopoulos, "An Associative RAM-Based CAM and Its Application to Broad-Band Communications System," *Trans. Neural Networks,* vol. 9, no. 5, pp. 1036–1041.

[15] S. V. Kartalopoulos, "Applicability of RAM-based CAMs in ATM Communications Systems," Globecom'98, Sydney, Nov. 1998.

[16] S. V. Kartalopoulos, "Global Multi-Satellite Networks," International Communications Conference '97, Montreal, Canada, June 1997.

[17] S. V. Kartalopoulos, "A Manhattan Fiber Distributed Data Interface Network," Globecom'93, Houston, TX, Dec. 2–5, 1993.

[18] S. V. Kartalopoulos, "Disaster Avoidance in the Manhattan Fiber Distributed Data Interface Architecture," Globecom'90, San Diego, Dec. 2–5, 1990.

[19] S. V. Kartalopoulos, "A Plateau of Performance?" Guest Editorial, *IEEE Commun. Mag.,* Sept. 1992, pp. 13–14.

[20] S. V. Kartalopoulos, "Neural Networks in Communications Systems," Tutorial, Globecom'91, Phoenix, AZ, Dec. 2–5, 1991.

[21] S. V. Kartalopoulos, "Temporal Fuzziness in Communications Systems," WCCI'94, ICNN, Orlando, FL, July 2, 1994.

[22] D. N. Knisely, S. Kumar, S. Laha, and S. Nanda, "Evolution of Wireless Data Services: IS-95 to cdma2000," *IEEE Commun. Mag.,* vol. 36, no. 10, 1998, pp. 140–149.

[23] S. Kumar and S. Nanda, "A Simulation Technique to Study CDMA System Performance with Integrated Voice and Data Services," Advanced Simulation Techniques 1998, Boston, MA, April 5–9, 1998.

[24] J. Lane, "Is ATM a Miracle or Another Terrible Mistake?" *Telephony,* Oct. 24, 1994, pp. 28–38.

[25] K. A. Lutz, "A Scalable ATM Switching System Architecture," *IEEE J. Selected Areas Commun.,* vol. 9, no. 8, 1991, pp. 1299–1307.

[26] M. A. Marsan, A. Bianco, E. Leonardi, A. Morabito, and F. Neri, "All-Optical WDM Multi-Rings with Differentiated QoS," *IEEE Commun. Mag.,* vol. 37, no. 2, 1999, pp. 58–66.

[27] B. Miller, "Satellites Free the Mobile Phone," *IEEE Spectrum,* March 1998, pp. 26–35.

[28] D. O'Shea, "Voice and Data: Riding in Tandem on ATM," *Telephony,* March 11, 1996, pp. 40–49.

[29] H. G. Perros, "Call Admission Control Schemes: A Review," *IEEE Commun. Mag.,* vol. 34, no. 11, 1996, pp. 82–91.

[30] J. G. Proakis, "Adaptive Equalization for TDMA Digital Mobile Radio," *IEEE Trans. Veh. Tech.,* vol. 40, no. 2, May 1991, pp. 333–341.

[31] M. De Prycker, *Asynchronous Transfer Mode: Solutions for Broadband ISDN,* 3rd ed., Prentice-Hall, Englewood Cliffs, NJ, 1995.

[32] D. Raychaudhuri, "Wireless ATM Networks: Architecture, System Design and Prototyping," *IEEE Pers. Commun.,* vol. 3, no. 4, 1995, pp. 42–49.

[33] G. Ellis, "Internet Protocol: The Future Route for Telephony?", *EDN Magazine,* Nov. 19, 1998, pp. 62–78.

[34] M. Veeraraghavan, "An Alternative Approach to Call/Processing Control in Broadband Switching Systems," *IEEE Commun. Mag.,* vol. 33, no. 11, 1995, pp. 90–96.

[35] E. Witte-Zigura, "Architectures for ATM Switching Systems," *IEEE Commun. Mag.,* vol. 31, no. 2, 1993, pp. 28–48.

STANDARDS

[1] ANSI/IEEE Standard 802.3, "Local Area Networks; Carrier Sense Multiple Access with Collision Detection," IEEE, New York, 1985.

[2] ATM Forum, "ATM User-Network Interface [UNI] Specification," version 3.1, July 21, 1994.

[3] ATM Forum, "ATM User-Network Interface [UNI] Signaling," version 4.0, May 1996.

[4] ATM Forum, "ATM Private Network Node Interface (PNNI)," version 1.0, Mar. 1996, with "PNNI Available Bit Rate Addendum," Jan. 1997.

[5] ATM Forum, "ATM Data Exchange Interface (DXI)," June 15, 1993.

[6] ATM Forum, "BISDN Inter-Carrier Interface (B-ICI)," version 2.0, Dec. 1995; with "B-ICI 2.0 Addendum 2.1," Nov. 1996.

[7] ATM Forum, "Integrated Local Management Interface (ILMI)", version 4.0, Sept. 1997.

[8] ATM Forum, "Interim Inter-Switch Signaling Protocol (IISP)," version 1.0, Dec. 1994.

[9] ATM Forum, "Inverse Multiplexing over ATM (IMA)," version 2.0, July 1997.

[10] ATM Forum, "Audio/Visual Multimedia Service (AMS)," version 1.0, Jan. 1996.

[11] ATM Forum, "Voice and Telephony Over ATM (VTOA) to the Desktop," version 1.0, May 1997.

[12] ATM Forum, "Multi-Protocol over ATM (MPOA)," version 1.0, July 1997.

[13] ATM Forum, "LAN Emulation over ATM Specification," version 1, Feb. 1995.

[14] ATM Forum, "Traffic Management," version 4.0, Apr. 1996; with "Traffic Management Available Bit Rate Addendum," Jan. 1997.

[15] Bellcore, GR-2842-CORE, "ATM Service Access Multiplexer (SAM) Generic Requirements," 1996.

[16] Bellcore, GR-2869-CORE, "Generic Requirements for Operations Based on the TMN Architecture," 1995.

[17] Bellcore, TR-TSV-000772, "Generic System Requirements in Support of Switched Multi-megabit Data Service," issue 1, May 1991.

[18] Bellcore, TR-TSV-001239, "Generic System Requirements for Low Speed SMDS Access," issue 1, Dec. 1993.

[19] ETSI 300 612-1, "Digital Cellular Telecommunications System (Phase 2): Network Management (NM); Part 1," Aug. 1996.

[20] ETSI 300 612-2, "Digital Cellular Telecommunications System (Phase 2): Network Management (NM); Part 2," Aug. 1996.

[21] ETSI TC-RES 06921, "High Performance Radio Local Area Network (HIPERLAN): Functional Specification," draft prETS 300 652, Sophia Antipolis, France, July 1995.

[22] Frame Relay Forum FRF.3: Multiprotocol Encapsulation Implementation Agreement, 1993.

[23] Frame Relay Forum FRF.4: Frame Relay User-to-Network SVC Implementation Agreement, 1994.

[24] Frame Relay Forum FRF.5: Frame Relay/ATM Implementation Agreement, 1994.

[25] Frame Relay Forum FRF.8: Frame Relay/ATM PVC Multicast Service Interworking Implementation Agreement, 1995.

[26] Frame Relay Forum FRF.10: SVCs at the NNI Implementation Agreement, 1996.

[27] Frame Relay Forum FRF.12: Frame Relay Fragmentation Agreement, 1997.

[28] IEEE 802-11.1997, "IEEE Standard for Wireless LAN Medium Access Control and Physical Layer Specification," June 1997.

[29] ISO/IEC 14496-6 CD, "Delivery Multimedia Integration Framework, DMIF," May 1998.

[30] ITU-T Recommendation E.164, "The International Public Telecommunication Numbering Plan," May 1997.

[31] ITU-T Recommendation G.804, "ATM Cell Mapping into Plesiochronous Digital Hierarchy (PDH)," 1998.

[32] ITU-T Recommendation G.805, "Generic Functional Architecture of Transport Networks," Nov. 1995.

[33] TU-T Recommendation G.822, "Stage 1, Stage 2 and Stage 3 Description of the Q3 Interface—Performance Management," May 1994.

[34] ITU-T Recommendation G.823, "Stage 2 and Stage 3 Functional Specifications for Traffic Management," July 1996.

[35] ITU-T Recommendation I.312/Q.1201, "Principals of Intelligent Network Architectures," 1992.

[36] ITU-T Recommendation I.365.1, "Frame Relaying Service Specific Convergence Sublayer (FR-SSCS)," 1993.

[37] ITU-T Recommendation I.432, "B-ISDN User-network Interface—Physical Layer Specification," March 1993.

[38] ITU-T Recommendation I.555, "Frame Relaying Bearer Service Core Features," Dec. 1995.

[39] ITU-T Recommendation Q.933, "DSS1 Signaling Specification for Frame Mode Basic Call Control," 1992.

[40] ITU-T Recommendation X 213, "Information Technology—Open System Interconnection—Network Service Definition," Addition of the Internet protocol address format identifiers, August 1997.

[41] ITU-T Recommendation Y.100, "GII Overview," Oct. 1997.

[42] ITU-T Recommendation Y.110, "GII Principles and Framework Architecture," Oct. 1997.

[43] ITU-T Recommendation Y.120, "GII Scenario Methodology," June 1998.

[44] ITU-T Standard H.323, "Packet-Based Multimedia Communications Systems—version 2," Jan. 1998.

[45] J. Postel, RFC 793, "Internet Protocol (IP)," Sept. 1981.

[46] J. Postel, RFC 793, "Transmission Control Protocol (TCP)," Sept. 1981.

[47] J. Heinanen, RFC 1483, "Multiprotocol Encapsulation over ATM Adaptation Layer 5," 1993.

[48] M. Laubach, RFC 1577, "Classical IP and ARP over ATM," Jan. 1994.

[49] M. Perez, F. Liaw, D. Grossman, A. Mankin, E. Hoffman, and A Malis, RFC 1755: "ATM Signaling Support for IP over ATM," Feb. 1995.

[50] G. Armitage, RFC 2022, "Support for Multicast over UNI 3.0/3.1 based ATM Networks," Nov. 1996.

[51] J. Postel, RFC 2200, STD-1: "Internet Official Protocol Standards," June 1997.

[52] S. Shenker, C. Partridge, and R. Gueriz, RFC 2212, "Specification of Guaranteed Quality of Service," Sept. 1997.

[53] SMDS Interest Group, SIG-TS-001/1991, "SMDS Data Exchange Interface Protocol," revision 3.2, Oct. 22, 1991.

[54] SMDS Interest Group, SIG-TS-008/1994, "Protocol Interface Specification for Implementation of SMDS over an ATM-based Public UNI," revision 31, May 3, 1994.

[55] TIA IS-707, "Data Services Standard for Wideband Spread Spectrum Cellular System," 1995.

[56] TIA TSB.91, "Sattelite ATM Networks: Architectures and Guidelines," 1995.

[57] *www.atis.org/sif/sifhom.htm,* Web site that contains updated activities on common applications, network architectures and testing methods, CIT/OS platform definitions, information models, and implementation.

[58] *www.atmforum.com/atmforum/specs/approved.html,* Web site that contains all approved specifications by ATM Forum.

[59] *www.atmforum.com/atmforum/specs/specwatch.html,* Web site that contains all currently prepared specification by ATM Forum.

[60] *www.dmtf.org,* Web site of Desktop Management Task Force.

[61] *www.gsc.etsi.fr/,* Web site for Global Standards Collaboration (GSC).

[62] *www.iana.org,* Internet Assigned Number Authority (IANA) web page.

[63] *www.ieee.org,* Web site of the IEEE.

[64] *www.ieee-pin.org* and *http://stdsbbs.ieee.org/groups/index.html,* Web sites of IEEE P1520 standards initiative for programmable network interfaces.

[65] *www.nfoec.com,* Web site of National Fiber Optic Engineers Conference.

[66] *www.omg.org,* Web site of Object Management Group.

[67] *www.tinac.com,* Web site for Telecommunications Information Networking Architecture.

[68] *http://comet.columbia.edu/opensig,* Web site of project OPENSIG at Columbia University.

[69] *http://www.t1.org*

LIST OF ABBREVIATIONS

10BaseT   10 Mbps over twisted pair; an Ethernet (IEEE 802.3) standard
100BaseT   100 Mbps over twisted pair; an Ethernet (IEEE 802.3) standard
1000BaseT   1000 Mbps over twisted pair; an Ethernet (IEEE 802.3ab) standard
2B1Q   Two-bits-to-one Quartenary
2FSK   Two-level frequency shift keying
2W   Two wire
4FSK   Four-level frequency shift keying
7B8B   Seven bit to eight bit
AA   Adaptive antenna
AAL   ATM adaptation layer
ABR   Available bit rate
AC   Authentication counter; alternating current
ACD   Automatic call distribution system
ACIS   Advanced Cellular Internet Service
ACK   Acknowledgment
ACSE   Association control service element
ACTS   Advanced Communications Technology and Services
ADBF   Advanced DBF
ADC   Analog-to-digital conversion
ADM   Add-drop multiplexer
ADPCM   Adaptive differential PCM
ADSL   Asymmetric DSL
ADTS   Automated digital terminal equipment system
AFI   Authority format identifier
AFNOR   Association Francaise de Normalisation

AH   Applications header

AIS   Alarm indication signal; also called blue alarm

AIU   Access interface unit

AIX   Advanced interactive executive

ALTS   Alternative local transmission system

AM   Administration module; amplitude modulation

AMAC   American Market Awareness and Education Committee

AMF   Asian Multimedia Forum

AMI   Alternate mark inversion (technique)

AMPS   Advanced Mobile Phone Service

AN   Access node

ANSI   American National Standards Institute

AP   Access point; adjunct processor

APC   Adaptive predictive coding

APD   Avalanche photo detector; access procedure of the D channel; advanced photodiode

APDPCM   Adaptive predictive DPCM

APDU   Application protocol data unit; authentic protocol data unit

APEC   Asian Pacific Economic Cooperation

APII   Asia-Pacific Information Infrastructure

APMAC   Asian Pacific Market Awareness and Education Committee

APS   Automatic protection switching

ARIB   Association of Radio Industries and Business

ARM   Access resource management

ARP   Address resolution protocol

ARQ   Automatic repeat request

ASBC   Adaptive subband coding

AS&C   Alarm, surveillance, and control

ASE   Application service element

ASK   Amplitude shift key

ASP   Adjunct service point

ATM   Asynchronous transfer mode

ATU   ADSL transceiver unit

ATU-C   ATU central office

ATU-R   ATU remote terminal

AU   Administrative unit

AU-AIS   Administrative unit AIS

AUG   Administrative unit group

AU-LOP Administrative unit loss of pointer

AU-N Administrative unit level N

AU-NDF Administrative unit new data flag

AUP Administrative unit pointer

AU-PJE Administrative unit pointer justification event

AWGN Additive white gaussian noise

B6ZS Bipolar with six-zero substitution (see BnZS)

B8ZS Bipolar with eight-zero substitution (see BnZS)

BAF Burst allocation function

BAS Broadband access signaling

BBE Background block error

BBER Background block error ratio

BCC Block check character; blocked-calls-cleared

BCCH Broadcast control channel

BCD Binary coded decimal; blocked-calls-delayed

BDCS Broadband digital cross-connect system

BDMA Band division multiple access

BECN Backward error congestion notification

BER Bit error rate; basic encoding rules

BICI Broadband Inter-Carrier Interface

BITS Building Information Timing Supply

BFSK Binary FSK

BIM Byte-interleaved multiplexer

BIP Bit-interleaved parity

BIP-8 Bit-interleaved parity-8 field

BISDN Broadband Integrated Services Digital Network

BLER Block error rate

BLSR Bidirectional line-switch ring

BnZS Bipolar with n-zero substitution, $n = 3, 6, 8$

BPF Band-pass filter

B-PISN Broadband Private Integrated Services Network

Bps Bits per second

BPSK Binary PSK

BRI Basic rate interface

BS Burst second

BSHR Bidirectional shelf healing ring

BSI British Standards Institution

BSS Broadband switching system; basic service set

BT   Burst tolerance

BV   Bipolar violation

C-N   Container level N, $N = 11, 12, 2, 3, 4$

CAC   Connection admission control

CAM   Content addressable memory

CAP   Carrierless amplitude phase; competitive access provider

CAS   Channel associated signaling

CAT5   Category 5

CB   Channel bank

CBMS   Computer-based message system

CBR   Constant bit rate

CC   Composite clock

CCAF   Call control agent system

CCC   Clear channel capability

CCF   Call control function

CCITT   Consultative Committee International Telegraph and Telephone (renamed ITU)

CCM   Cross-connect multiplexing

CCR   Current cell rate

CCSN   Common channel signaling network

CDMA   Code division multiple access

CDPD   Cellular digital packet data

CDR   Call detail record

CDV   Cell delay variation

CDVT   Cell delay variation tolerance

CEI   Connection endpoint identifier

CEIGU   Channel estimation and interference generation unit

CELP   Code excited linear prediction

CENELEC   Comit Europ en de Normalisation Electrotechnique

CEPT-n   Conference of European Posts and Telecommunications-level n (see E1)

CER   Cell error ratio

CES   Circuit emulation service

CEU   Committed end user

CFP   Contention-free period

CGSA   Cellular Geographic Serving Area

CI   Concatenation indication

CICS   Customer information control subsystem

CIM   Common information model

CIR   Committed information rate

CIT   Craft interface terminal

CIU   Channel interface unit

CLASS   Custom local area signaling services

CLEC   Competitive local exchange carrier

CLLI   Common language location identifier

CLNP   Conectionless network layer protocol

CLP   Cell loss priority

CLR   Cell loss rate

CLTP   Connectionless transport layer protocol

CM   Communications module

CMI   Coded mark inversion

CMIP   Common management information protocol

CMISE   Common management information service element

CMIS/P   Common management information service/protocol

CMOS   Complementary metal-oxide-semiconductor

CMR   Cell mis-insertion rate

CMRTS   Cellular Mobile Radio Telephone System

CNM   Customer network management

CNTRL   Control

CO   Central office

CODEC   Coder-decoder

COFDM   Coded orthogonal frequency-division multiplexing

COP   Connection-oriented protocol

CORBA   Common object request broker architecture

COSMIC   Coherent multistage interference canceller

COT   Central office terminal

COTS   Commercial off-the-shelf technology/equipment

CP   Control point; connection point

CPCS   Common part convergence sublayer

CPDU   Computer protocol data unit

CPE   Customer premises equipment

CPFSK   Continuous-phase FSK

CPN   Calling party's number

CPR   Current-period register

CRBS   Cell relay bearer service

CRC   Cyclic redundancy code

CRM Cell rate margin
CRS Cell relay service
CS Convergence sublayer
CS-PDU Convergence sublayer-PDU
CSA Carrier serving area
CSES Consecutive severely errored seconds
CSI Convergence sublayer indicator
CSMA/CD Carrier sense multiple access/collision detection
CSR Current-second register
CSU Channel Service Unit
CT-2 Cordless Telephone version 2
CTD Cell transfer delay
CTI Computer-telephony integration
CU Channel unit
CV Coding violation
CVSDM Continuous variable slope delta modulation
DACS Digital access and cross-connect system
DAMA Demand assignment multiple access
D-AMPS Digital AMPS
DARPA Defense Advanced Research Project Agency
DBF Digital beam forming
DC Direct current
DCB Digital channel bank
DCC Data country code; data communications channel; digital clear channel
DCE Data circuit-terminating equipment
DCF Distributed coordination function
DCME Digital compression multiplex equipment
DCN Data communication network
DCOM Distributed component object model
DCS Digital cross-connect system
DDCMP Digital data communications message protocol
DDD Direct distance dialing
DDE Dynamic data exchange
DDS Digital Data Service
DECT Digital European Cordless Telecommunications System
DES Data encryption standard
DFI Domain format identifier

DHCP   Dynamic host configuration protocol

DIN   Deutsches Institut fuer Normung EV

DIU   Digital interface unit

DLC   Digital loop carrier

DLCI   Data link connection identifier

DLL   Delay-lock tracking group

DM   Delta modulation

DMT   Discrete multitone (modulation)

DMTF   Desktop Management Task Force

DNHR   Dynamic nonhierarchical routing

DOA   Direction of arrival

DPA   Dynamic packet assignment

DPBX   Digital PBX

DPCM   Differential pulse code modulation

DPDU   Data link PDU

DPE   Distributed processing environment

DPSK   Differential PSK

DQDB   Distributed queue dual bus

DR   Digital radio

DSAP   Destination service access point

DSBSC   Double side band suppressed carrier

DS-CDMA   Direct sequence CDMA

DSI   Digital speech interpolation

DSL   Digital subscriber line

DSLAM   Digital subscriber line access multiplexer

DS-SMF   Dispersion-shifted single-mode fiber

DS-N   Digital signal level N, $N = 0, 1, 2, 3$

DSP   Domain-specific part; digital signal processor

DSSS   Direct-sequence spread spectrum

DSU   Data service unit

DSX-N   Digital signal cross-connect point for DS-N signals

DTE   Data terminal equipment

DTMF   Dual-tone multifrequency

DTS   Digital termination service

DWDM   Dense wavelength division multiplexing

DXC   Digital cross connect

DXI   Data exchange interface

E1   A wideband digital facility at 2.048 Mbps, aka CEPT-1

E3   A broadband digital facility at 34.368 Mbps, aka CEPT-3

E4   A broadband digital facility at 139.264 Mbps, aka CEPT-4

EA   Address extension

EBC   Errored block count

EBCDIC   Extended Binary Coded Decimal Interchange Code

EC   Echo canceller

ECC   Embedded communication channel

ECMA   European Association for Standardizing Information and Communication Systems

ECSA   Exchange Carriers Standards Association

EDC   Error detection code

EDCC   Error detection and correction code

EDFA   Erbium-doped fiber amplifier

EDI   Electronic data interchange

EFCN   Explicit forward congestion notification

EFI   Errored frame indicator

EFS   Error-free second

EIA/TIA   Electronics Industry Association/Telecommunications Industry Association

EIM   External interface module

EIR   Excess information rate; Equipment Identity Register

ELAN   Emulated LAN

EMA   Expectation maximization algorithm

EMAC   European, Middle East, and Africa Market Awareness and Education Committee

EMI   Electromagnetic interference

EML   Element management layer

EMS   Element management system

ENEQ   Unequipped

E/O   Electrical to optical

EOC   Embedded-operations channel

EPD   Early packet discard

EQTV   Extended quality TV

ES   Errored second

ESCON   Enterprise systems connection

ESF   Extended superframe format

ESR   Errored seconds ratio

ESI   End-system identifier
ETRI   Electronics and Telecommunications Research Institute
ETSI   European Telecommunications Standardization Institute
FACCH   Fast associated control channel
FACH   Forward access channel
FAS   Frame alignment signal
FBG   Fiber Bragg gratings
FC   Functional component; failure count
FCC   Federal Communications Commission
FCS   Frame check sequence
FD   Frame discard
FDD   Frequency-division duplex
FDDI   Fiber-distributed data interface
FDI   Feeder distribution interface
FDM   Frequency-division multiplexing
FDMA   Frequency-division multiple access
FEBE   Far-end block error
FECN   Forward error congestion notification
FEC   Forward error correction
FEP   Front-end processor
FER   Frame error rate
FERF   Far-end receive failure
FEXT   Far-end crosstalk
FFT   Fast fourier transform
FH   Frequency hopping
FHSS   Frequency-hopped spread spectrum
FIFO   First in, first out
FITL   Fiber in the loop
FM   Frequency modulation
FOA   First office application
FOTS   Fiber-optic transmission system
FPS   Fast packet switching
FR   Frame relay
FRAD   Frame relay assembler/disassembler
FRF   Frame Relay Forum
FRAMES   Future radio wideband multiple-access system
FRI   Frame relay interface
FRS   Frame relay service

FRSP   Frame relay service provider
FSK   Frequency shift keying
FTAM   File transfer and access method
FTP   File Transfer Protocol
FTTC   Fiber to the curb
FTTH   Fiber to the home
FUNI   Frame user network interface
FWA   Fixed wireless access
FX   Foreign exchange
Gbps   Gigabits per second, =1000 Mbps
GCRA   Generic cell rate algorithm
GDMO   Guidelines for the definition of managed objects
GEO   Geosynchronous Earth Orbit
GFC   Generic flow control
GI   Group identification
GII   Global Information Infrastructure
GMPCS   Global Mobile Personal Communications Satellite
GNE   Gateway network element
GPS   Global Positioning System
GRIN   Graded index for fiber
GSC   Global Standards Collaboration
GSM   Global System for Mobile Communications
gTLD   Global top-level domain
GUI   Graphical user interface
HCDS   High-capacity digital services
HCS   Hierarchical cell structure
HDB3   High-density bipolar three-zero substitution
HDBn   High-density bipolar n zeroes allowed
HDLC   High-level data link control
HDSL   High-bit-rate digital subscriber line
HDTV   High-definition TV
HDX   Half-duplex
HEC   Header error control
HFC   Hybrid fiber coax
HIPERLAN   High-performance radio local area network
HIPPI   High-speed serial interface
HLR   Home location register
HO   High order

HPF   High-pass filter

HP-PLM   High-order payload label mismatch

HP-RDI   High-order RDI

HP-REI   High-order REI

HP-TIM   High-order TIM

HP-UNEQ   High-order path unequipped

HTML   Hyper-Text Markup Language

HTR   Hard to reach

HTU   HDSL terminal unit

HVC   High-order virtual container

IANA   Internet Assigned Number Authority

IBSS   Independent basic service set

IC   Integrated circuit; interference canceller

ICC   Interstate Commerce Commission

ICD   International code designator

ICI   Intercarrier interface; intercarrier interface

ICIP   Inter-Carrier Interface Protocol

ICR   Initial cell rate

ID   Identifier

IDI   Initial-domain identifier

IDL   Interface Definition Language

IDLC   Integrated digital loop carrier

IDP   Initial-domain part

IDSL   ISDN DSL

IEC   Interstate Electrotechnical Commission

IEEE   Institute of Electrical and Electronics Engineers

IETF   Internet Engineering Task Force

IFFT   Inverse fast Fourier transform

ILEC   Incumbent local exchange carrier

ILMI   Interim local management interface

IM   Inverse multiplexer; intelligent multiplexer

IMA   Inverse multiplexing over ATM

IMAC   Isochronous medium-access controller

IMS   Information Management System

IMT-2000   International Mobile Telecommunications-2000

IN   Intelligent network

IOF   Interoffice framework

IP   Internet Protocol; intelligent peripheral

IPgn   Internet Protocol next generation
IPNNI   Integrated PNNI
IPv6   Internet Protocol version 6
IPX   Inter-network Packet Exchange
IR   Infrared
IrDA   Infrared Data Association
ISA   Industry Standard Architecture
ISDN   Integrated Services Digital Network
ISI   Intersymbol interference
ISM   Intelligent or integrated synchronous multiplexer
ISO   International Standards Organization
ISOC   Internet Society
ISP   Internet service provider
ITSP   Internet telephony service provider
ITU   International Telecommunications Union
ITU-D   ITU Development Sector
ITU-R   ITU Radio-communications Sector
ITU-T   ITU Telecommunications Standardization Sector
IW   Interworking
IWF   Interworking function
IWU   Interworking unit
IXC   Interexchange carrier
JIDM   Joint Inter Domain Management Group
JIT   Jitter transfer function
JMAPI   Java Management API
JTC1   Joint Technical Committee 1 (ISO/IEC)
Kbps   Kilobits per second, =1000 bps
KTN   Kernel transport network
LAC   Link access control
LAN   Local area network
LANE   Local area network emulation
LAPD   Link access protocol for the D channel
LAPF   Link access protocol for frame relay
LATA   Local access and transport area
LB   Loopback
LBC   Laser bias current
LCD   Loss of cell delineation
LCM   Least common multiplier

LCN   Logical channel number
LCV   Line coding violation
LD   Long distance
LEC   Local exchange carrier
LED   Light-emitting diode
LENO   Originating line equipment number
LENT   Terminating line equipment number
LES   Line-errored seconds
LEOS   Low Earth Orbit Satellite
LF   Line feed
LLC   Logical link control
LO   Low order
LOF   Loss of frame
LOH   Line overhead
LOM   Loss of multiframe
LOP   Loss of pointer
LO-PLM   Low-order PLM
LO-RDI   Low-order RDI
LO-REI   Low-order REI
LO-RFI   Low-order remote failure indication
LOS   Loss of signal
LO-TIM   Low-order TIM
LO-UNEQ   Low-order UNEQ
LPC   Linear prediction coding
LPF   Low-pass filter
LPRC   Longitudinal redundancy check
LSAP   Link Service Access Point
LSB   Least significant bit
LSES   Line-severed errored seconds
LSS   Loss of sequence synchronization
LSSU   Link status signaling unit
LTE   Line-terminating equipment
LU   Logical unit
LVC   Low-order virtual container
LVDS   Low-voltage differential signal
M1   Level 1 multiplexer
M11c   Two DS1 multiplexers for T1c rates
M12   Level 1-to-2 multiplexer

M2 Level 2 multiplexer

M23 Level 2-to-3 multiplexer

M13 Level 1-to-3 multiplexer

MAC Media access control

MAF Management application function

MAI Multiple access interference

MAN Metropolitan area network

Mbps Megabits per second, =1000 Kbps

MBS Maximum burst rate

MCF Message communications function

MCR Maximum cell rate

MCS Multicast server

MCTD Mean cell transfer delay

MD Mediation device

MDF Main distribution frame

MEOS Medium Earth Orbit Satellite

MF Mediation function; matching filter

MI Management information

MIB Management Information Base

MLM Multilongitudinal mode

MLSE Maximum-likelihood sequence estimator

MMDS Multichannel multipoint distribution service

MO Managed object

MONET Multiwavelength optical networking

MoU Memorandum of understanding

MPEG Motion Picture Experts Group

MPOA Multiprotocol over ATM

MS-AIS Multiplex section AIS

MSB Most significant bit

MSC Mobile switching center

MSDSL Multirate SDSL

MS-FERF Multiplex section FERF

MSK Minimum shift keying

MSN Manhattan Street Network

MSO Multiple system operator

MSOH Multiplexer section overhead

MS-RDI Multiplex section remote defect indication

MS-REI Multiplex section remote error indication

MSRN   Mobile station roaming number
MSS   Mobile Satellite Service
MSTE   Multiplex section-terminating equipment, also called LTE
MSU   Message signal unit
MTBF   Mean time between failure
MTIE   Maximum time interval error
MTJ   Maximum tolerable jitter
MTP   Message transfer part
MTSO   Mobile telephone switching office
MUD   Multiuser detection
MUX   Multiplexer
MVL   Multiple virtual lines
NANP   North American Numbering Plan
NAP   Network access provider
NAU   Network addressable unit
NCP   Network control point; network control program
NDF   New data found
NDIS   Network driver interface specification
NE   Network element
NEBS   Network equipment building system
NEF   Network element function
NEXT   Near-end crosstalk
NHRP   Next hop resolution protocol
NIC   Network interface card
NID   Network interface device; network information database
NIST   National Institute for Standards and Testing
NIU   Network interface unit
NLSS   Non-locally-switched special
NML   Network management layer
NMS   Network management system
NNI   Network-to-network interface
NOB   Network operator byte
NPC   Network parameter control
NPDU   Network protocol data unit
NPI   Null pointer indication
NRM   Network resource management
NRZ   Nonreturn to zero
NSA   Non–service affecting

NSAP   Network Service Access Point of the OSI

NSN   Network service node

NSP   Network service provider

NT   Network termination

NTU   Network termination unit

OADM   Optical ADM

OAM   Operations, administration, and management

OAM&P   Operation, administration, maintenance and provisioning (services)

OC-N   Optical carrier level N

ODMA   Open distributed management architecture

ODP   Open distributed processing

O/E   Optical-to-electrical conversion

OEM   Original equipment manufacturer

OFA   Optical fiber amplifier

OFDM   Orthogonal frequency-division multiplexing

OFS   Optical fiber system

OH   Overhead

OLC   Optical loop carrier

OLE   Object linking and embedding

OMA   Object management architecture

OMAP   Operations, maintenance, and administration part

OMG   Object management group

ONU   Optical network unit

OOF   Out of frame

OOS   Out of synchronization

OPR   Optical power received

OPT   Optical power transmitted

ORL   Optical return loss

OS   Operating system

OSF   Operating system function

OSI   Open system interconnect

OSI-RM   Open system interconnect reference model

OSS   Operator service system

OUI   Organization unit identifier

OVSE   Orthogonal variable spreading factor

OXC   Optical cross-connect

PACS   Personal access communications system

PAD   Packet assembler and disassembler
PAM   Pulse amplitude modulation
PBX   Public Branch Exchange
PC   Payload container; protection channel; personal computer
PCM   Pulse code modulation
PCMCIA   Personal Computer Memory Card International Association
PCR   Peak cell rate
PCS   Personal Communication Services
PD   Propagation delay
PDH   Pleisiochronous digital hierarchy
PDI   Payload defect indication
PDU   Payload data unit
PE   Payload envelope
PEP   Product evolution planning
PER   Packet error rate
PHS   Personal Handy-phone Sytsem
PHY   Physical layer
PIM   Personal information manager
PIN   Positive-intrinsic-negative photodiode
PJ   Pointer justification
PJC   Pointer justification count
PKS   Public key cryptosystem
PLCP   Physical layer convergence protocol
PLL   Phase-locked loop
PLM   Payload label mismatch
PM   Performance monitoring
PMD   Physical medium dependent
PMO   Present method of operation
PN   Pseudorandom numerical sequence
PNNI   Private NNI
POH   Path overhead
PON   Passive optical network
POP   Point of presence
POTS   Plain Old Telephone Service
PP   Pointer processing
ppm   Parts per million
PPP   Point-to-point protocol
PPS   Path protection switching

PRBS   Pseudorandom binary sequence
PRC   Primary reference clock
PRI   Primary rate interface
PRK   Phase reversal keying
PRS   Primary Reference Source
PS   Protection switching
PSC   Public Service Commission; protection switching count
PSD   Protection switching duration; power spectral density
PSK   Phase shift keying
PSTN   Public Switched Telephone Network
PTE   Path-terminating equipment
PTI   Payload-type identifier
PTO   Public telephone operator
ptp   Peak to peak
PTT   Postal Telephone and Telegraph ministries
PUC   Path user channel
PVC   Permanent virtual channel
PVP   Permanent virtual path
QAM   Quadrature amplitude modulation
QDU   Quantizing distortion unit
QoS   Quality of service
QPSK   Quadrature PSK; quartenary PSK; quadriphase PSK
RAC   Remote-access concentrator
RACE   Research of Advanced Communications Technologies in Europe
RADSL   Rate adaptive DSL
RAI   Remote alarm indication
RBOC   Regional Bell Operating Company
RDF   Rate decrease factor
RDI   Remote defect indication, formerly FERF; also called yellow alarm
REI   Remote error indication
RF   Radio frequency
RFI   Remote failure indication; radio frequency interference
RIF   Rate interface factor
RM   Resource management
RMS   Root-mean-square
ROSE   Remote operation service element
RRM   Radio resource management
RSM   Remote switch module

RSOH   Regenerator section overhead
RSTE   Regenerator section-terminating equipment
RS-TIM   RS trace identifier mismatch
RSVP   Resource reservation setup protocol
RT   Remote terminal
RTS   Return to send; residual time stamp
RTT   Round-trip time; radio transmission technology
RTU   Remote termination unit
RZ   Return to zero
SA   Service affecting
SAAL   Signaling AAL
SACCH   Slow associated control channel
SAGE   Space-alternating generalized EMA
SAI   Serving area interface
SAP   Service access point
SAPI   Service Access Point Identifier
SAR   Segmentation and reassembly
SAR-PDU   SAR payload data unit
SAT   Supervisory audio tone
SATATM   Satellite ATM
SCAM   Supplemental channel assignment message
SCC   Specialized common carrier
SCCP   Signaling connection control unit
SCF   Service control function
SCI   Scalable coherent interface
SCO   Serving central office
SCP   Service control point
SCPC   Single channel per carrier
SCR   Sustainable cell rate
SCV   Section coding violation
SD   Signal degrade
SDCU   Satellite delay compensation unit
SDH   Synchronous Digital Hierarchy
SDLC   Synchronous data link control protocol
Σ/ΔPCM   Sigma-delta PCM
SDSL   Symmetric DSL
SDU   Service data unit
SEC   Synchronous equipment clock

SECB   Severely errored cell block
SEFS   Severely errored frame second
SES   Severely errored second
SESR   Severely errored seconds ratio
SF   Signal Fail; superframe; Spreading Factor
SHR   Self-healing ring
SIFS   Short interframe space
SIM   Subscriber identity module
SIP   SMDS interface protocol
SIR   Signal-to-interference ratio
SLC   Synchronous line carrier
SLM   Synchronous line multiplexer
SM   Switching module
SMASE   System management application service element
SMC   SONET minimum clock
SMDS   Switched multimegabit digital service
SMF   Single-mode fiber; service management function
SML   Service management layer
SMN   SONET management network; SDH management network
SMS   SDH management subnetwork
SN   Sequence number; serving node
SNA   Systems network architecture
SNAP   Subnet Access Protocol
SNC   Subnet connection
SNC/Ne   Subnetwork connection protection/intrusive end-to-end
  monitoring
SNC/Ns   Subnetwork connection protection/nonintrusive sublayer
  monitoring
SNCP   Subnetwork connection protection
SNI   Subscriber-to-network interface; SMDS network interface
SNICF   Subnetwork independent convergence function
SNMP   Simple network management protocol
SNP   Sequence number protection
SNR   Signal-to-noise ratio
SOCI   SONET Operations Communication Interface
SOH   Section overhead
SOHO   Small office/home office
SONET   Synchronous Optical Network

SP   Switching point

SPDU   Session protocol data unit

SPE   Synchronous payload envelope

SPRING   Shared protection ring

SR   Software radio

SRF   Specialized resource function

SRTS   Synchronous residual time stamp

SS7   Signaling system 7

SSAP   Source service access point (IEEE); session service access point (ISO)

SSB   Single sideband

SS-CDMA   Spread spectrum CDMA

SSCF   Service specific coordination function

SSCOP   Service specific connection oriented protocol

SSCP   System services control point

SSCS   Service specific CS

SSL   Secure socket layer

SSM   Synchronization status message

SSR   Side mode suppression ratio

SSU   Synchronization supply unit

STDM   Statistical TDM

STE   Section-terminating equipment; switching terminal exchange

STM-N   Synchronous transport module level N, $N = 1,4,16,64$

STP   Shielded twisted pair; signal transfer point

STS   Synchronous transport signal; Space-Time-Space switch

SVC   Switched virtual channel

SWAP   Shared wireless access protocol

SWC   Service wire center

T1   A digital carrier facility used to transmit a DS1 signal at 1.544 Mbps

T3   A digital carrier facility used to transmit a DS3 signal at 45 Mbps

TA   Terminal adapter

TASI   Time assignment speech interpolation

Tbps   Terabits per second, =1000 Gbps

TCAM   Telecommunications access method

TCAP   Transaction capabilities part

TCM   Tandem connection maintenance; trellis code modulation

TCP   Transmission control protocol

TCP/IP   TCP/Internet Protocol

TDD   Time-division duplex
TDE   Time-domain extinction
TDEV   Time deviation
TDM   Time-division multiplexing
TDMA   Time-division multiple access
TE   Terminal equipment
TEI   Terminal endpoint identifier
TH   Transport header
TIA   Telecommunications Industry Association
TIM   Trace identifier mismatch
TINA   Telecommunications Information Networking Architecture
  Consortium
TM   Traffic management; terminal mode
TMM   Transmission monitoring machine
TMN   Telecommunications Management Network
TOH   Transport overhead (SOH + LOH)
TP   Twisted pair; transport layer protocol
TPC   Transmit power control
T&R   Tip and ring
TS   Time stamp; time slot; traffic shaping
TSB   Telecommunications Systems Bulletin
TSE   Test sequence error
TSG   Timing signal generator
TSI   Time slot interchanger
TST   Time-space-time switch
TTA   Telecommunications Technology Association
TU   Tributary unit
TU-AIS   Tributary unit AIS
TU-LOP = tributary unit LOP
TUC   Total user cell number
TUCD   Total user cell difference
TUG-N   Tributary unit group N, $N = 2, 3$
TU-LOM   Tributary unit loss of multiframe
TU-N   Tributary unit level N, $N = 11, 12, 2, 3$
TU-NDF   Tributary unit NDF
UAS   Unavailable second
UAT   Unavailable time
UAWG   Universal ADSL Working Group

UBR   Unspecified bit rate
UCAID   University Corporation for Advanced Internet Development
UDC   Universal digital channel
UDP   User datagram protocol
UI   Unit interval
UME   UNI Management Entity
UMTS   Universal Mobile Telecommunications System
UNEQ   Unequipped
UNI   User-to-network interface
UPC   Usage parameter control
UPSR   Unidirectional path switch ring
URL   Uniform resource locator
USART   Universal synchronous/asynchronous receiver transmitter
USTIA   United States Telecommunications Industry Association
UTP   Unshielded twisted pair
UUID   Universal unique ID
VBR   Variable bit rate
VC   Virtual channel; virtual container
VCC   VC connection
VCCG   Voltage-controlled code generator
VCI   Virtual-circuit identifier
VC-N   Virtual container level N; $N = 11, 12, 2, 3$, or 4
VC-N-Mc   Virtual container level N, M concatenated virtual containers
VCS   Virtual-channel switching
VDSL   Very-high-bit-rate DSL
VF   Voice frequency
VGL   Voice grade line
VLAN   Virtual LAN
VLSI   Very large scale integration
VOD   Video on demand
VoIP   Voice over IP
VOIP   Video over IP
VP   Virtual path
VPC   VP connection
VPI   Virtual-path identifier
VPL   Virtual-path link
VPN   Virtual private network
VPS   Virtual-path switching

VR   Virtual radio

VT   Virtual tributary

VTAM   Virtual telecommunications access method

VTOA   Voice telephone over ATM

W3C   World Wide Web Consortium

WAN   Wide area network

WATM   Wireless ATM

WATS   Wide Area Telephone Service

WB-DCS   Wideband Digital Cross-connect System

WBEM   Web-Based Enterprise Management

W-CDMA   Wideband DS-CDMA

W-DCS   Wideband Digital Cross-connect System

WDM   Wavelength division multiplexing

WIPO   World Intellectual Property Organization

WLAN   Wireless LAN

WMSA   Weighted multislot averaging

WTR   Wait to restore

X.25   Packet switching international standard

xDSL   Any DSL

XOR   Exclusive OR logic function

ZBTSI   Zero-byte TSI

INDEX

ABOUT THE AUTHOR

Stamatios V. Kartalopoulos is currently with the Optical Networks Group of Lucent Technologies, Bell Labs Innovations. He holds a B.Sc. in Physics, a graduate Diploma in Electronics, and an M.Sc. and Ph.D. in Engineering Science.

His most recent contributions in the area of communications are in SONET/SDH and ATM systems, in ultrafast pattern recognition, and dense wavelength division multiplexing (DWDM). Since 1979 he has made technical contributions to digital loop carrier systems, local area networks, fiber networks, satellite systems, and intelligent signal processing including neural networks and fuzzy logic. Previous contributions are in the definition, development, and management of advanced real-time, high-speed communications architectures and their implementation with VLSI and/or microprocessors, and the definition and development of high-speed and robust communications protocols.

Dr. Kartalopoulos has recently taught SONET/SDH and ATM systems as well as neural networks and fuzzy logic in several seminars. Prior to AT&T, he taught undergraduate and graduate courses and conducted research on dynamic phenomena of optical materials, electro-optic devices, digital and analog computers, and searching algorithms.

Dr. Kartalopoulos is the author of *Understanding Neural Networks and Fuzzy Logic* (IEEE Press, 1996). In addition, he has published numerous articles and has been awarded many patents, several in optical communications systems. He has been a guest editor of the IEEE's Communications Magazine and an associate editor of the *Transactions on Neural Networks*. He has served as vice president of the IEEE Neural Network Council and was a member of the IEEE USA-Board.

A member of the IEEE, Dr. Kartalopoulos represents the Communications Society to the Technical Activities Board (TAB) New Technology Directions organization, and is a member of the IEEE Press Board. Prior to this, he chaired the Signal Processing and Electronics Committee. He also is a member of the Communications Society Transmission, Access, and Optical Systems Committee.